Graded examples in

Sets, Probability and Statistics

M. R. Heylings M.A., M.Sc.

Schofield & Sims Limited   Huddersfield

0 7217 2337 3

First printed 1986. Reprinted 1986.

Acknowledgements
The work on Simulation on pages 126 to 129 is based
on ideas from F.R. Watson's *A Simple Approach to
Simulation,* KMEP (Dept. of Education), University
of Keele.
The diagram on page 134 is reproduced from *Shaking
A Six* (*Statistics in Your World* series) published by
Foulsham Educational. Copyright — Schools Council
Publications.

The series **Graded examples in mathematics**
comprises:

Fractions and Decimals	0 7217 2323 3
Answer Book	0 7217 2324 1
Algebra	0 7217 2325 x
Answer Book	0 7217 2326 8
Area and Volume	0 7217 2327 6
Answer Book	0 7217 2328 4
General Arithmetic	0 7217 2329 2
Answer Book	0 7217 2330 6
Geometry and Trigonometry	0 7217 2331 4
Answer Book	0 7217 2332 2
Negative Numbers and Graphs	0 7217 2333 0
Answer Book	0 7217 2334 9
Matrices and Transformations	0 7217 2335 7
Answer Book	0 7217 2336 5
Sets, Probability and Statistics	0 7217 2337 3
Answer Book	0 7217 2338 1

In preparation:

Revision of Topics	0 7217 2339 x
Answer Book	0 7217 2340 3

Designed by Graphic Art Concepts, Leeds
Artwork by Barry & Tim Davies
Printed in England by Pindar Print Limited, Scarborough, North Yorkshire.

Author's Note

This series has been written and produced in the form of eight topic books, each offering a wealth of graded examples for pupils in the 11–16 age range; plus a further book of revision examples for fifth formers.

There are no teaching points in the series. The intention is to meet the often heard request from teachers for a wide choice of graded examples to support their own class teaching. The contents are clearly labelled for easy use in conjunction with an existing course book; but the books can also be used as the chief source of material, in which case the restrictions imposed by the traditional type of mathematics course book are removed and the teacher is free to organise year-by-year courses to suit the school. Used in this way, the topic-book approach offers an unusual and useful continuity of work for the class-room, for homework or for revision purposes.

The material has been tested over many years in classes ranging from mixed ability 11-year-olds to fifth formers taking public examinations. Some sections are useful for pupils of above average ability while other sections suit the needs of the less able, though it is for the middle range of ability that the series is primarily intended.

Contents

Sets

Other topics

Probability

Statistics

Symbols

$=$	is equal to
$\neq$	is not equal to
$\simeq$	is approximately equal to
$<$	is less than
$\leqslant$	is less than or equal to
$\not<$	is not less than
$>$	is greater than
$\geqslant$	is greater than or equal to
$\not>$	is not greater than
$\Rightarrow$	implies
$\Leftarrow$	is implied by
$\rightarrow$	maps onto
$\in$	is a member of
$\notin$	is not a member of
$\subset$	is a subset of
$\not\subset$	is not a subset of
$\cap$	intersection (or overlap)
$\cup$	union
A'	the complement (or outside) of set A
$\mathscr{E}$	The Universal set
$\varnothing$ or $\{\ \}$	the empty set
(x,y)	the co-ordinates of a point
$\begin{pmatrix} x \\ y \end{pmatrix}$	the components of a vector

The Greek alphabet

A	α	alpha
B	β	beta
Γ	γ	gamma
Δ	δ	delta
E	ε	epsilon
Z	ζ	zeta
H	η	eta
Θ	θ	theta
I	ι	iota
K	κ	kappa
Λ	λ	lambda
M	μ	mu
N	ν	nu
Ξ	ξ	xi
O	o	omicron
Π	π	pi
P	ρ	rho
Σ	σ, ς	sigma
T	τ	tau
Y	υ	upsilon
Φ	ϕ, φ	phi
X	χ	chi
Ψ	ψ	psi
Ω	ω	omega

Sets

Symbols and diagrams

Part 1 Introduction

1 A set is a group of objects or symbols which have something in common. Which is the odd-one-out in each of these groups? Give your reasons.

a

b

c

d

e a, e, i, o, t, u

f metre, mile, kilometre, gram, inch

g circle, rectangle, cuboid, triangle, quadrilateral

h light bulb, television, pencil, cassette player, washing machine

i Pam, Bob, David, Liz, Steve

j whale, cow, man, eagle, dog

k metre, mile, kilometre, centimetre, millimetre

l 2, 4, 8, 9, 14, 18

m 3, 6, 8, 9, 12, 15

n 10, 15, 17, 25, 30, 35

o $\frac{1}{2}, \frac{3}{4}, \frac{2}{3}, \frac{9}{8}, \frac{1}{5}$

p 181 808 916 42 69

q cow, dog, pig, hare, rat

r cow, dog, pig, hen, rat

s cow, dog, pig, cat, rat

2 Name another member of these sets.

a {Joan, Jean, Janice, ...}

b {Herbert, Albert, Cuthbert, ...}

c {2, 4, 6, 8, 10, ...}

d {Mercury, Earth, Venus, Uranus, ...}

e {Pennines, Grampians, Pyrenees, Rockies, ...}

f {madam, toot, radar, pip, ...}

g {triangle, square, rectangle, circle, ...}

h {5, 15, 40, 45, ...}

i {a, at, ate, late, ...}

j {Dorset, Cumbria, Kent, ...}

k {arts, tars, star, ...}

l {Brahms, Chopin, Vivaldi, ...}

Symbols and diagrams

3 Describe these sets in words.
   a {2, 4, 6, 8, 10, 12, ...}
   b {England, Wales, Scotland, Northern Ireland}
   c {Jack, John, James, Julian, ...}
   d {5, 10, 15, 20, 25, 30, ...}
   e {Matthew, Mark, Luke, John}
   f {Sunday, Monday, Tuesday, Wednesday, Thursday, Friday, Saturday}
   g {1, 4, 9, 16, 25, 36, ...}
   h {1, 2, 5, 10, 20, 50, 100}
   i {Europe, Asia, Africa, Oceania, North America, South America}
   j {R, O, Y, G, B, I, V}

4 Name the pairs of equal sets.
   A = {the vowels}
   B = {odd numbers less than 10}
   C = {days of the weekend}
   D = {1, 2, 5, 10, 20, 50, £1}
   E = {1, 3, 5, 7, 9}
   F = {amounts of British coins}
   G = {a, e, i, o, u}
   H = {Saturday, Sunday}

5 Which of these sets have (i) an *infinite* number of members
                            (ii) a *finite* number of members?
   a {all even numbers}
   b {even numbers between 3 and 33}
   c {the days of the week}
   d {all fractions}
   e {people who live in Durham}
   f {January, February, March, April, ...}
   g {N, NE, E, SE, S, SW, ...}
   h {10, 20, 30, 40, 50, ...}
   i {Avon, Bucks., Berks., Cumbria, ...}
   j {a, b, c, d, e, f, ...}
   k {α, β, γ, δ, ...}
   l {$\frac{1}{2}$, $\frac{2}{3}$, $\frac{3}{4}$, $\frac{4}{5}$, $\frac{5}{6}$, ...}
   m {0.1, 0.01, 0.001, 0.0001, ...}
   n {all decimal numbers between 3 and 4}

A class of school pupils have these names.

Jane Taylor	Anita Kelly	David Jones	Aziz Awan
Amanda Williams	John Thwaites	Andrew Summers	Ann Haywood
Tina Hawkins	Megan Jones	Carol Williams	John Martin
Ann Summers	Fatima Patel	Michael Daly	Robert Openshaw

List the members of the class in these sets.
   a {boys with the same first name}
   b {the surnames of more than one pupil}
   c {girls with the same first name}
   d {pupils with surnames beginning with H}
   e {the names of girls with first name and surname of the same length}
   f {the first five girls alphabetically by surname}

Symbols and diagrams

7 List all the members of these sets, remembering that no member need be written more than once.
  a {even numbers between 5 and 15}
  b {the last six letters of the English alphabet}
  c {the first six letters of the Greek alphabet}
  d {the letters used in the word MISSISSIPPI}
  e {the first six multiples of 6}
  f {the capital cities of the four countries of the United Kingdom}
  g {the five oceans of the world}
  h {square numbers less than 101}
  i {the letters used in the word MATHEMATICS}
  j {the planets between the Earth and the Sun}
  k {the colours used in traffic-lights}
  l {the three longest rivers in the British Isles}

Part 2   Venn diagrams

1 Here are square S, triangle T and circle C, overlapping each other.

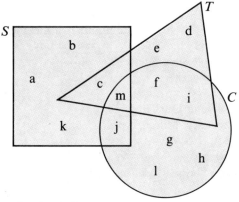

Which letters are   a   in the circle
                    b   in the triangle
                    c   where the triangle and circle overlap
                    d   in the square
                    e   in the square but not in the circle
                    f   where the square, triangle and circle all overlap?

2   This diagram shows the members of two clubs.
Inside circle A are all the members of the riding club.
Inside circle B are all the members of the swimming club.

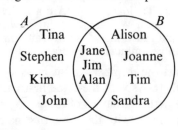

  a   Of which club is Sandra a member?
  b   Of which club is John a member?
  c   Who are members of both clubs?
  d   Who is in the riding club but not in the swimming club?
  e   Which girls are in the swimming club but not in the riding club?

Symbols and diagrams

3   Circle *G* contains the names of a
    group of girl friends and circle *F*
    contains the names of the brothers
    and sisters in one family.

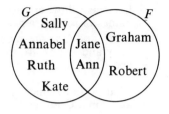

a   How many girls are friends with each other?
b   How many children are in the family?
c   How many sisters are in the family?
d   How many brothers are in the family?
e   Is Sally Robert's sister?
f   Who are Graham's sisters?
g   How many girls are not members of the family?

4   The sentence "Set *X* has members 1, 2, 3 and 4"
    can be written in short as

$$X = \{1, 2, 3, 4\}.$$

    Write set *Y* in the same way.

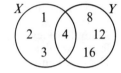

5   Write the members of each set in these Venn diagrams using this shorthand.

a

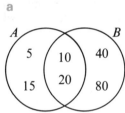

b

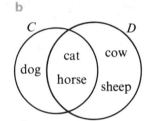

c

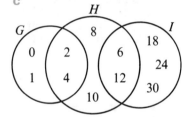

d

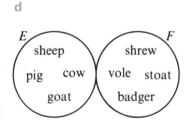

e

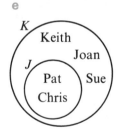

f

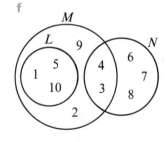

g

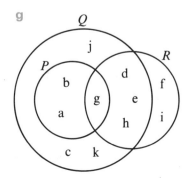

h

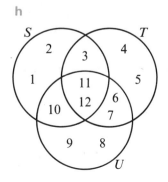

11

Symbols and diagrams

6 Copy this Venn diagram to show the members of the tennis club *T* and the football club *F*. Use the following information to write the names of seven friends in their correct sets.

Barry and Eric are members of both the tennis club and the football club. Alan, Judy and Diana are members of the tennis club, but not the football club. Frank and Garry are in the football club, but not the tennis club.

7 Charles and Pamela are the parents of Sophie, Ben and Tina. Copy and complete this Venn diagram where F = {members of the family} and C = {children in the family} .

8 Draw a similar diagram for your family or your friend's family.

9 A smallholder keeps a few sheep and pigs and has two cows. There are also foxes, rabbits and mice on his land.
Draw a Venn diagram for the sets W = {wild animals}
and E = {animals he might eat}.
Write the animals mentioned in their correct positions on the diagram.

10 In a group of office workers, Sandra, Helen and John can both type and take shorthand. Angela, Fiona and Pat can type but know no shorthand. Donald ca~ take shorthand but cannot type.
Draw a Venn diagram to illustrate this information.

Part 3   is a member of

1 The symbol ∈ means "is a member of"
            and ∉ means "is not a member of".
Say whether these statements are *true* or *false*.

a June ∈ {months of the year}
b June ∈ {girls' names}
c John ∈ {girls' names}
d Mark ∉ {girls' names}
e Neptune ∉ {planets}
f Neptune ∈ {Ancient Greek go~
g Saturday ∈ {days of the week}
h i ∈ {vowels}
i 2 ∉ {even numbers}
j 13 ∈ {prime numbers}
k tennis ∉ {international sports}
l Lancashire ∈ {English countie~
m 10p ∈ {British copper coins}
n $\frac{2}{4}$ ∉ {fractions equal to $\frac{1}{2}$}

2 This diagram shows three sets.
N = {whole numbers up to 15}
E = {even numbers up to 15}
P = {prime numbers up to 15}

Say whether these statements are *true* or *false*.

a 4 ∈ E
b 9 ∈ N
c 13 ∈ P
d 6 ∈ P
e 8 ∉ P
f 13 ∉ E
g 11 ∈ N
h 2 ∈ E
i 2 ∉ P
j 2 ∉ N

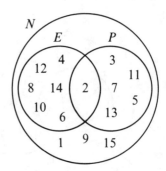

Symbols and diagrams

3 This diagram shows three sets.
N = {whole numbers up to 15}
E = {multiples of 2 up to 15}
F = {multiples of 3 up to 15}

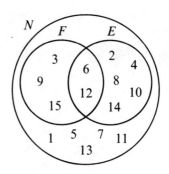

Copy and complete each of
these statements.

a $\quad 3 \in \ldots$ b $\quad 3 \notin \ldots$
c $\quad 5 \in \ldots$ d $\quad 5 \notin \ldots$
e $\quad 8 \in \ldots$ f $\quad 8 \notin \ldots$
g $\quad 6 \in \ldots$ h $\quad 15 \notin \ldots$
i $\quad 13 \in \ldots$ j $\quad 10 \notin \ldots$

4 Follow the patterns in these sets and say whether the statements are *true* or
false.

a $\quad \frac{6}{12} \in \{\frac{1}{2}, \frac{2}{4}, \frac{3}{6}, \frac{4}{8}, \frac{5}{10}, \ldots\}$

b $\quad \frac{10}{40} \in \{\frac{1}{4}, \frac{2}{8}, \frac{3}{12}, \frac{4}{16}, \frac{5}{20}, \ldots\}$

c $\quad \frac{6}{7} \in \{\frac{1}{2}, \frac{2}{3}, \frac{3}{4}, \frac{4}{5}, \frac{5}{6}, \ldots\}$

d $\quad 100 \notin \{1, 4, 9, 16, 25, 36, 49, \ldots\}$

e $\quad \frac{1}{64} \notin \{1, \frac{1}{2}, \frac{1}{4}, \frac{1}{8}, \frac{1}{16}, \frac{1}{32}, \ldots\}$

f $\quad -9 \in \{1, -2, 3, -4, 5, -6, \ldots\}$

g $\quad 242 \in \{1, 3, 9, 27, \ldots\}$

h $\quad 89 \in \{12, 23, 34, 45, 56, \ldots\}$

i $\quad \frac{1}{100} \notin \{1, \frac{1}{4}, \frac{1}{9}, \frac{1}{16}, \frac{1}{25}, \ldots\}$

j $\quad \frac{13}{14} \in \{\frac{1}{2}, \frac{3}{4}, \frac{5}{6}, \frac{7}{8}, \frac{9}{10}, \ldots\}$

k $\quad 22 \in \{1, 2, 4, 7, 11, \ldots\}$

l $\quad 80 \in \{0, 3, 8, 15, 24, 35, 48, \ldots\}$

Part 4   Intersection

1 The symbol $\cap$ is used to denote the **intersection** (or *overlap*) of two sets.
So $A \cap B$ means "the intersection (or overlap) of sets A and B".

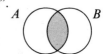

Copy and complete this statement $A \cap B = \{\ldots\}$
for each of these Venn diagrams.

a

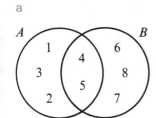

b

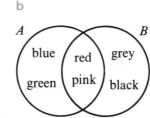

c

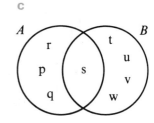

d

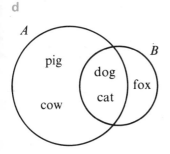

e

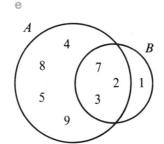

f

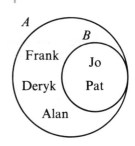

Symbols and diagrams

2 Copy and complete these statements.

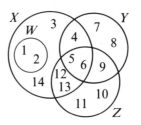

  a $X \cap Y = \{\ldots\}$
  b $Y \cap Z = \{\ldots\}$
  c $X \cap Z = \{\ldots\}$
  d $W \cap X = \{\ldots\}$
  e $X \cap Y \cap Z = \{\ldots\}$
  f $W \cap Y = \{\ldots\}$

3

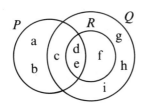

Copy and complete these statements.
  a $P \cap R = \{\ldots\}$
  b $P \cap Q = \{\ldots\}$
  c $Q \cap R = \{\ldots\}$
  d $P \cap Q \cap R = \{\ldots\}$
  e   Which two intersections are equal?

4 a Copy this diagram of sets A and B where $A = \{1, 2, 3, 4, 5\}$ and $B = \{2, 4, 6, 8\}$.
Look for the intersection of the two sets and then write all members of both sets in their correct positions on your diagram.

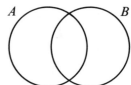

  b   Copy and complete this statement.
$A \cap B = \{\ldots\}$

5 a Use a similar diagram for sets Y and Z where $Y = \{a, b, c, d, e\}$ and $Z = \{a, e, i, o, u\}$.
Write the members of both sets on your diagram.
  b   Copy and complete the statement $Y \cap Z = \{\ldots\}$.

6

  a   Copy this diagram of sets P and Q where $P = \{2, 4, 6, 8, 10, 12\}$ and $Q = \{4, 8, 12\}$.
Write the members of both sets on your diagram.
  b   Copy and complete the statement $P \cap Q = \{..$

7 a Use a similar diagram for the sets $R = \{e, f, g, h, i\}$ and $S = \{e, i\}$. Write the members of both sets on your diagram.
  b   Copy and complete the statement $R \cap S = \{\ldots\}$.

8 Choose the correct diagram from these three for each pair of sets A and B.
Copy the diagram of your choice and write in the members of the two sets.
In each case, write the set $A \cap B$.

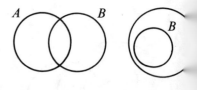
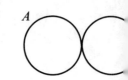

  a $A = \{1, 2, 3, 4\}$ and $B = \{3, 4, 5, 6, 7\}$
  b $A = \{2, 4, 6, 8, 10\}$ and $B = \{10, 15, 20\}$
  c $A = \{3, 6, 9, 12, 15\}$ and $B = \{3, 9\}$
  d $A = \{5, 10, 50, 100, 500, 1000\}$ and $B = \{5, 50, 500\}$
  e $A = \{1, 3, 5, 7\}$ and $B = \{2, 4, 6, 8\}$
  f $A = \{\frac{1}{2}, 1, 2, 4\}$ and $B = \{1\frac{1}{2}, 3, 6, 12\}$

Symbols and diagrams

9 If E = {European countries}
and S = {English-speaking countries}, draw a
Venn diagram and write in these countries.

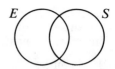

France   New Zealand   Scotland   Denmark

Choose three other countries and write one in each part of your diagram.

10 Draw a Venn diagram for the sets S = {seas of the world} and C = {colours}.
Enter these on your diagram.

brown   red   green   yellow

Choose three other members and write one in each part of the diagram.

11 Draw a Venn diagram for the sets
F = {animals found on farms} and
P = {animals kept as pets}.
Enter these on your diagram.

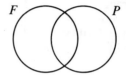

cows   hamsters   dogs   sheep

Write three other entries, one in each part of the diagram.

12 Given that T = {towns in Britain} and
S = {British seaside resorts}, draw a Venn
diagram and enter these names.

Derby   Blackpool   Halifax   Torquay

Write another three towns of your choice on your diagram.

3 If W = {whole numbers less than 12} and E = {even numbers less than 12},
draw a Venn diagram to show these sets and write in all their members.
List the members of the set W ∩ E.

4 Without drawing any diagram, list the members of A ∩ B when
- a   A = {letters in the first half of the alphabet}   B = {vowels}
- b   A = {whole numbers between 10 and 20}   B = {all odd numbers}
- c   A = {all prime numbers}   B = {whole numbers between 4 and 30}
- d   A = {multiples of 3 less than 30}   B = {multiples of 4 less than 30}.

5 Describe in words the set A ∩ B when
- a   A = {all butterflies}   B = {all white objects}
- b   A = {all greetings cards}   B = {articles in the Christmas post}
- c   A = {burrowing animals}   B = {animals which eat grass}
- d   A = {vehicles built in Britain}   B = {four-wheel-drive vehicles}.

Copy this diagram of sets P, Q and R. Write in
all the members of the sets using the following
information.
P ∩ Q = {b, c}   P = {a, b, c}
Q ∩ R = {f, g}   Q = {b, c, d, e, f, g, h}

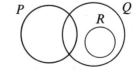

Copy this diagram of sets X, Y and Z.
Write in all the members of the sets
using the following information.
X ∩ Y = {3, 4}   X = {1, 2, 3, 4, 8}
Y ∩ Z = {3, 5, 6}   Y = {3, 4, 5, 6, 7}
X ∩ Z = {3, 8}   Z = {3, 5, 6, 8, 9}

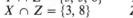

15

Symbols and diagrams

18 This map of Europe shows the sets
   N = {member countries of NATO, excluding Canada and USA}
   C = {member countries of the EEC or "Common Market"}.

List the members
of $N \cap C$.

B	Belgium
D	West Germany
DK	Denmark
E	Spain
F	France
G	Greece
GB	Great Britain
I	Italy
IRL	Ireland
IS	Iceland
L	Luxembourg
N	Norway
NL	Netherlands
P	Portugal
T	Turkey

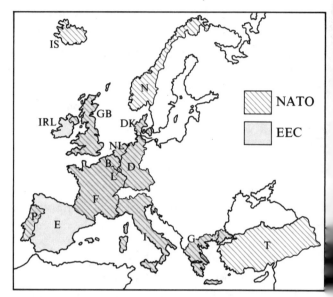

19 An overhead projector or any other
   bright light can be used to combine the
   colours of different transparencies.
   If R = {all reds}, Y = {all yellows} and
   B = {all blues}, how would you describe
   a $R \cap Y$ b. $B \cap Y$.
   c Copy this diagram and label as
      many intersections as you can.

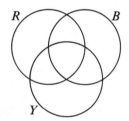

Part 5 Union

The symbol $\cup$ denotes the *union* of two sets.
$A \cup B$ means "the union of sets A and B" and includes
everything that is in both A and B joined together.

1 Copy and complete the statement $A \cup B = \{\ldots\}$ for each of these Venn
   diagrams.

a

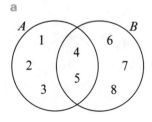

b

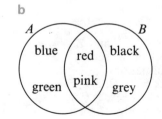

c

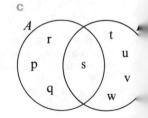

Symbols and diagrams

d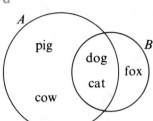

e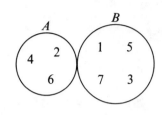

f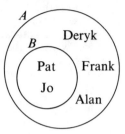

2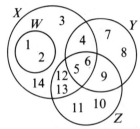

Use this diagram to copy and complete these statements.

a $Y \cup Z = \{\ldots\}$
b $X \cup Y = \{\ldots\}$
c $X \cup Z = \{\ldots\}$
d $W \cup Y = \{\ldots\}$
e $W \cup Z = \{\ldots\}$
f $X \cup W = \{\ldots\}$

3 Copy and complete these statements.

a $P \cup R = \{\ldots\}$
b $P \cup Q = \{\ldots\}$
c $Q \cup R = \{\ldots\}$
d $P \cup Q \cup R = \{\ldots\}$
e Which two unions are equal?

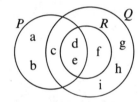

4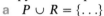

A   **B**

a Copy this Venn diagram of the sets A and B where $A = \{2, 4, 6, 8, 10\}$ and $B = \{4, 8, 12, 16, 20\}$. Write in the members of both sets in their correct positions.
b Copy and complete the statement $A \cup B = \{\ldots\}$.

5 a Copy this diagram of the sets $Y = \{q, r, s, t, u\}$ and $Z = \{a, e, i, o, u\}$ and write in the members of both sets.

b Copy and complete the statement $Y \cup Z = \{\ldots\}$.

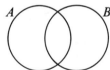

6 a Copy this diagram and enter the members of the sets $A = \{5, 10, 15, 20, 25, 30\}$ and $B = \{10, 20, 30\}$.

b Copy and complete the statement $A \cup B = \{\ldots\}$.

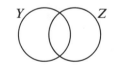

Draw a similar diagram for the sets $P = \{a, b, c, d, e\}$ and $Q = \{a, e\}$ and write the members of the set $P \cup Q$.

a Copy this diagram and enter the members of the sets $M = \{2, 3, 5, 7, 11\}$ and $N = \{1, 4, 6, 8, 9, 10\}$.

b Copy and complete the statement $M \cup N = \{\ldots\}$.

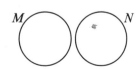

Draw a similar diagram for the sets $Y = \{fox, hare, vole\}$ and $Z = \{dog, cat\}$ and write down the members of the set $Y \cup Z$.

17

Symbols and diagrams

10 For each pair of sets A and B
    choose the correct diagram from
    these three.
    Copy the diagram of your choice
    and write in the members of the two
    sets.
    In each case, write the members of
    set $A \cup B$.

a $A = \{9, 10, 19, 20, 29\}$ and $B = \{10, 15, 20, 25\}$
b $A = \{a, e, i, o, u, y\}$ and $B = \{u, v, w, x, y, z\}$
c $A = \{1, 2, 3, 4\}$ and $B = \{11, 12, 13, 14\}$
d $A = \{a, b, c, d, e\}$ and $B = \{x, y, z\}$
e $A = \{0, 1, 2, 4, 8, 16\}$ and $B = \{2, 4, 8\}$
f $A = \{m, a, t, h, s\}$ and $B = \{m, a, t\}$

11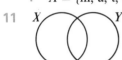
    If $X = \{$whole numbers between 0 and 10$\}$ and
    $Y = \{$even numbers between 3 and 19$\}$, draw a
    Venn diagram and write the members of $X \cup Y$.

12 Draw a similar diagram for the sets $P = \{$multiples of 3 which are less than 31$\}$
    and $Q = \{$multiples of 5 which are less than 31$\}$.
    List the members of $P \cup Q$.

13 Malcolm, Jane, Ewen and Sonia are members of a youth group Y. The two
    boys, Malcolm and Ewen, are also members of a sports club S. Other members
    of the sports club S include Aslam, Paul and Stephen.
    Draw a Venn diagram for the two sets Y and S and list the members of $Y \cup S$.

14 All the children in a small class at a primary
    school are taken home by bus, though some still
    have further to walk.
    Barry, Pam, Tracy and Bob go all the way home
    by bus, but Ann, Eric and Sadie still have some
    way to walk.
    Copy this diagram where $B = \{$children who travel on the bus$\}$
    $\qquad\qquad\qquad$ and $W = \{$children who use the bus and then walk$\}$.
    Enter the names of the children and list the members of $B \cup W$.

15 Look at the map of Europe in question **18** on page 16 and list the members
    of $N \cup C$.

16 Without drawing any diagrams, describe in words the set $A \cup B$ when
    a $A = \{$even numbers less than 100$\}$ $\qquad$ $B = \{$odd numbers less than 100$\}$
    b $A = \{$vowels in the alphabet$\}$ $\qquad\qquad$ $B = \{$consonants in the alphabet$\}$
    c $A = \{$cars with left-hand drive$\}$ $\qquad\quad$ $B = \{$cars with right-hand drive$\}$
    d $A = \{$letters before N in the alphabet$\}$
    $\qquad\qquad\qquad\qquad\qquad\qquad$ $B = \{$letters after K in the alphabet$\}$
    e $A = \{$whole numbers between 1 and 51
    $\qquad\qquad\qquad\qquad\qquad\qquad$ $B = \{$whole numbers between 21 and 106
    f $A = \{$letters before F in the alphabet$\}$
    $\qquad\qquad\qquad\qquad\qquad\qquad$ $B = \{$letters before J in the alphabet$\}$
    g $A = \{$left-handed people$\}$ $\qquad\qquad\quad$ $B = \{$people who wear spectacles$\}$.

18

Symbols and diagrams

17 Copy this Venn diagram of the sets P and Q.
Write in all the members of the sets using the
following information.
$P \cap Q = \{4\}$ $P = \{1, 2, 3, 4\}$
$P \cup Q = \{1, 2, 3, 4, 5, 6\}$

18 Copy this Venn diagram of the sets A, B and C.
Write in all the members of the sets using the
following information.
$A \cap B = \{s, t\}$ $C = \{u, v\}$
$A \cup C = \{s, t, u, v, x, y\}$
$A \cup B = \{s, t, u, v, w, x, y, z\}$

Part 6 is a subset of

1 $A \subset B$ means that "A is a subset of B" where on a
Venn diagram A lies entirely inside B.
$X \not\subset Y$ means that "X is not a subset of Y".
Say whether these statements are *true* or *false*.
  a {dogs} $\subset$ {animals}
  b {wellington boots} $\subset$ {footwear}
  c {Sandra, Susan, Sheila} $\subset$ {boys' names}
  d {Saturday, Sunday} $\subset$ {months of the year}
  e {daffodils} $\not\subset$ {autumn flowers}
  f {cups, saucers} $\not\subset$ {crockery}
  g {giraffes} $\not\subset$ {African animals}
  h {The Bible} $\not\subset$ {religious books}
  i {hockey, chess} $\subset$ {international games}
  j {oak, ash, pine} $\not\subset$ {British trees}

2 Pair these sets and subsets and write a statement for each pair.
For example, $F \subset A$.
$A = \{$all girls' names$\}$ $F = \{$Joanne, Carole, Angela$\}$
$B = \{$Mars, Jupiter, Pluto$\}$ $G = \{$Glasgow, Hull, Dover$\}$
$C = \{$all marsupials$\}$ $H = \{$gods whose names gave the days of the week$\}$
$D = \{$ports of Britain$\}$ $I = \{$kangaroo, platypus, wallaby$\}$
$E = \{$Roman gods$\}$ $J = \{$Woden, Thor$\}$

3 Say whether these statements are *true* or *false*.
  a {p, q} $\subset$ {p, q, r, s} b {m, n} $\subset$ {j, k, l, m, n}
  c {7, 8, 9} $\not\subset$ {1, 2, 3, 4, 5} d {1, 2, 3} $\not\subset$ {1, 2, 3, 4, 5, 6, 7}
  e {w, x, y} $\not\subset$ {u, v, w, x} f {4, 5} $\not\subset$ {4, 5, 8, 10}
  g {2, 3} $\not\subset$ {1, 2, 3, 4} h {0, 1, 10} $\subset$ {0, 1, 10, 11, 100}

4 Choose *one* of these three statements to describe each diagram.
$X \subset Y$ $X \not\subset Y$ $Y \subset X$

 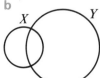 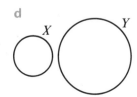

Symbols and diagrams

5 Copy this diagram of the sets $P = \{s, t, u, v, w\}$ and $Q = \{s, t, u\}$ and enter all the members of P and Q on your diagram.
Label the diagram *either* $Q \subset P$ *or* $P \subset Q$.

6

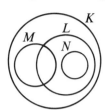

Say whether these statements are *true* or *false*.

a $N \subset L$ b $M \subset K$
c $N \not\subset M$ d $L \subset K$
e $M \subset L$ f $N \not\subset K$

7 This map shows the sets
$E = \{$English counties$\}$ and
$M = \{$midland counties$\}$.
Which *one* of these three statements is correct?

a $M \not\subset E$ b $E \subset M$ c $M \subset E$

8

This map of the set E of European countries shows three subsets:
$S = \{$Scandinavian countries$\}$
$Be = \{$Benelux countries$\}$
$Ba = \{$Balkan countries$\}$.
Which of these statements are correct?

a $S \subset E$ b $Be \not\subset E$
c $Ba \subset E$ d $S \not\subset E$
e $E \subset Ba$ f $Be \subset E$

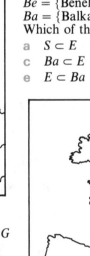

9 The second map of Western Europe E shows the German-speaking countries G and the region called Bavaria, B.
Which of these statements are correct?

a $G \subset E$ b $B \subset G$
c $B \not\subset E$ d $E \subset G$
e $G \not\subset E$ f $B \subset E$

10 a Draw three circles, labelled C, E and B to indicate the sets
$C = \{$all breeds of cattle$\}$, $E = \{$European breeds of cattle$\}$ and
$B = \{$British breeds of cattle$\}$.

b Say whether these statements are *true* or *false*.
(i) $E \subset C$ (ii) $E \subset B$ (iii) $B \subset C$ (iv) $B \subset E$

c Shade that part of your diagram which indicates European breeds which are not British.

Symbols and diagrams

11 **a** Draw three labelled circles for the sets C = {all cats},
D = {domesticated cats} and T = {tabby cats}.

b Say whether these statements are *true* or *false*.
(i) $T \subset D$ (ii) $C \subset D$ (iii) $D \subset C$ (iv) $T \subset C$

c Shade that part of your diagram which indicates wild undomesticated cats.

12 **a** Copy this diagram for
N = {whole numbers from 1 to 12}.
Draw arrows from one number to another
using the relation "... add 2 equals ...".

b Note that you have divided (or *partitioned*) N
into two subsets.
List the members of each subset. How would
you describe the members of these subsets?

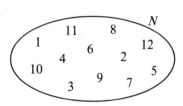

13 Draw the diagram for set N again.
Join members of N by arrows using the relation "... add 3 gives ...".
This partitions N into three subsets.
List the members of each subset.

14 Draw another diagram for N and partition it using the relation
"... add 4 equals ...". List the members of each subset.

15 If M = {whole numbers from 1 to 30} and it is partitioned using the relation
"... add 5 equals ...", can you list the members of all the subsets *without*
drawing any diagram?

Part 7 The number of members in a set

1 $n(A)$ means "the number of members in set A" and answers the question "How
many members has set A?"
What is the value of $n(A)$ when A is

a {days in the week}   **b** {months in a year}
c {even numbers between 1 and 21}   **d** {odd numbers between 0 and 20}
e {suits in a pack of cards}   **f** {faces on an ordinary dice}
g {letters in the English alphabet}   **h** {different coins in British money}
i {different letters in HUDDERSFIELD}   **j** {square numbers between 10 and 15}
k {seasons in the year}   **l** {colours in the rainbow}
m {countries in the United Kingdom}   **n** {counties bordering on Cornwall}?

2 Say whether these statements are *true* or *false*.
a $n(X) = 5$ **b** $n(Y) = 4$
c $n(Z) = 4$ **d** $n(X \cap Y) = 2$
e $n(X \cup Y) = 9$

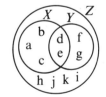

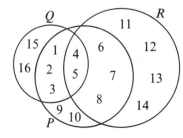

Find the value of
a $n(Q)$ **b** $n(R)$
c $n(Q \cap R)$ **d** $n(Q \cup R)$
e $n(P)$ **f** $n(P \cap R)$
g $n(P \cup R)$ **h** $n(P \cap Q)$
i $n(P \cup Q)$ **j** $n(P \cup Q \cup R)$.

Symbols and diagrams

4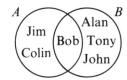

This diagram shows two sets of boys, A and B. If we are interested only in the *number* of boys and not their actual names, this diagram can be drawn with only a cross for each boy.

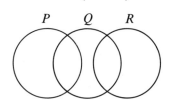

An even simpler diagram just has the *number* of boys entered—but take care to remember that 2, 1 and 3 are not the *members* of sets A and B, but the *number* of members.

a Copy this diagram of sets L and M and complete it using this information.
$$n(L \cap M) = 2 \quad n(L) = 10 \quad n(M) = 6$$
b What is the value of $n(L \cup M)$?

5 Copy this Venn diagram of sets P, Q and R. Complete it using this information.
$$n(P \cap Q) = 3 \quad n(P) = 5$$
$$n(Q \cap R) = 1 \quad n(R) = 4 \quad n(Q) = 7$$
Find the value of
a $n(P \cup Q)$ b $n(Q \cup R)$
c $n(P \cup R)$ d $n(P \cup Q \cup R)$.

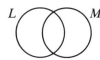

6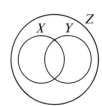

Copy this Venn diagram and complete it using this information.
$$n(X \cap Y) = 5 \quad n(X) = 7 \quad n(Y) = 9 \quad n(Z) = 1$$
Find the values of $n(X \cup Y)$ and $n(X \cup Z)$.

7 Copy this diagram and complete it using the following information.
$$n(A \cap C) = 2 \quad n(C) = 5 \qquad n(A \cap B) = 6$$
$$n(B) = 12 \qquad n(A \cup B) = 17$$
Find the values of $n(A)$ and $n(A \cup C)$.

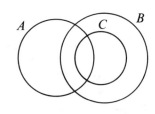

8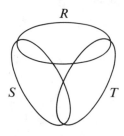

Copy and complete this diagram using th following information.

$n(R \cap S) = 4$	Find the values
$n(R \cap T) = 3$	
$n(S \cap T) = 2$	a $n(S \cup T)$
$n(R) = 10$	b $n(T)$
$n(R \cup S) = 13$	c $n(R \cap S \cap$ ⸍
$n(R \cup T) = 12$	d $n(R \cup S \cup$

9 a Copy this diagram of sets Y and Z.
If $n(Y \cup Z) = 12$ and $n(Y) = 8$ and $n(Z) = 6$, find the value of $n(Y \cap Z)$ and write it in your diagram. Then complete the rest of the diagram.

b Draw a new diagram and repeat with $n(Y \cup Z) = 23$, $n(Y) = 13$ and $n(Z) = 20$.

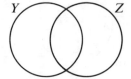

Symbols and diagrams

10 *L* and *M* are two sets where n(*L*) = 12 and n(*M*) = 10.
  a Draw a Venn diagram of *L* and *M* where n(*L* ∩ *M*) = 3.
     Write the value of n(*L* ∪ *M*).
  b Draw a Venn diagram of *L* and *M* where *L* intersects (or overlaps) *M*
     completely, i.e. where *M* ⊂ *L*.
     Write the value of n(*L* ∪ *M*).
  c Draw a Venn diagram of *L* and *M* where *L* and *M* do not intersect
     (or overlap) at all.
     Write the value of n(*L* ∪ *M*).

11 *P* and *Q* are two sets where n(*P*) = 6 and n(*Q*) = 4.
    Draw two Venn diagrams to show *P* and *Q* when their intersection is
  a as large as possible
  b as small as possible.
    In each case, write the value of n(*P* ∪ *Q*).

12 Copy and complete this diagram from the information given.

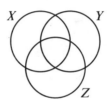

n(*X* ∩ *Y* ∩ *Z*) = 2
n(*X* ∩ *Y*) = 8   n(*X*) = 12
n(*X* ∩ *Z*) = 5   n(*Y*) = 13
n(*Y* ∩ *Z*) = 3   n(*Z*) = 8
Find the value of
  a n(*X* ∪ *Y*)   b n(*Y* ∪ *Z*)
  c n(*X* ∪ *Z*)   d n(*X* ∪ *Y* ∪ *Z*).

Part 8   The Empty set

The Empty set is the set which has NO members.
It can be written as *either* { } *or* ∅.

1 Which of these are Empty sets?
  a {boys who are called Pamela}
  b {living people over 1000 years old}
  c {circles with three corners}
  d {English counties beginning with L}
  e {red daffodils}
  f {rivers on which London stands}
  g {islands which are not surrounded by water}
  h {summer months}
  i {mountains higher than Mount Everest}
  j {days with 24 hours in them}

2 Without drawing any Venn diagrams, find
  a *P* ∩ *Q* when *P* = {1, 4, 7, 9} and *Q* = {1, 4, 5, 6}
  b *E* ∩ *F* when *E* = {a, f, k, t} and *F* = {e, g, m, n}
  c *R* ∩ *S* when *R* = {0, 1, 2, 3} and *S* = {4, 5, 6, 7}
  d *S* ∩ *T* when *S* = {a, b, c, d, e} and *T* = {d, e, f, g, h}
  e *Y* ∩ *Z* when *Y* = {10, 20, 30, 40} and *Z* = {11, 21, 31, 41}
  f *A* ∩ *B* when *A* = {p, q, r, s} and *B* = {w, v, u, t, s}
  g *L* ∩ *M* when *L* = {9, 8, 19, 18} and *M* = {7, 6, 17, 16}.

Symbols and diagrams

3 Describe in words the intersection $A \cap B$ of these pairs of sets.
- a $A = \{\text{people with fair hair}\}$ $B = \{\text{people with blue eyes}\}$
- b $A = \{\text{people with brown eyes}\}$ $B = \{\text{people with blue eyes}\}$
- c $A = \{\text{animals with fur}\}$ $B = \{\text{animals which hunt}\}$
- d $A = \{\text{winter months}\}$ $B = \{\text{summer months}\}$
- e $A = \{\text{4-door cars}\}$ $B = \{\text{left-hand-drive cars}\}$
- f $A = \{\text{4-door cars}\}$ $B = \{\text{2-door cars}\}$
- g $A = \{\text{sports using a ball}\}$ $B = \{\text{sports using a racquet}\}$
- h $A = \{\text{houses with a telephone}\}$ $B = \{\text{houses with a garage}\}$

4 Say whether these statements are *true* or *false*.
- a $M = \{4, 5, 6, 7\}$
- b $N = \{6, 7\}$
- c $L = \{1, 2, 3\}$
- d $L \cap M = \varnothing$
- e $M \cap N = \{6\}$
- f $L \cap N = \varnothing$

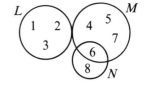

5

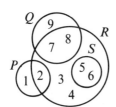

Use this Venn diagram to list the members of these sets.
- a Q
- b R
- c $Q \cap R$
- d $P \cap Q$
- e $P \cap R$
- f $P \cap S$
- g $Q \cap S$
- h $P \cap Q \cap S$

6 Say whether these statements are *true* or *false*.
- a $K \cap N = \varnothing$
- b $L \cap M = \varnothing$
- c $K \cap M = \varnothing$
- d $K \cap L \neq \varnothing$
- e $M \cap N \neq \varnothing$
- f $L \cap N \neq \varnothing$

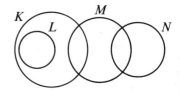

7

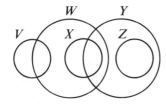

Say whether these statements are *true* or *fals*
- a $X \cap Z = \varnothing$
- b $V \cap X = \varnothing$
- c $V \cap W \neq \varnothing$
- d $V \cap Y \neq \varnothing$
- e $X \cap Y = \varnothing$
- f $Y \cap Z = \varnothing$
- g $W \cap Y \neq \varnothing$
- h $W \cap Z = \varnothing$
- i $W \cap X = \varnothing$

Part 9   The Universal set

1 The Universal set $\mathscr{E}$ is that set which includes all the members of all sets involved
a particular problem.
On a Venn diagram, it is drawn as a *rectangle*, rather than a circle, and all membe
of all sets are thus written inside the rectangle.
Suggest a possible Universal set from which each of these sets could have come
- a {Pekinese, corgi, poodle, collie}
- b {swift, tern, lapwing, warbler}
- c {lemon, grapefruit, orange}
- d {oxygen, hydrogen, argon, xeno
- e {cobra, viper, python}
- f {6, 14, 92, 154, 208}
- g $\{\frac{2}{4}, \frac{3}{6}, \frac{4}{8}, \frac{5}{10}, \frac{6}{12}, \frac{7}{14}\}$
- h {coal, peat, wood, coke}
- i {beret, cap, trilby, Homburg}
- j {biro, quill, pencil, brush}
- k {Wordsworth, Auden, Keats, Shelley}
- l {Jane Austen, Graham Greene DH Lawrence, R L Stephenso

Symbols and diagrams

2 These four Universal sets have several members written inside them.
The members can be divided into various subsets.
List the members of each of these subsets and describe them in words.
For example,
{Ann, Alice, Annabel, Annette, Anita} = {Girls' names with the initial A}.

a	b	c	d
$\mathscr{E}$ Annabel Mark Annette Anita Morris Melvin Alice Ann Michael Matthew	$\mathscr{E}$ ash carrot pine rose bean crocus lupin birch oak turnip pea	$\mathscr{E}$ France Austria Cumbria Greece Devon Scotland Italy Kent Cheshire Yorkshire	$\mathscr{E}$ Thames Ouse Snowdon North Nevis Irish Scafell Severn Baltic Mediterranean

3 Copy this diagram where
$\mathscr{E}$ = {all animals}
F = {farm animals} and
P = {animals beginning with P}.
Write these members in the correct places on your diagram. cow panther pig lion wolf

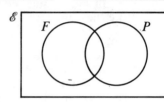

4 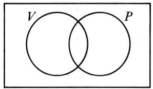 Copy this diagram where
$\mathscr{E}$ = {all things to eat}
V = {vegetables} and
P = {food beginning with P}.
Write these members in their correct places.
beans peas jam plums sugar

5 This Venn diagram has
$\mathscr{E}$ = {names of all living creatures}
R = {names beginning with R}
P = {names of people} and
B = {boys' names}.
Copy the diagram and write these members in their correct places.
Mary Tim Robert Rosemary Fido Rover

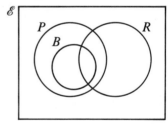

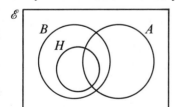 This Venn diagram has
$\mathscr{E}$ = {all sports}
H = {sports needing an implement for hitting}
B = {sports needing a ball} and
A = {sports which use animals}.
Copy the diagram and write these members in their correct places.
tennis rugby athletics show-jumping polo skiing

Copy this diagram and write these members:
buttercup snowdrop daffodil daisy lilac dandelion
given that
$\mathscr{E}$ = {all flowers}
Y = {yellow flowers}
S = {spring flowers} and
D = {flowers with the initial D}.

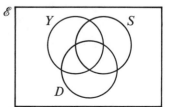

25

Symbols and diagrams

8 This diagram shows these sets:
   $\mathscr{E}$ = {all whole numbers}
   J = {even numbers}
   K = {numbers exactly divisible by 3} and
   L = {numbers exactly divisible by 4}.
   Write these members on your diagram.
   14 9 18 15 8 22 1 23 12 30 7 32

9 Draw your own diagram for these sets, deciding first whether sets R and Y intersect.
   $\mathscr{E}$ = {all colours}　　R = {all kinds of red}　　Y = {all kinds of yellow}
   Write these colours on your diagram.
   crimson daffodil pink blue lemon black

10 Draw your own diagram for the sets $\mathscr{E}$ = {all whole numbers},
   F = {all square numbers} and G = {numbers between 10 and 40}.
   Write these numbers on your diagram.
   9 39 36 1 12 7 81 42

11 Draw a diagram for these sets, taking care to see which sets intersect.
   $\mathscr{E}$ = {all whole numbers}　　G = {numbers greater than 100}
   F = {even numbers}　　　　　　H = {numbers less than 60}
   Write these numbers on your diagram.
   84 3 101 102 56 92 93 77

12 Draw a Venn diagram for $\mathscr{E}$ = {all names of people}
                           P = {names with the initial B}
                           Q = {boys' names with the initial B}.
   Insert these names on your diagram.
   Bill Gary Brenda Mary Bert Beryl Andrew

13

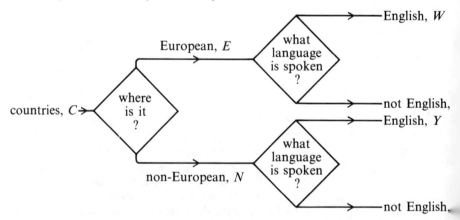

The countries of the world can be divided into groups in many ways.

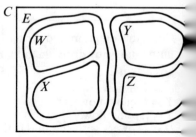

  a Copy this Venn diagram and use the flow diagram to write these six countries in their correct subsets.
     Australia France Scotland China USA Italy

  b Which of the four subsets W, X, Y or Z do you think will have the *largest* number of countries?

Symbols and diagrams

c   Which subset do you think will contain
the *smallest* number of countries?

d   List *all* the members of subset *W*.

14

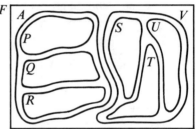

Animal, *A* → where does it live ? → below the surface, *P*

→ at the surface, *Q*

→ above the surface, *R*

forms of life, *F* → which form ?

Vegetable, *V* → where does it live ? → below the surface, *S*

→ at the surface, *T*

→ above the surface, *U*

All forms of life can be classified in many
different ways. This flow diagram shows one
possibility.
Copy the Venn diagram and use the flow
diagram to insert these six life-forms.
fox seagull seaweed mistletoe cabbage
herring

5

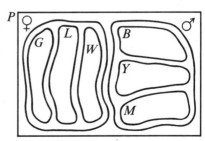

male, ♂ → what age group ? → boys, *B*

→ youths, *Y*

→ men, *M*

people, *P* → male or female ?

female, ♀ → what age group ? → girls, *G*

→ young ladies, *L*

→ women, *W*

This flow diagram divides the universal set of
all people *P* into six subsets.
Copy the Venn diagram and write in the
names of these six people.
George (age 45)   Lorna (age 18)
Kate (age 3)   Andrew (age 19)
Mary (age 52)   Tony (age 4)

27

Symbols and diagrams

Part 10 The complement of a set

1   A' is the set of members **not** included in set A, and is called the **complement** of set A.
On a Venn diagram, the complement of set A is the region
outside A.

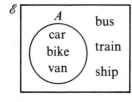

Describe in words the complement A' of set A if

a	$\mathscr{E}$ = {all children}	A = {all boys}
b	$\mathscr{E}$ = {all coins}	A = {all copper coins}
c	$\mathscr{E}$ = {all your toes}	A = {toes on your right foot}
d	$\mathscr{E}$ = {the seasons}	A = {spring, summer}
e	$\mathscr{E}$ = {days of the week}	A = {Monday, Tuesday, Wednesday}
f	$\mathscr{E}$ = {all books}	A = {hardback books}
g	$\mathscr{E}$ = {all whole numbers}	A = {odd numbers}
h	$\mathscr{E}$ = {whole numbers between 1 and 11}	A = {odd numbers}
i	$\mathscr{E}$ = {letters of the alphabet}	A = {consonants}
j	$\mathscr{E}$ = {whole numbers between 0 and 20}	A = {prime numbers}
k	$\mathscr{E}$ = {all roads}	A = {motorways}.

2   Use the Venn diagrams to list the members of these sets.

a	A	b	A'
c	B	d	B'
e	C'	f	D'
g	E'	h	$(D \cup E)'$
i	$(D \cap E)'$	j	H'
k	F'	l	G'
m	$(F \cap G)'$	n	$(F \cup G)'$
o	J'	p	$(I \cup J)'$
q	$(J \cap K)'$	r	$(I \cup J \cup K)'$
s	$(I \cup K)'$	t	$(I \cap K)'$
u	M'	v	$(L \cap N)'$
w	$(L \cap M)'$	x	$(M \cup N)'$
y	$\mathscr{E} \cap M$	z	$(\mathscr{E} \cap M)'$

3   Say whether these statements are *true* or *false*.

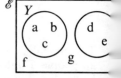

a $Y' = \{d, e, f, g, h\}$ b $Z' = \{f, g, h\}$
c $(Y \cup Z)' = \{f, g, h\}$ d $Y' \cap Z = \{d, e\}$
e $Y \cap Z' = \{a, b, c, f, g, h\}$ f $Y' \cup Z' = \{f, g, h\}$
g $(Y \cap Z)' = \mathscr{E}$ h $Y' \cap Z' = \{f, g, h\}$

4   Say whether these statements are *true* or *false*.

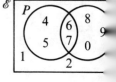

a $P' = \{0, 1, 2, 3, 8, 9\}$ b $Q' = \{1, 2, 3, 4, 5, 6, 7\}$
c $(P \cup Q)' = \{4, 5, 8, 9, 0\}$ d $(P \cap Q)' = \{4, 5, 8, 9, 0\}$
e $P' \cap Q = \{8, 9, 0\}$ f $P \cap Q' = \{4, 5\}$
g $P' \cup Q' = \{1, 2, 3\}$ h $P' \cap Q' = \{1, 2, 3\}$

Symbols and diagrams

5 Write the members of these sets.
  a A' b B'
  c $(A \cup B)'$ d $(A \cap B)'$
  e $A' \cap B$ f $A \cap B'$
  g $A' \cup B'$ h $A' \cap B'$

6 Write the members of these sets.
  a C' b D'
  c $D' \cap C$ d $C' \cup D$
  e $(C \cup D)'$ f $(C \cap D)'$
  g $C' \cup D'$ h $C' \cap D'$

7 Write the members of these sets.
  a M' b N'
  c $(M \cup N)'$ d $(M \cap N)'$
  e $M' \cap N$ f $M \cap N'$
  g $M' \cup N'$ h $M' \cap N'$

8 If $\mathscr{E} = \{$all people$\}$, $G = \{$all girls$\}$ and $B = \{$all boys$\}$,
  describe in words   a G' b B' c $(G \cup B)'$.

9 If $\mathscr{E} = \{$all whole numbers$\}$, $P = \{$even numbers$\}$ and
  $Q = \{$numbers less than 50$\}$,
  describe in words   a P' b Q' c $P' \cap Q$.

0 If $\mathscr{E} = \{$all members of the medical professions$\}$, $X = \{$all doctors$\}$
  and $Y = \{$all dentists$\}$,
  describe in words   a X' b Y' c $(X \cup Y)'$.

Look at the map of Europe in question **18** on page 16.
List all the members of   a $N' \cap C$
                       b $N \cap C'$.
  c Write the names of any two European countries which are members
    of $(N \cup C)'$.

Shading Venn diagrams

Relations between sets can be illustrated on a Venn diagram. Without knowing the individual members of any set, we can represent the set by shading part of the diagram.

Part 1

1 Copy each of these diagrams *twice* and shade in that part of each diagram which indicates the given set.

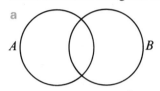
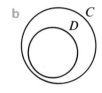
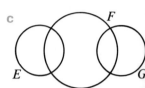

a (i) $A \cap B$
(ii) $A \cup B$

b (i) $C \cap D$
(ii) $C \cup D$

c (i) $E \cup F$
(ii) $F \cap (E \cup G)$

2 Copy this diagram three times.
Shade in these sets.
a $(P \cap R) \cup Q$ b $P \cap R \cap Q$
c $P \cap (Q \cup R)$

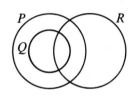

3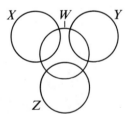

Copy this diagram four times and shade in thes sets.
a $X \cup (Y \cap Z)$ b $(X \cup Y) \cap Z$
c $X \cap Y \cap Z$ d $(X \cap Y) \cup (X \cap Z)$

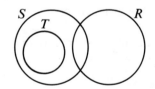

4 Copy this diagram twice.
Shade in these sets.
a $(S \cap R) \cup T$ b $(S \cup R) \cap T$

5

For each set given here, copy the diagram a shade in the required region.
a $X \cup W \cup Z$ b $W \cap (X \cup Y)$
c $X \cup Y \cup Z$ d $W \cap (X \cup Y \cup Z)$

Part 2   Complements of sets

1 For each part, copy this Venn diagram and shade in the required set.
a $(A \cup B)'$ b $(A \cap B)'$
c $A' \cap B$ d $A \cup B'$

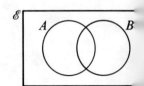

Shading Venn diagrams

2 For each part, copy this Venn diagram and shade
   in the required set.

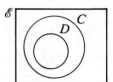

   a $(C \cup D)'$ b $(C \cap D)'$
   c $D' \cap C$ d $C' \cup D$

3

Copy this diagram twice and shade in these sets.
   a $(S \cup R) \cap T'$ b $(T \cup R)' \cap S$

4 Copy this diagram four times and shade in these
   sets.

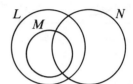

   a $(L \cup N) \cap M'$ b $(M \cup N) \cap L'$
   c $(M \cup N)' \cap L$ d $(M \cap N)' \cap L$

5

Copy this diagram four times and shade in these
sets.
   a $(X \cup Y) \cap Z'$ b $(X \cap Y) \cap Z'$
   c $(X \cup Y)' \cap Z$ d $(X \cap Y)' \cap Z$

6 Copy this diagram four times and shade in these
   sets.

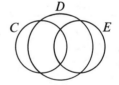

   a $(C \cup E)' \cap D$ b $(C \cup E) \cap D'$
   c $(C \cap E)' \cap D$ d $(C \cup D)' \cap E$

De Morgan's Laws

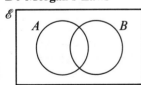

Copy this diagram four times and shade in these
sets.
   a $(A \cap B)'$ b $(A \cup B)'$
   c $A' \cup B'$ d $A' \cap B'$

By looking at your four answers, write two equations connecting them.

rt 3 Applications

For each of these pairs of sets:
   (i) use this simple Venn diagram and label
       the circles
   (ii) shade the required set.

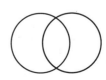

   a $M = \{$all men$\}$
      $S = \{$all people over 60 years old$\}$
      Shade $\{$men under 60 years old$\}$.
   b $F = \{$all flying creatures$\}$ $B = \{$all birds$\}$
      Shade $\{$birds which do *not* fly$\}$.

Shading Venn diagrams

c C = {all cricketers}
   F = {all footballers}   Shade {cricketers who do *not* play football}.

d C = {all cats}
   W = {all wild animals}   Shade {wild cats}.

e P = {all ports}
   T = {all towns on rivers}   Shade {ports on rivers}.

Copy each of the following diagrams and shade the required set.

2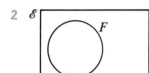

$\mathcal{E}$ = {all children in your school}
F = {all first-year children}

Shade {children *not* in their first year}.

3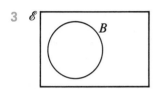

$\mathcal{E}$ = {all colours}
B = {all bright colours}

Shade {dull colours}.

4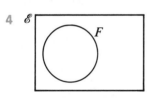

$\mathcal{E}$ = {everyone in the world}
F = {people who speak only French}

Shade {those who speak languages other than French}.

5

W = {wild animals}
D = {dogs}   Shade {working dogs}.
P = {pets}

6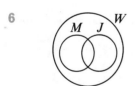

W = {all women}
M = {mothers}   Shade $\left\{\begin{array}{l}\text{jobless women}\\\text{with no children}\end{array}\right\}$.
J = {women with jobs}

7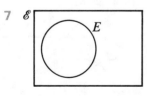

$\mathcal{E}$ = {all whole numbers}
E = {even numbers}   Shade {odd numbers}.

8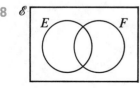

$\mathcal{E}$ = {all whole numbers}
E = {even numbers}   Shade $\left\{\begin{array}{l}\text{odd numbers whic}\\\text{are }not\text{ multiples of}\end{array}\right.$
F = {multiples of 5}

Revision of symbols

The symbols used are summarised in this table.

Symbols	Meanings	Venn diagrams
$\mathscr{E}$	the Universal set	
$A \cup B$	the union of sets A and B	
$A \cap B$	the intersection (or overlap) of sets A and B	
$2 \in A$	2 is a member of set A	
$3 \notin A$	3 is **not** a member of set A	
$B \subset A$	B is a subset of A	
$C \not\subset A$	C is **not** a subset of A	
A'	the complement (or outside) of A	
$n(A)$	the number of members in A	
$\varnothing$ or { }	the Empty set	

Part 1

Write the next three members of these sets.
a $P = \{1, 11, 21, 31, \ldots, \ldots, \ldots\}$
b $Q = \{1, 2, 4, 8, 16, 32, \ldots, \ldots, \ldots\}$
c $R = \{1, 3, 5, 7, 9, \ldots, \ldots, \ldots\}$
d $S = \{a, c, e, g, i, \ldots, \ldots, \ldots\}$
e $T = \{0, -2, -4, -6, \ldots, \ldots, \ldots\}$

Write the number of members in each of these sets.
a   {months in the year after July}
b   {days in the week}
c   {British coins in common usage}
d   {vowels in the English alphabet}
e   {months beginning with J}
f   {even numbers between 5 and 25}

Write the value of n(A) when
a $A = \{$odd numbers between 10 and 24$\}$
b $A = \{$multiples of 3 between 1 and 25$\}$
c $A = \{$months containing the letter R$\}$
d $A = \{$English counties beginning with the letter Z$\}$.

Give a name to each of these sets.
a   {Joan, June, Julie, Jane, Janet, ...}
b   {Shropshire, Somerset, Sussex, ...}
c   {2, 4, 6, 8, 10, ...}
d   {6, 12, 18, 24, 30, ...}
e   {m, n, o, p, q, ..., z}
f   {Austria, France, Denmark, Spain, Norway, ...}
g   {1, 4, 9, 16, 25, 36, 49, ...}

Revision of symbols

5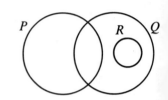

Copy and complete

a a ∈	b d ∈ ...
c j ∈ ...	d f ∉ ...
e h ∉ ...	f i ∈ ...
g c ∉ ...	h L = {...}
i L ∩ M = {...}	j L ∪ M = {...}
k M ∩ N = {...}	l L ∩ M ∩ N = {...}
m n(N) = ...	n n(L ∪ N) = ...
o n(L ∩ N) = ...	p n(L ∪ M ∪ N) = ...

6 Copy and complete this Venn diagram where
$R = \{2, 4, 8\}$
$Q = \{1, 2, 3, 4, 5, 6, 7, 8\}$
$P = \{3, 6, 9, 12\}$.

Complete these statements.

a $P \cap Q = \{...\}$
b $Q \cup R = \{...\}$
c $R \subset ...$
d $P \cap R = ...$

7

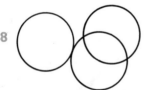

This Venn diagram illustrates the sets
$A = \{y, z\}$
$B = \{v, w, x, y, z\}$
$C = \{\ldots\ v, w, x, y, z\}$.

Copy the diagram, label the circles, and write in all the members of the sets.
Which of these statements are *true* and which are *false*?

a $n(A) = 2$ b $n(C) = 9$
c $A \subset B$ d $A \subset C$
e $y \notin B$ f $w \in C$
g $A \cap B = \{y, z\}$ h $A \cap C = \{y, z\}$

8

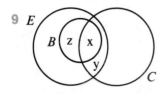

Copy this Venn diagram of the sets
$X = \{1, 3, 5, 7, 9\}$
$Y = \{2, 4, 6, 8, 10\}$
$Z = \{10, 20, 30, 40\}$.

Label the circles and write in all the members of the sets.
Which of these statements are *true* and which are *false*?

a $Y \cap Z = \{10\}$ b $X \cup Y = \{$all whole numbers from 1 to 10$\}$
c $2 \in X$ d $10 \notin Z$
e $X \cap Y = \varnothing$ f $Y \cap Z \neq \varnothing$
g $n(X \cap Z) = 0$ h $n(Y \cup Z) = 9$

9

$C = \{$all capital cities$\}$
$E = \{$European cities$\}$
$B = \{$British cities$\}$
The three letters x, y, z stand for the three cities,
London, York, Paris.
Which letter stands for which city?

10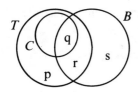

$T = \{$all trees$\}$
$C = \{$all conifers$\}$
$B = \{$British flowers and trees$\}$
The letters p, q, r, s stand for oak, teak, fir, bluebell.
Which letter stands for which tree or flower?

11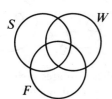

$F = \{$spring flowers$\}$
$W = \{$white flowers$\}$
$S = \{$flowers with names beginning with S$\}$
Copy this Venn diagram and write in these names.
daffodil snowdrop daisy sunflower

2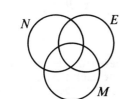

$N = \{$whole numbers from 1 to 10$\}$
$E = \{$even numbers$\}$
$M = \{$multiples of 3$\}$
Copy this Venn diagram and write in these numbers.
7 15 4 20 6 30

3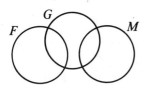

$F = \{$flowers$\}$
$G = \{$girls' names$\}$
$M = \{$months$\}$
Copy this Venn diagram and write in these names.
June Lucy Rose March Crocus

This Venn diagram represents these three sets:
$\{$first-year pupils$\}$
$\{$junior pupils$\}$
$\{$all pupils in the school$\}$.
Match the letters X, Y and Z with the three sets.

This Venn diagram represents these three sets:
$\{$all dogs$\}$
$\{$all cats$\}$
$\{$all collies$\}$.
Match the letters R, S and T with the three sets.

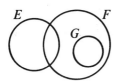

The three sets $\{$all yellow objects$\}$
$\{$all daffodils$\}$
$\{$all butterflies$\}$
are represented on this diagram.
a Match the letters E, F and G with the sets.
b Copy the diagram and shade that part which represents $\{$butterflies which are not yellow$\}$.

35

Revision of symbols

17 Copy each diagram and shade that part of the diagram which illustrates the given set.

a $A \cup B$ b $C \cap D$ c $E \cap F$
d $G \cup H$ e $L \cap M \cap N$ f $P \cap Q \cap R$

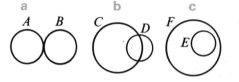

18

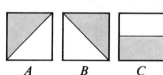

The shaded parts of these squares give the sets of points A, B and C inside each square.
Draw six squares and shade these sets of points.

a $A \cap B$ b $A \cup B$
c $A \cap C$ d $A \cup C$
e $(A \cup B) \cap C$ f $A \cap B \cap C$

19

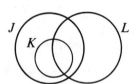

X   Y   Z

The shaded parts of these triangles give the sets of points X, Y and Z inside each triangle.
Draw six triangles and shade these sets of points

a $X \cap Y$ b $X \cup Y$ c $X \cap Z$ d $X \cup Z$
e $X \cap Y \cap Z$ f $X \cup Y \cup Z$

Part 2

1 Copy this Venn diagram and write in the members of these sets.
$L = \{3, 6, 9, 12, 15, 30\}$
$M = \{2, 4, 6, 8, 10, 12, 30\}$
$N = \{5, 10, 15, 25, 30\}$

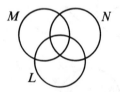

2

Copy this Venn diagram and write in the members of these sets.
$J = \{2, 4, 6, 8, 12\}$
$K = \{2, 4\}$
$L = \{2, 8, 16, 32\}$

Say whether these statements are *true* or *false*.
a $4 \in K$ b $8 \notin J$ c $K \cap L = \{4, 8\}$
d $K \cap J = \{2, 4\}$ e $n(K \cup L) = 5$ f $n(J \cap L) = 1$

3 Design a Venn diagram to illustrate these sets. Write in all the members on your diagram.
$A = \{1, 2, 3, 4, 5, 6\}$ $B = \{2, 4, 6, 8, 10\}$
Copy and complete.   a $A \cap B = \{...\}$ b $5 \in ...$ c $8 \notin ...$
                       d $n(A) = ...$ e $n(A \cup B) = ...$

4 Design a Venn diagram for these sets. Write in all the members on your diagram.
$P = \{2, 4, 6, 8, 18\}$
$Q = \{3, 6, 9, 12, 15, 24\}$
$R = \{12, 24\}$

Revision of symbols

Copy and complete.

a $P \cap Q = \ldots$ b $P \cap R = \ldots$ c $P \cup R = \ldots$ d $n(Q) = \ldots$

e $n(Q \cap R) = \ldots$ f $15 \in \ldots$ g $24 \notin \ldots$ h $R \subset \ldots$

5   Design a Venn diagram for these sets and write in all the members on your diagram.

$X = \{6, 7, 8\}$

$Y = \{1, 2, 3, 4, 6, 8\}$

$Z = \{1, 3, 5, 9\}$

Say whether these statements are *true* or *false*.

a $X \cap Y = \{6, 8\}$ b $X \cap Z = \varnothing$ c $n(Z) = 4$

d $n(X \cup Y) = 5$ e $n(Y \cup Z) = 10$ f $6 \in X$

g $3 \notin Z$ h $\{1, 3\} \subset Z$

6   Design a Venn diagram for these sets and write in all the members on your diagram.

$L = \{a, e, i\}$

$M = \{a, b, c, d\}$

$N = \{a, b, c, d, e, f, g, h, i\}$

Say whether these statements are *true* or *false*.

a $L \cap M = \{a\}$ b $n(L \cup M) = 7$ c $e \in L$

d $i \notin M$ e $L \subset N$ f $M \not\subset N$

g $n(L \cap N) = 2$ h $L \cap N = \{a\}$

7   $Y = \{5, 10, 15, 20, 25, 30\}$ $Z = \{10, 20, 30\}$

Without drawing a Venn diagram say whether these statements are *true* or *false*.

a $Y \cap Z = \{10, 20, 30\}$ b $n(Y \cup Z) = 9$ c $20 \in Y \cap Z$

d $Z \subset Y$ e $Y \subset Z$

8   $P = \{1, 2, 3, 4, 5\}$ $Q = \{2, 4, 6, 8, 10\}$

Without drawing a Venn diagram, copy and complete.

a $P \cap Q = \{\ldots\}$ b $P \cup Q = \{\ldots\}$

c $n(P \cup Q) = \ldots$ d $n(P \cap Q) = \ldots$

$A = \{p, q, r, s\}$ $B = \{t, u, v, w\}$ $C = \{r, s, t, u, v\}$

Without drawing a Venn diagram, copy and complete.

a $A \cap C = \ldots$ b $B \cap C = \ldots$

c $A \cap B = \ldots$ d $A \cup B = \ldots$

e $B \cup C = \ldots$ f $n(A \cup C) = \ldots$

g $n(A \cap B) = \ldots$

$E = \{\text{all even numbers}\}$ $F = \{\text{whole numbers from 11 to 21}\}$

a   Write the members of $E \cap F$.   b   Write the value of $n(E \cap F)$.

$Y = \{\text{multiples of 5 less than 31}\}$ $Z = \{\text{multiples of 3 less than 31}\}$

Write the members of   a Y b Z

                      c $Y \cap Z$ d $Y \cup Z$.

Write the values of   e $n(Y \cap Z)$ f $n(Y \cup Z)$.

$W = \{\text{multiples of 3 less than 37}\}$ $X = \{\text{multiples of 4 less than 37}\}$

Write the members of   a W b X

                      c $W \cap X$ d $W \cup X$.

Write the values of   e $n(W \cap X)$ f $n(W \cup X)$.

Revision of symbols

13 A = {odd numbers less than 24} B = {multiples of 3} C = {multiples of 5}
Write the members of   a $A \cap B$ b $A \cap C$ c $A \cap B \cap C$.
Write the values of   d $n(A \cap B)$ e $n(A \cap C)$ f $n(A \cap B \cap C)$.

14 Design a Venn diagram for these sets.
C = {all coins} P = {all pennies} M = {all money}
Shade that part of the diagram which represents {notes}.

15 Design a diagram for these sets.
B = {all blue objects}
F = {all flowers}
S = {all snowdrops}
Shade that part of your diagram which represents
{flowers which are not blue}.

16 Design a Venn diagram for these sets.
W = {all countries in the world}
C = {all Commonwealth countries}
A = {all Asian countries}
Write these members on your diagram.
Canada China France India

17 $\mathscr{E}$ = {months of the year} T = {months of 31 days}
R = {months named after a Roman emperor} J = {months with the initial J}
Say whether these statements are *true* or *false*.
a $n(J) = 2$ b $n(R) = 2$
c $n(R') = 10$ d $R \subset T$
e $J \subset T$ f T' = {April, September, November}
g $R \cap J$ = {July}   h $T \cup J = \mathscr{E}$

18 You may wish to draw diagrams to help you solve these problems.
a If $n(A) = 6$, $n(B) = 10$ and $n(A \cup B) = 12$, find $n(A \cap B)$.
b If $n(C) = 8$, $n(D) = 15$ and $n(C \cup D) = 20$, find $n(C \cap D)$.
c If $n(E) = 7$, $n(F) = 9$ and $n(E \cap F) = 3$, find $n(E \cup F)$.
d If $n(G) = 5$, $n(H) = 8$ and $n(G \cap H) = 4$, find $n(G \cup H)$.
e If $n(I) = 3$, $n(J) = 7$, and $n(I \cap J) = 3$, find $n(I \cup J)$.

19 Simplify
a $A \cap A$ b $A \cup A$ c $A \cup \varnothing$ d $A \cap \varnothing$.

20 Draw a Venn diagram to illustrate each of these statements.
a $A \subset B$ b $C \cap D = \varnothing$
c $E \cap F = F$ d $G \cup H = H$
e $I \cap J \neq \varnothing$ f $n(K) + n(L) = n(K \cup L)$
g $n(M \cap N) = n(M)$

21 Draw *one* Venn diagram to satisfy all this information.
$A \subset B$ $A \cap C = \varnothing$ $C \not\subset B$

22 Draw *one* Venn diagram to satisfy this information.
$P \cap Q \neq \varnothing$ $P \cup Q \subset R$

23 Draw *one* Venn diagram to satisfy this information.
$n(X \cap Y) = 0$ $n(X \cap Z) \neq 0$ $n(Y \cap Z) \neq 0$

Revision of symbols

Part 3 Involving complements

1 If $\mathscr{E}$ = {all children} and L = {left-handed children}, describe in words the set L'.

2 If $\mathscr{E}$ = {all photographs} and N = {black and white photographs}, describe in words the set N'.

3 If $\mathscr{E}$ = {whole numbers} and P = {even numbers}, describe in words the set P'.

4 If $\mathscr{E}$ = {all British coins} and R = {copper coins}, describe in words the set R'.

5 If $\mathscr{E}$ = {days of the week} and M = {days beginning with T or S}, list the members of the set M'.

6 If $\mathscr{E}$ = {whole numbers from 1 to 10} and Q = {multiples of 3}, list the members of the set Q'.

7 Describe in words the universal set $\mathscr{E}$ for each set A and its complement A'.
a A = {left-handed children}
A' = {right-handed children}
b A = {the land areas of the world}
A' = {areas of the world covered by sea}
c A = {even numbers between 1 and 101}
A' = {odd numbers between 0 and 100}
d A = {the northern hemisphere}
A' = {the southern hemisphere}
e A = {Eastern Europe}
A' = {Western Europe}
f A = {candidates who pass an exam}
A' = {candidates who fail an exam}

8 If A = {0, 4, 8, 12, 16} and A' = {5, 10, 15}, list the members of $\mathscr{E}$ in order.

9 If P = {3, 6, 9, 12, 15, 18} and P' = {0, 7, 14, 21}, list the members of $\mathscr{E}$ in order.

10 Copy and complete.

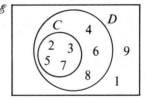

a $4 \in \ldots$
b $6 \notin \ldots$
c $C \subset \ldots$
d $C \cap D = \{\ldots\}$
e $n(C \cap D) = \ldots$
f $D' = \{\ldots\}$
g $n(D') = \ldots$
h $C' = \{\ldots\}$
i $C' \cap D = \{\ldots\}$
j $n(C' \cap D) = \ldots$

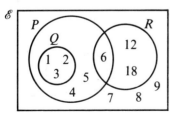

Say whether these statements are *true* or *false*.
a $5 \in P$
b $6 \notin R$
c $Q \subset P$
d $P \cap R = \{4, 5, 6\}$
e $Q \cap R = \emptyset$
f $P' = \{7, 8, 9, 12, 18\}$
g $R' = \{4, 5, 7, 8, 9\}$
h $(P \cup R)' = \{7, 8, 9\}$
i $n(P \cap R)' = 7$
j $n(Q \cup R) = 5$
k $n(Q \cup R)' = 5$

For each part, copy the diagram and shade the given set.

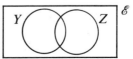

a $Y \cap Z$
b $(Y \cap Z)'$
c $Y \cup Z$
d $(Y \cup Z)'$
e $Y' \cap Z$
f $Y \cap Z'$

Revision of symbols

13 For each part, copy the diagram and shade the given set.

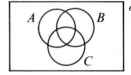

    a Q' b P' c $P \cap Q$
    d $P' \cap Q$ e $P \cap Q'$

14 For each part, copy the diagram and shade the given set.

    a $(A \cup B) \cap C$ b $(A \cup B) \cap C'$
    c $(A \cup B) \cup C'$ d $(A \cap B) \cup C$
    e $(A \cup B \cup C)'$ f $A' \cap (B \cup C)$

15 $\mathscr{E} = \{a, b, c, d, e, f, g, h, i\}$
   $A = \{a, e, i\}$
   $B = \{$the letters of the word "beach"$\}$
   List the members of these sets without drawing any diagram.
    a A' b B' c $A \cup B$
    d $(A \cup B)'$ e $A \cap B$ f $(A \cap B)'$

16 $\mathscr{E} = \{$the first ten letters of the alphabet$\}$
   $M = \{$vowels$\}$
   $N = \{$the letters of the word "cabbage"$\}$
   List the members of these sets without drawing any diagram.
    a M' b N' c $M \cup N$
    d $(M \cup N)'$ e $M \cap N$ f $(M \cap N)'$

17 $\mathscr{E} = \{$all points inside an equilateral triangle$\}$ and sets A and B are given by these shaded regions.

   Draw diagrams to show these sets.
    a A' b B' c $A' \cap B$ d $A' \cup B$
    e $A \cap B'$ f $A \cup B'$ g $A' \cap B'$ h $(A \cup B)'$
   What conclusion do you draw from your answers to **g** and **h**?

18 $\mathscr{E} = \{$all points inside a square$\}$ and sets P and Q are given by these shaded regions.

   Draw diagrams to illustrate these sets.
    a P' b Q' c $P' \cap Q$ d $P' \cup Q$
    e $P \cap Q'$ f $P \cup Q'$ g $P' \cap Q'$ h $(P \cup Q)'$

19 Match these six sets with the shading in the six diagrams **a** to **f**.
    $A \cap B$ $A' \cap B$ $A \cap B'$ $(A \cap B)'$ $A \cup B$ $(A \cup B)'$

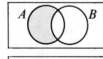

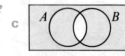

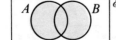
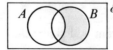

Classification

1

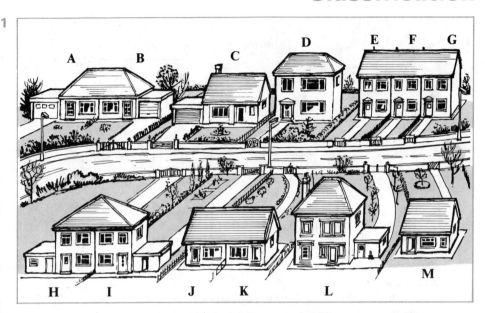

This picture shows a street in which there are many different types of houses, labelled **A** to **M**, which can be classified into different sets.
List the members of these sets.

a {detached dwellings}
b {semi-detached dwellings}
c {detached bungalows}
d {semi-detached bungalows}
e {dwellings with garages}
f {bungalows with garages}
g {detached bungalows with garages}
h {terraced houses}
i {terraced houses with garages}

2 Here are the flags of several countries. ("Blue" is shown in *heavy* colour; "red" in *light* colour; "white" without colour.)
List the members of these sets.

a $C = $ {flags with crosses}   b $H = $ {flags with horizontal stripes}
c $V = $ {flags with vertical stripes}   d $R = $ {flags with some red in them}
e $B = $ {flags with some blue in them}   f $C \cap R$ g $C \cap B$
h $R \cap B$ i $H \cap R$ j $V \cap R$ k $H \cap B$ l $V \cap B$
m $C \cap R \cap B$ n $H \cap R \cap B$ o $V \cap R \cap B$

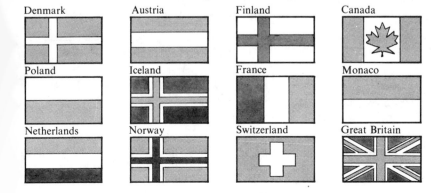

41

Classification

3

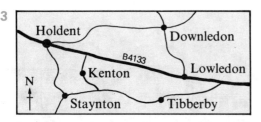

0   miles   5

This map shows six villages which have the amenities and populations given in this table.

Village	Population	Churches	Primary schools	Secondary schools	Garages	Post offices	Food shops
Downledon	320	1	1	0	0	0	1
Holdent	3640	4	2	1	4	1	12
Kenton	34	0	0	0	0	0	0
Lowledon	57	1	0	0	1	0	0
Staynton	152	1	0	0	0	0	1
Tibberby	1240	2	1	0	1	1	2

Answer these questions.

a Which village has the largest population?

b Which is the only village without a church?

c A family with children of primary and secondary school age move into the area. If the children are to walk to school, in which village must they live?

d Mr & Mrs Bond have a daughter who walks to primary school. List the villages in which they might live.

e Which village is approximately ten times bigger than Kenton?

f Which village is approximately a hundred times bigger than Kenton?

g Which village *not* on the main road B4133, has the largest population?

h Mr Pitt lives in a village which has no school and no garage, but it does have a church. Where does he live?

i Mrs Marchand wants to buy a house in a village which has a church, a post office and a food shop. Where should she look?

j Mr & Mrs Elton live in a village which has a church and a primary school and lies to the south of the B4133. Where do they live?

List the members of these sets.

k {villages with a population less than 500}

l {villages with a primary but no secondary school}

m {villages with both a garage and a post office}

n {villages with a church but no primary school}

Copy and complete these Venn diagrams by writing in the six village names.

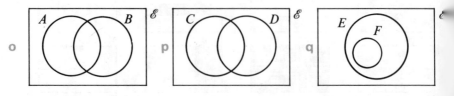

ℰ = {villages on the map}
A = {villages with a garage}
C = {villages on the B4133}
E = {villages with a primary school}

B = {villages with a primary school}
D = {villages with a food shop}
F = {villages with a post office}

Classification

4 The towns of Dinchurch, Overton and
   Netherby are shown on this map which also
   shows wooded areas and land more than
   200 metres above sea-level. The various
   regions are labelled A to L.
   List the lettered regions which indicate

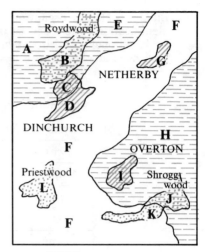

a the built-up areas
b the woodlands
c woodlands over 200 m
d woodlands which border on a built-up
   area
e built-up areas under 200 m.

   Give the name of:

f the town which is partly above and
   partly below the 200 m contour
g the woodland which crosses the 200 m
   contour
h the woodland which is totally above the
   200 m contour
i the town which lies above the 200 m
   contour.

Key: ▭ Land over 200 m
      ▨ Built-up areas
      ▦ Woodland

List the lettered regions which are members of these sets.

j {all regions over 200 m}
k {all regions under 200 m}
l {regions under 200 m} ∩ {built-up areas}
m {regions under 200 m} ∩ {woodlands}
n {woodlands} ∩ {built-up areas}

5 This diagram shows an area of the
   Pennines in northern England where fields
   are separated by dry-stone walls. The
   railway runs along the edge of the flat river
   valley, separating lowland fields on one side
   from highland fields on the other side.
   These fields have sheep or cattle in them, or
   are empty.

   How many lowland fields contain

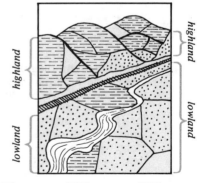

a sheep   b cattle   c no stock at all?

   How many highland fields contain

d sheep   e cattle   f no stock at all?

Key: ▭ sheep   ▦ cattle   ▭ empty

g Copy this Venn diagram
   where ℰ = {all fields}
         H = {highland fields}
   and   L = {lowland fields}.
   Enter your answers for **a** to **f** on the
   diagram.
h Can you make any deduction about
   where farmers tend to keep sheep and
   where they tend to keep cattle?

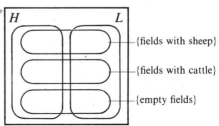

Classification

6 Biologists classify organisms to produce order out of chaos and make
identification easier. The set of organisms which have a vertebral column
(or backbone) is called **vertebrata**. It is divided into subsets, called **classes**, which
have been labelled A to F in this table.

Vertebrata

	Scientific name	Common name
A	Cyclostomata	Jawless fish
B	Pisces	True fish
C	Amphibia	Amphibians
D	Reptilia	Reptiles
E	Aves	Birds
F	Mammalia	Mammals
	X Monotremes	Egg-laying
	Y Marsupials	Having a pouch
	Z Eutherians	Having a placenta

Say whether these statements are *true* or *false*.
a cod $\in B$ b crocodile $\in D$ c gull $\in E$
d bat $\in E$ e beetle $\in D$ f snake $\in D$
g dog $\in F$ h ostrich $\in E$ i whale $\in B$
j dinosaur $\in D$ k whale $\in F$ l frog $\in C$
Copy and complete these statements.
m shark $\in$ ...   n sparrow $\in$ ...   o pike $\in$ ...
p lion $\in$ ...   q trout $\in$ ...   r monkey $\in$ ...
s lizard $\in$ ...   t squirrel $\in$ ...   u duck $\in$ ...
v koala bear $\in$ ...   w turtle $\in$ ...   x ape $\in$ ...
y newt $\in$ ...
z Copy this Venn diagram which shows the six
classes and note that the class **mammalia** is
subdivided into three subsets X, Y and Z.
Write these names on your diagram.
toad   haddock
wren   tortoise
kangaroo   platypus
man   lamprey

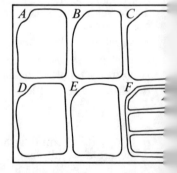

7 This diagram shows a calendar for events in the history of the earth which is
called a *geological time scale*. Rocks and their fossils can be dated because ar
radioactivity in them decays with time, so that older rocks have less
radioactivity in them than younger rocks. Studying the fossils from different
has made it possible to follow the evolution of plants and animals over millic
of years.

Classification

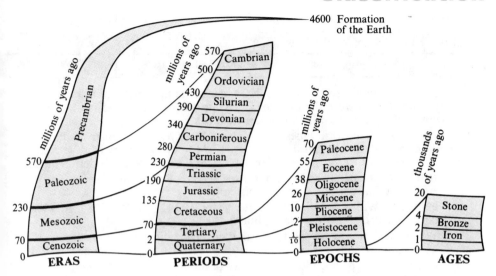

a   Radioactive materials in meteorites and rocks from the moon suggest a date for the formation of the Earth. How many years ago was this?

b   The first 85% of the history of the Earth produced no abundant fossils. What name is given to this **era**?

c   **Paleozoic** means "ancient life", **Mesozoic** means "middle life" and **Cenozoic** means "modern life". How long did each of these **eras** last?

d   Into how many subsets or periods is the **Paleozoic era** divided?

e   Primitive fish with backbones first appeared in the **Ordovician period**. How long did this **period** last?

f   Plants and primitive animals first invaded land from the sea about 420 million years ago. During what period was this?

g   The first trees and amphibians appeared about 380 million years ago. During what **period** was this?

h   Reptiles displaced amphibians as the dominant group during the **Permian period**. How many years did this period last?

i   Into how many subsets or **periods** is the **Mesozoic era** divided?

j   Dinosaurs first appeared at the start of the **Triassic period** and dominated the earth until they disappeared mysteriously at the end of the **Cretaceous period**. What name is given to this **era** and how long did it last?

k   Primitive mammals first appeared about 180 million years ago. During what **period** was this?

l   Modern types of mammals began to appear about 70 million years ago. What **era** started at this time and how many periods is it divided into?

m   The first monkeys appeared about 35 million years ago. In which **epoch** was this?

n   The mammoth became extinct and early man (hominids) began to dominate the earth at the start of the **Quaternary period**. How long ago was this, and what is the name of the **epoch** which started this **period**?

o   Four ice ages occurred in the **epoch** which started 2 million years ago. What is the name of this **epoch**? (The last of these ice ages is still receding today.)

p   Modern man (homo sapiens) first began to appear about 20 000 years ago. What was the first material from which he made his tools?

q   If modern man (homo sapiens) has been on the earth 20 000 years, use a calculator to express this time as a percentage of the age of the earth.

45

Classification

8

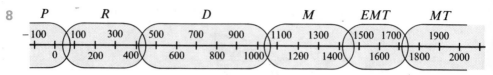

This number ladder from − 100 to 2000 represents the period of time in British history from just before the birth of Christ up to the present. Historians group years together into sets which overlap each other.

P = {years in Prehistoric times} R = {years of Roman Britain}
D = {years of the Dark Ages} M = {years of the Middle Ages}
EMT = {years in Early Modern Times} MT = {years in Modern Times}

a Before the Romans arrived, no written records were kept of events in Britain. What period of time is this called?

b Hadrian's Wall was built during the years AD 122 to AD128. In what period of British history was it built?

c When the Romans started to leave, their civilization in Britain began to fall apart. A new and very different age dawned. What was its name?

d About what time did the Roman way of life in Britain disappear?

e In the middle of the Dark Ages, Anglo-Saxon England was Europe's major artistic workshop producing many beautiful objects, women had civil rights never again held in England until very recently and Christian missionaries were sent to a heathen Europe. In what years, approximately, did all this occur?

f The greatest king of all England, Denmark and Norway was King Knut (or Canute) who was alive about 1000 years ago. Towards the end of what age did he live?

g One of the main events which heralded a new age was King Harold's defeat at Hastings in AD 1066 after his march from victory over the Scandinavians in Yorkshire. What name do we give to this new age?

h The feudal system imposed in England by the Normans began to give way to central government by strong kings in the 1400's. During what age did this feudal system operate?

i Sir Francis Drake continued to play bowls on Plymouth Hoe in 1588 as the Spanish Armada approached. In what age did this occur?

j The rise of parliamentary government in the late 1600's and the dawn of the Industrial Revolution in the early 1700's heralded a new age. What is its name?

k In 1945 atomic bombs were dropped on the Japanese cities of Hiroshima and Nagasaki and hundreds of thousands of people were killed. In what age did this occur?

9

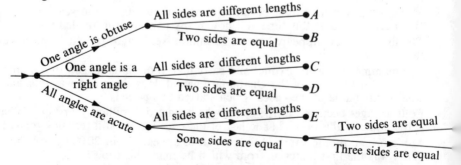

This tree diagram can be used to classify triangles by looking firstly at their angles and then at their sides. There are seven categories labelled A to G.

Classification

a A **scalene** triangle has all its sides of different lengths. Which *three* of these seven categories give scalene triangles?

b An **isosceles** triangle has at least two of its sides equal in length. Which *four* of these categories give isosceles triangles?

c An **equilateral** triangle has all three sides of equal length. Which *one* category gives these triangles?

d Which category gives right-angled isosceles triangles?

e Which category gives obtuse-angled isosceles triangles?

f Here are seven triangles. Name the correct category for each one.

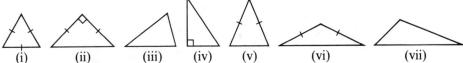

(i)   (ii)   (iii)   (iv)   (v)   (vi)   (vii)

g This Venn diagram shows
$\mathscr{E} = \{$all triangles$\}$
divided vertically according to the angles of the triangle and horizontally according to its sides. Note that equilateral triangles form a subset of isosceles triangles, giving a total of **nine** subsets.

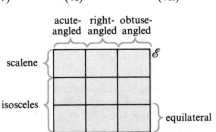

Copy the diagram, draw the seven triangles of part **f** in their correct subsets and write the letter of their category from the tree diagram. What can you say about the two remaining subsets on your diagram?

h

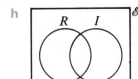

$\mathscr{E}$ Copy this Venn diagram where
$\mathscr{E} = \{$all triangles$\}$,
$R = \{$right-angled triangles$\}$
and $I = \{$isosceles triangles$\}$.
Write the letters **C, D, E, F**
to represent these four triangles in their correct positions.

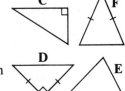

i This Venn diagram shows
$\mathscr{E} = \{$all triangles$\}$,
$I = \{$isosceles triangles$\}$
$E = \{$equilateral triangles$\}$ and
$O = \{$obtuse-angled triangles$\}$.
Draw five triangles to illustrate
the regions v, w, x, y and z.

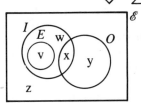

0 Quadrilaterals can be grouped into overlapping sets.
Consider $P = \{$parallelograms$\}$, $R = \{$rectangles$\}$,
        $Rh = \{$rhombi$\}$, $K = \{$kites$\}$
    and $S = \{$squares$\}$.
Copy each of these Venn diagrams and draw the given quadrilaterals on *your* diagram in their correct places.

a
Draw

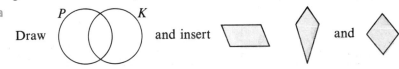

and insert   and

47

Classification

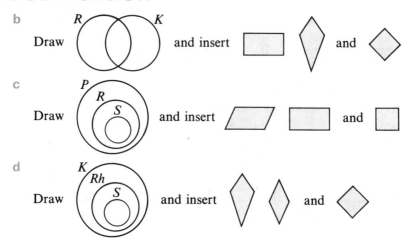

b Draw [R K diagram] and insert ▭ ◇ and ◈

c Draw [P R S diagram] and insert ▱ ▭ and ▢

d Draw [K Rh S diagram] and insert ◇ ◇ and ◈

Are these statements *true* or *false*?

e $P \cap K = Rh$ f $R \cap K = S$ g $S \subset R$

h $P \subset R$ i $Rh \subset K$ j $Rh \subset S$

k The above information can all be shown on one Venn diagram, where $\mathscr{E} = \{\text{all parallelograms}\}$.

Match the letters u to z on the diagram with these shapes numbered from 1 to 6.

  1   2   3   4   5   6

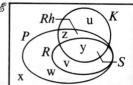

11 a Copy this number square showing the set of integers from 1 to 100.
Shade the set $M_2 = \{\text{multiples of 2}\}$.
Use a second colour to shade the set $M_3 = \{\text{multiples of 3}\}$.
List the members of $M_2 \cap M_3$ and describe them in words.

1	2	3	4	5	6	7	8	9	10
11	12	13	14	15	16	17	18	19	20
21	22	23	24	25	26	27	28	29	30
31	32	33	34	35	36	37	38	39	40
41	42	43	44	45	46	47	48	49	50
51	52	53	54	55	56	57	58	59	60
61	62	63	64	65	66	67	68	69	70
71	72	73	74	75	76	77	78	79	80
81	82	83	84	85	86	87	88	89	90
91	92	93	94	95	96	97	98	99	100

b On another number square, shade the sets M_4 and M_5 in different colours.
List the members of $M_4 \cap M_5$ and describe them in words.

c On another number square, shade M_2 and M_9 in different colours.
List the members of $M_2 \cap M_9$ and describe them in words.

d Without drawing any other diagrams, list the members of
(i) $M_2 \cap M_5$ (ii) $M_5 \cap M_6$ (iii) $M_3 \cap M_{10}$.

e If $\mathscr{E} = \{\text{integers from 1 to 20}\}$, copy these three Venn diagrams and write in all the members of the sets in their correct positions.

(i) 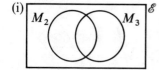   (ii) 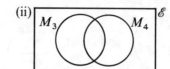   (iii)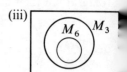

Classification

f Copy this Venn diagram and insert these numbers.
4 5 6 7 10 12 15 20 30 36 60 62

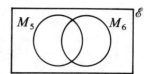

g

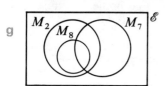

Copy this Venn diagram and insert these numbers.
2 3 4 5 7 8 10 14 16 40 49 50 56

h Copy this Venn diagram and insert these numbers.
1 2 3 4 5 6 7 8 9 10 15 20 25 30

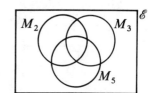

2 This Venn diagram can be used to divide $\mathscr{E}$ = {all numbers} into various subsets.
Numbers greater than 0 are positive, those less than 0 are negative, but 0 itself is neither positive nor negative.
Rational numbers are those which can be written as a ratio or fraction.
Irrational numbers cannot be written as a ratio or fraction.
On the diagram
I = {integers or whole numbers}
and Z = {zero}.

positive numbers   negative numbers

rational numbers

irrational numbers

a Copy this diagram and write these numbers in their correct places.

$$2\tfrac{1}{2} \quad 2 \quad -3 \quad -\tfrac{1}{4} \quad 0 \quad \sqrt{3} \quad -\pi \quad -\sqrt{5} \quad 0.5 \quad 1 \quad -6 \quad \frac{\pi}{2}$$

b If R = {rational numbers}, describe the set R' in words.
c If I = {integers}, describe the set I' in words.
d If P = {positive numbers}, N = {negative numbers} and Z = {zero}, describe the set $P \cup N \cup Z$.

Say whether these statements are *true* or *false*.

e $6 \in R$ 　　 f $6 \in P$ 　　 g $6 \in I$ 　　 h $-5 \in R$
i $-5 \in P$ 　 j $-5 \in I$ 　 k $\tfrac{2}{3} \in R$ 　 l $\tfrac{2}{3} \in N$
m $\tfrac{2}{3} \in I$ 　 n $0 \in P$ 　　 o $0 \in R$ 　　 p $\pi \in R$
q $\pi \in R'$ 　 r $\pi \in P$ 　　 s $\sqrt{2} \in R$ 　 t $\sqrt{3} \in I$

Some computers can be fed information on cards punched with holes, but you do not need a computer to use this idea to classify and sort information.
Each member of your class needs a piece of card with ten holes 2 cm apart and 1 cm from an edge as shown on this diagram.

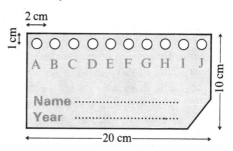

Classification

Write your name and year, and then answer these ten question A to J which match the ten holes on your card.
If you answer a question **no**, then you leave the hole alone.
If you answer a question **yes**, then you make the hole into a slit.

A Are you a girl?
B Do you have any brothers at school?
C Do you have any sisters at school?
D Do you eat school lunch?
E Do you bring sandwiches for lunch?
F Do you go home for lunch?
G Do you walk all the way to school?
H Do you travel by car to school?
I Do you travel by bus to school?
J Do you cycle to school?

Your card might look like one of these.
Write a few sentences to describe these four pupils.

a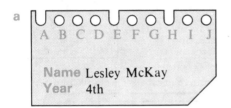

b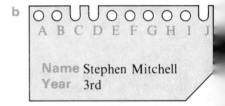

c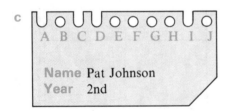

d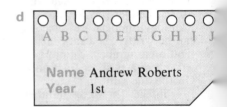

Collect all the cards of the class into one pile with them all facing the same way.
Take a knitting needle and push it through one set of holes to extract the set of pupils who answered **no** to that particular question.
Do this to find these sets of pupils in your class.

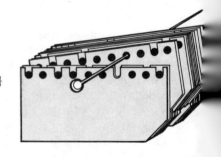

e {those who have brothers in the school}
f {those who take a school lunch}
g {those who go home for lunch}
h {those who cycle to school}
i {all the girls in the class}
j {all the boys in the class}

You will need to use the needle more than once to find these sets of pupils.

k {the girls who have sisters in the school}
l {those who walk to school and also go home for lunch}
m {those who come by car and also go home for lunch}
n {the boys who bring their own sandwiches for lunch}
o {the boys who cycle to school and go home for lunch}
p {the girls who travel by bus and have brothers at school}
q {those who have *either* brothers *or* sisters at school}
r {those who have *both* brothers *and* sisters at school}

50

Problems using sets

Part 1   Problems with two sets

Draw a Venn diagram of two overlapping circles, as shown here, to help you solve each of these problems.

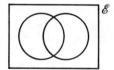

1   In a class of pupils, 9 take both French and biology; 6 take French but not biology; 8 take biology but not French and 5 take neither of these subjects. How many pupils are in the class?

2   Not all the supermarkets in a town sell wine, but 6 of them sell both red and white wine. Two sell only red wine and three sell only white wine. If four supermarkets sell no wine at all, find the number of supermarkets in the town.

3   On a small estate there are 22 houses which do not have a car. Five houses have both a British and a foreign car; 17 houses have just a British car; and 14 have just a foreign car. Find how many houses are on the estate.

4   In a group of schoolfriends, 12 like both homework and television but 3 like neither of these. Eight like television but not homework, and one likes homework but not television. How many friends are in the group?

5   Twelve boys travel on the same bus to school. Three of them support both Rovers and City; four support just Rovers; and two support just City. How many of the boys are not interested in either of these football teams?

6   During the 30 days of September, it both rained and was sunny on 12 days. It was sunny but did not rain on 10 days; and it rained when the sun did not shine on 5 days. On how many days was there neither rain nor sun?

7   There are 20 houses on Mewough Lane. Eight houses have neither a cat nor a dog; four houses have only a cat; and five houses have only a dog. How many houses have both a cat and a dog?

8   A newspaper boy delivers two kinds of newspaper, the Daily Post and the Daily Mercury, to a street of fifty houses. Six houses take both newspapers and 15 houses take no newspaper. If 22 houses take only the Daily Post, how many buy only the Daily Mercury?

9   In a group of 25 British businessmen, two can speak fluently in both French and German, and 17 can speak neither of these languages. If one speaks German but not French, find how many speak French but not German.

10   On a school trip, 12 pupils want to visit the zoo and 10 want to visit the castle, including 8 pupils who want to visit both. If two do not want to visit either the zoo or the castle, find how many children are on the school trip.

11   24 new houses are built on an estate. Ten families which move into them have a boy and eight families have a girl. These include 5 families which have both a boy and a girl. How many of these houses will have no children living in them?

12   In the hills around Penthwaite there are 35 small farms. 28 of them have some sheep and 18 have some cattle—including 15 farms which have both sheep and cattle. How many of these farms have neither sheep nor cattle?

13   All six of Mrs. Wilson's children like either white or brown bread or both. If four of them like white bread and five of them like brown bread, how many like *both* white *and* brown?

14   All ten houses in a row have in their gardens either daffodils or primroses or both. If eight have daffodils and five have primroses, how many have *both* daffodils *and* primroses?

15   All sixteen tourists in a coach party took either colour or black & white photographs. If 14 took them in colour and 5 took them in black & white, how many took *both* types of photographs?

Problems using sets

16 In another party of tourists, 5 had been to neither Rome nor Paris. 12 had been to Paris and 10 had been to Rome. If there are 20 people in the party, how many had been to both these cities?

17 At a "Bring and Buy" Sale 16 people brought something, 24 people bought something and 3 people neither brought nor bought anything. If 36 people went to the sale, how many of them both brought and bought?

18 In a class of 25 pupils, 3 did not pass either their maths or their science exam. 16 passed in maths, and 18 passed in science. How many passed
   a in both maths and science
   b in maths but not science?

19 In a primary school of 120 children, 34 have neither a brother nor a sister. 59 have a brother and 55 have a sister. How many have a brother but no sister?

20 50 children are asked if they own a bicycle or a record player. 20 said they had only a record player and 18 said they had only a bicycle. The number with neither of these was equal to the number with both. Find how many children had
   a both a bicycle and a record player   b a bicycle.

Part 2   Further problems

Draw a Venn diagram to help to solve each of these problems.

1 In a group of friends, 8 like orange squash and 4 like lemonade. These numbers include 3 who like both drinks. If 2 of the group like neither drink, how many friends are there in the group?

2 In another group, 8 pupils at a school study history and 7 study geography. These numbers include 6 who take both subjects. If there are 3 in the group who take neither history nor geography, how many pupils are there in the group?

3 Police make a random check on cars travelling along a road. 21 cars had no faults with their tyres or their lights, but 12 cars had faulty tyres and 6 had faulty lights. These numbers include 2 cars with both faulty tyres and faulty lights. How many cars did the Police stop?

4 In a small village, 24 houses have both gas and electricity, 3 houses have only gas, and 12 houses have only electricity. Every house has at least one of these services. How many houses are there in the village?

5 One rainy morning, 18 pupils in a class at a school came with their raincoats. Of these 18, six also had umbrellas. Four came with umbrellas but no raincoats and seven brought neither raincoats nor umbrellas. How many pupils are in this class?

6 19 people watch television one evening. 14 watch BBC programmes and 15 watch ITV programmes. How many watch both channels?

7 In a group of 20 children, 15 pass their maths exam and 17 pass their English exam. How many pass both their maths and their English exams, if no child fails both?

8 27 people go on holiday by train via either London or York. 22 pass through London and 17 pass through York. How many pass through both cities?

9 In a class of 30 students, 20 take physics, 15 take chemistry and 2 take neither of these subjects. How many students take both of them?

10 A boy delivers 62 newspapers in one street, either the Daily Post or the Daily Mercury. 39 houses take the Daily Post and 26 houses take the Daily Mercury. If 15 houses take neither of these papers,
   a how many houses take both of them
   b how many houses are there in the street?

Problems using sets

11 In a group of 30 boys, 24 like cycling of whom 19 do not like hiking. If 4 of the 30 do not like either cycling or hiking, how many like hiking?

12 In a group of 22 boys, 15 play football and 13 play basketball. 3 of the boys play neither of these games. How many play both games?

13 In a school with 294 fifth-formers, 80 are members of the Music Society. 35 belong to both the Music and Photographic Societies. 152 fifth-formers belong to neither of these societies. How many members are there in the Photographic Society?

14 Of the 140 firms in a town, 35 do not manufacture anything. 90 make goods for overseas markets, of which 82 also make goods for the home market. How many firms sell goods only for the home market?

15 An office advertises for a clerk and receives 85 applications. 74 of them have qualifications in either shorthand or typing or both. 46 have qualifications in both shorthand and typing, and 25 can type but not do shorthand. How many of the applicants

 a have no qualification in either shorthand or typing

 b can do shorthand but not typing?

16 Of the 133 countries in the Organisation of International Aid, 121 either give aid or receive aid, 15 countries both give and receive aid, and 74 only receive aid. How many countries

 a neither give nor receive aid

 b give aid?

17 53 young people apply for a post with an engineering firm. 49 of them have experience of either woodwork or metal work or both. 42 have experience of metal work and 40 have experience of woodwork. How many of the applicants have experience of

 a neither wood nor metal work

 b both wood and metal work?

18 One evening at a hospital, attention was given to several people involved in accidents, 14 of whom needed surgery. Road accidents accounted for 12 patients and of these 12, 10 needed surgery. If 11 people had been in non-road accidents, how many people were given attention altogether?

19 To get a certain qualification, candidates have to pass each of two exams. 70% of the candidates passed paper I and 10% failed paper I but passed paper II. If 50% of the candidates passed paper II, how many

 a passed paper I but failed paper II

 b gained their qualification?

20 There are 21 men and 23 women in a room. Of these people, 17 are wearing glasses. If 10 men do not wear glasses, how many women do not wear them?

Part 3 Problems with three sets

For each of these problems, draw a Venn diagram as shown here, to help you find a solution.

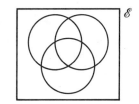

In a group of 48 fourth-formers, 15 study biology, geography and French, 18 study both geography and French, 23 study both biology and French, and 25 study both biology and geography.

Problems using sets

38 out of the 48 study biology; 32 study geography; and 27 study French.
Find the number who

a study biology but neither geography nor French
b study both geography and French but not biology
c do not study any of these three subjects.

2 A driving-test centre have 90 people taking their test during one day. The people who fail do so on three possible points: reversing, using the mirror, turning at road junctions.
6 fail on all three counts; 10 fail because of mirror use and turning at road junctions; 9 fail because of mirror use and reversing; 8 fail because of reversing and road junctions.
A total of 19 fail due to their reversing; 24 fail due to their turning at junctions; 16 fail due to their use of the mirror. Find

a the total number of people who fail
b the number of people who pass
c the number of people who fail just because of their use of the mirror
d the number of people who fail but not because of their reversing.

3 A survey shows that in a group of 50 people, 3 watched television programmes during the morning, afternoon and evening. 4 watched both morning and afterr programmes; 5 watched both afternoon and evening programmes; 7 watched bot morning and evening programmes.
11 watched programmes during the morning; 8 watched during the afternoon an 32 watched during the evening.

Find how many people watched television

a sometime   b not at all   c only during the evening
d both in the afternoon and the evening but not in the morning.

4 200 commuters were asked what kind of transport they used to get to work in the morning. 3 people said they used train, car and bus. 6 people used a train and a car, 23 used a train and a bus, 3 used a car and a bus. Altogether 43 used a train, 65 used a car and 105 used a bus.

a How many people used only a train to get to work?
b How many used both a car and a bus but not a train?
c How many used either a train or a bus (or both) but not a car?
d How many did not use any of these three forms of transport?

5 A group of 100 people were asked which of the three services (gas, electricity and telephone) they had in their houses. 65 said they had gas, 93 said they had electricity and 77 said they had a telephone.
64 said they had both electricity and gas; 76 said they had both electricity and telephone; 53 said they had gas and a telephone. 52 people said they had all three services.
How many people had

a none of these services
b both electricity and gas but no telephone
c either electricity or gas (or both)
d either electricity or gas (but not both)?

6 A school employs 120 teachers and the fifth-form do a survey about the numbers of cars the teachers own and whether they are British, Continental or Japanese.
36 have British cars; 31 have Continental cars; 23 have Japanese cars. 7 have both a British and a Continental car; 3 have both a Continental and a Japane car; 4 have both a British and a Japanese car.

Problems using sets

2 teachers have three cars, one of each type. How many teachers have

a   no cars

b   only British cars

c   either a British or a Continental car (or both)

d   either a British or a Continental car (or both) but not a Japanese car?

7   A youth club offers table tennis, snooker and dancing to its 42 members during one evening. 35 play table tennis; 30 play snooker; 20 dance.
26 play both table tennis and snooker; 16 play snooker and also dance; 20 play table tennis and dance.
If 16 members take part in all three of these activities, find how many

a   took part in none of these activities

b   played either table tennis or snooker (or both)

c   played either table tennis or snooker (but **not** both)

d   took part in just one activity.

8   At an international scientific convention attended by 82 scientists, 64 could speak English, 33 could speak French and 24 could speak German.
25 could speak both French and English; 14 could speak both French and German; 23 could speak both English and German; and 14 could speak all three languages.
How many

a   could speak none of these languages

b   could not speak English

c   spoke either English or German but not French

d   spoke both German and French but not English?

9   In a class of 28 primary school children, 8 had a dog as a pet, 4 had a cat and 9 had a budgie. No child had both a budgie and a cat; only one child had both a dog and a cat; 3 children had both a dog and a budgie.
Find how many

a   none of these as pets   b   either a dog or a cat but not a budgie

c   both a dog and a cat but not a budgie   d   just one type of pet.

0   Third-formers in a certain school have to say which of these three subjects they like—art, music and craft.
23 say they like all three subjects; 37 say they like both music and art; 33 say they like both art and craft; only 1 says she likes music and craft but not art.
51 say they like craft, and 71 say they like either music or craft (or both). 7 say they like only art, and 8 say they like none of these subjects.
How many third-formers

a   are there altogether   b   like art   c   like art but not craft

d   like just music?

Part 4   Problems using algebra

Example

In a group of 22 people, 5 like neither tea nor coffee. The number which likes only tea is one more than that which likes only coffee. Twice as many people like both drinks as those who like only coffee.
Let x = the number who like only coffee and find its value.

The completed Venn diagram gives $x + 1 + 2x + x + 5 = 22$

$$4x + 6 = 22$$
$$4x = 16$$
$$x = 4$$

Problems using sets

1 In a group of 29 friends, 2 do not play either
   tennis or badminton and 6 play only tennis. The
   number who play both games is twice the number
   who play only badminton.
   Let x = the number of those who play only
   badminton and find
   a the value of x
   b the number who play both games.

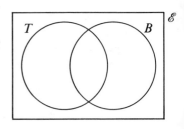

2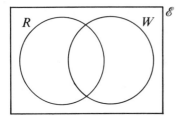

   A garage sells 20 different models of cars, of
   which 8 have neither radios nor heated windows
   fitted. 4 models have both these fittings. The
   number with heated windows only is three times
   that with radios only.
   Let x = the number with only radios, and find
   a the value of x
   b the number of models with heated windows
      but not radios.

3 Of the 48 couples living on an estate, 14 have no
   children. The number of couples with both boys
   and girls is double the number with boys only.
   The number with girls only is two more than that
   with boys only.
   Let x = the number with boys only and find
   a the value of x
   b how many couples have either just boys or
      just girls.

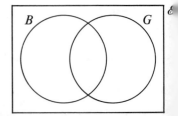

4 A man has an orchard of 18 different types of apple trees. There are 3 types of
   apple which can be neither eaten nor cooked. The number of those which can be
   either eaten or cooked is three times the number of those which can only be
   eaten. The number of types which can only be cooked is five more than those
   which produce only eaters.
   Let x = the number of types which produce only eaters and find
   a the value of x
   b how many types cannot be eaten.

5 A publisher produces 100 titles in either hardback or paperback, though some
   titles can have both types of cover.
   The number produced in paperback only is 6 more than the number in both
   types of cover.
   There are 4 more titles in hardback only than in both hardback and paperback
   Let x = the number produced in both types of cover, and find
   a the value of x
   b the total number of titles in paperback.

6 A shop sells 75 styles of shoe, of which 8 styles are made from neither synthetic
   materials nor leather. The number made from only leather is 8 less than the
   number made from only synthetic materials. The number made from a mixture
   synthetic materials and leather is 15 more than the number made from only
   synthetic materials.
   Let x = the number made from only synthetic materials, and find
   a the value of x   b how many styles have some leather in them.

Problems using sets

7   A class of 32 pupils sits a maths and an English exam. The number that passes
both exams equals the number that fails both exams. The number that passes
English only is double the number that passes both. Twelve pupils pass maths
but not English.
Let x = the number that passes both exams and find
a   the value of x
b   the number that fails maths
c   the number that passes just one of these two subjects.

8   In a group of 31 friends, 15 like Pop music but not Classical music. The number
that likes both types equals the number that likes neither type. The number
that likes only Classical is two less than the number that likes both types.
Let x = the number of friends that like both Classical and Pop. Find
a   the value of x
b   how many like Classical music
c   how many do not like Pop music.

9   The 75 pupils of a primary school have the chance to learn to swim or play the
piano. Those who can do both number five more than those who can only
play the piano. The number who can only swim was five times the number who
can only play the piano. The number who can do neither was two less than
the number who can only play the piano.
Let x = the number who can only play the piano. Find
a   the value of x
b   the number of pianists
c   the number of non-swimmers.

0   A builder sells 54 houses, some with fitted carpets and some with
double glazing. The number of those houses with neither of these extras is
double the number of houses with both of them. There are six more houses with
double glazing only than houses with both extras supplied. There are two more
houses with fitted carpets only than houses with double glazing only.
Let x = the number of houses with both extras supplied. Find
a   the value of x
b   the number of houses sold with double glazing
c   the number of houses sold with no fitted carpets.

1   In a class of 33 pupils, all but 2 of them took at
least one of the three subjects, maths, English and
German. 18 took English, 17 took maths
and 22 took German. 11 took both English and
maths ; 10 took both maths and German;
and 13 took both English and German.
Let x = the number of pupils who took all three
subjects.
Copy this Venn diagram and write in it the above
information using x.

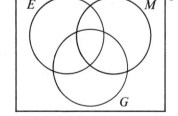

a   Write an equation for x and solve it.
b   How many pupils do both German and maths but not English?
c   How many pupils do either German or maths (or both) but not English?

106 people were asked when they had watched television the previous day.
20 said they had seen no television; 17 had watched some programmes during
the morning; 47 had watched during the afternoon and 58 had watched
during the evening..20 had watched in both afternoon and evening; 14 had
watched in both morning and afternoon; 6 had watched in both morning and
evening.

Problems using sets

Let x be the number which had watched some programmes at all times of the day. Copy this Venn diagram and write in it the above information using x.

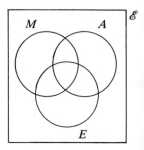

a Write an equation for x and solve it.
b How many people had watched programmes during both morning and afternoon?
c How many people had watched programmes during either morning or afternoon but not evening?

13 An exam was split into three parts, A, B and C, and 93 candidates took the exam All of them attempted some part of the exam.
67 candidates attempted part A; 46 attempted part B; and 40 attempted part C.
28 candidates tried both parts A and B; 8 tried both parts B and C;
and 26 tried both parts A and C.
Let x = the number of candidates who tried all three parts.
Copy this Venn diagram and write in it the above information using x.

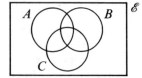

a Write an equation for x and solve it.
b How many candidates did not try part C?
c How many candidates tried part C but not part B?

14 There are 89 boys in the first year. Two boys are excused all games. 43 play hockey, 42 play football, 47 play tennis. 15 play both tennis and hockey; 17 play both tennis and football; 21 play both hockey and football.
Let x = the number of boys who play all three games.
a Draw a Venn diagram and write on this information using x.
b Construct an equation for x and solve it.
c How many boys play both football and tennis but not hockey?
d How many boys do not play football?

15 In one week at an MOT testing station, 102 cars were tested and 34 passed. The rest failed the MOT test due to defective brakes, lights or steering. 30 had faulty brakes, 30 faulty steering and 33 defective lights. 7 failed on both lights and steering; 10 failed on both lights and brakes; 11 failed on both brakes and steering.
Let x = the number that failed on all three counts.
a Draw a Venn diagram and write on this information using x.
b Construct an equation for x and solve it.
c How many failed because of either their lights or brakes or both?
d How many had good lights but still failed?

16 A sports club with 100 members puts out three teams, A, B and C, and everyon plays in at least one team. This table shows the number of members who playe for these teams during the season.

Team	A	B	C	A&B	B&C	C&A
Number of members	50	40	60	20	18	15

Let x = the number of members who played in all three teams.
a Use a Venn diagram to find the value of x.
b Find how many members played only for team C.
c How many played for either A or B (or both) but not for C?

Problems using sets

17　A wine shop sells white, red and rosé wines. It has 66 customers one morning, of whom 3 do not buy any wines.
35 customers buy white wine; 26 buy red wine and 16 buy rosé. 8 customers buy both red and white wines; 2 buy both red and rosé wines; and 6 buy both white and rosé.
Let x = the number of customers who buy all three kinds of wine.
  a　Use a Venn diagram to find the value of x.
  b　How many people buy white wines but not red wines?
  c　How many do not buy any rosé wine?

18　A supermarket stocks plain, self-raising and brown flour. Out of 147 shoppers, 102 do not buy any flour at all. 23 shoppers buy plain flour; 17 buy self-raising flour and 18 buy brown flour.
6 shoppers buy both plain and self-raising flour; 3 buy both brown and self-raising flour; and 4 buy both plain and brown flour.
Let x = the number of shoppers who buy all three kinds of flour. Find
  a　the value of x
  b　how many shoppers do not buy any plain flour at all
  c　how many buy just one kind of flour.

19　A London firm has 64 employees of whom only 3 do not use bus, tube or taxi to get to work.
2 employees use all three forms of transport; 4 use both taxi and bus; 17 use both taxi and tube.
In all, 21 use a taxi, 44 use the tube.
  a　Draw a Venn diagram and fill in as much information as possible.
  b　Find how many people use only a bus.
  c　If one quarter of those who use the tube use *only* the tube, find how many use both tube and bus but not a taxi.

20　At a conference of 100 people, there are 29 English women and 23 English men. Of the English, 4 are doctors and 24 are either men or doctors. There are no foreign doctors. How many women doctors are there?

Part 5　Symbolic problems

1　If n(A ∩ B) = 6, n(B) = 10 and n(A ∪ B) = 21, find n(A).

2　If n(C ∩ D) = 3, n(C) = 12 and n(C ∪ D) = 19, find n(D).

3　If n(E ∩ F) = 8, n(E) = 8 and n(E ∪ F) = 12, find n(F).

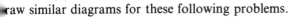

Draw similar diagrams for these following problems.

4　If n(G ∩ H) = 5, n(G) = 7 and n(H) = 12, find n(G ∪ H).
5　If n(I ∩ J) = 9, n(I) = 14 and n(J) = 19, find n(I ∪ J).
6　If n(K) = 6, n(L) = 8 and n(K ∪ L) = 10, find n(K ∩ L).
7　If n(M) = 12, n(N) = 5 and n(M ∪ N) = 14, find n(M ∩ N).
8　If n(P) = 24, n(Q) = 16 and n(P ∪ Q) = 31, find n(P ∩ Q).
9　If n(R' ∩ S) = 6, n(R) = 9 and n(S) = 12, find
  a　n(R ∪ S)　　b　n(R ∩ S)　　c　n(R ∩ S').
10　If n(T' ∩ V) = 14, n(T) = 20 and n(V) = 17, find
  a　n(T ∪ V)　　b　n(T ∩ V)　　c　n(T ∩ V').
If n(W' ∩ X) = 6, n(W ∩ X) = 2 and n(W ∩ X') = 7, find
  a　n(W)　　b　n(X)　　c　n(W ∪ X).

Problems using sets

12 If $n(Y' \cap Z) = 4$ and $n(Y \cap Z') = 7$ and $n(Y \cup Z) = 20$, find
   a $n(Y)$ b $n(Z)$ c $n(Y \cap Z)$.

13 If $n(A' \cap B) = 7$ and $n(B) = 11$ and $n(A \cup B) = 18$, find
   a $n(A)$ b $n(A \cap B)$ c $n(A \cap B')$.

14 If $n(C' \cap D) = 21$ and $n(C \cap D') = 20$ and $n(C \cup D) = 45$, find
   a $n(C)$ b $n(D)$ c $n(C \cap D)$.

15 If $n(E) = 7$ and $n(E \cup F) = 12$ and $n(E \cap F') = 3$, find
   a $n(F)$ b $n(E \cap F)$ c $n(E' \cap F)$.

16 Given that $n(G \cap H) = 7$ $n(G) = 12$
                 $n(H) = 19$ $n(\mathscr{E}) = 35$,
   use this Venn diagram to find
   a $n(G \cup H)$
   b $n(G \cup H)'$.

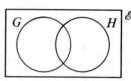

17 Given that $n(I \cap J) = 12$ $n(I) = 23$
                 $n(J) = 15$ $n(\mathscr{E}) = 28$,
   use this Venn diagram to find
   a $n(I \cup J)$
   b $n(I \cup J)'$.

18 Given that $n(K \cap L) = 8$ $n(K) = 12$
                 $n(K \cup L) = 19$ $n(K \cup L)' = 11$,
   use this Venn diagram to find
   a $n(L)$
   b $n(K' \cap L)$.

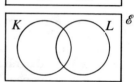

Draw similar diagrams for the following problems.

19       $n(M' \cap N) = 6$ $n(M \cap N') = 8$
         $n(M \cup N) = 20$ $n(M \cup N)' = 3$
         Find the values of   a $n(M)$ b $n(M)'$.

20       $n(P' \cap Q) = 13$ $n(P) = 20$
         $n(P \cap Q) = 9$ $n(P)' = 15$
         Find the values of   a $n(Q)$ b $n(Q)'$.

21       $n(R' \cap S) = 7$ $n(R)' = 9$
         $n(S)' = 10$ $n(R \cup S) = 20$
         Find the values of   a $n(R)$ b $n(\mathscr{E})$.

22       $n(T \cup V)' = 6$ $n(V)' = 9$
         $n(T) = 12$ $n(\mathscr{E}) = 22$
         Find the values of   a $n(T \cap V)$ b $n(T' \cup V)$.

Lines, regions and spaces

Part 1   Points on lines

1   This diagram shows two
    sets of points on a number
    line, which can be described
    by writing

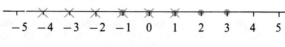

$P = \{x : x \text{ is integer and } -1 \leqslant x \leqslant 3\}$ for the set shown using dots,
and
$Q = \{x : x \text{ is integer and } -4 \leqslant x \leqslant 1\}$ for the set shown using crosses.
Write these sets in the same way   a $P \cup Q$ b $P \cap Q$.

2   The set of points M is shown on this number line using dots and the set N is
    shown using crosses.

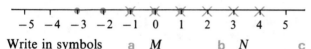

Write in symbols   a M b N c $M \cup N$ d $M \cap N$.

3   A is the set of points shown
    by dots and B is the set of
    points shown using crosses.
    Write in symbols

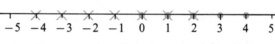

a A b B c $A \cup B$ d $A \cap B$.

4   For each of these number lines, P is the set of points indicated by dots and Q is
    the set of points indicated by crosses.
    Write in symbols   (i) P (ii) Q (iii) $P \cup Q$ (iv) $P \cap Q$.

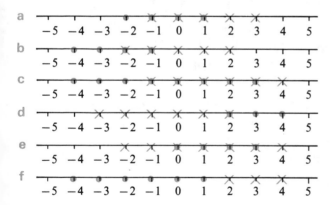

Draw your own number lines from -5 to 5 and illustrate these pairs of sets
using dots and crosses.
In each case, use symbols to describe   (i) $M \cup N$ (ii) $M \cap N$.

a $M = \{x : x \text{ is integer and } -2 \leqslant x \leqslant 2\}$
    $N = \{x : x \text{ is integer and } 0 \leqslant x \leqslant 4\}$

b $M = \{x : x \text{ is integer and } -3 \leqslant x \leqslant 1\}$
    $N = \{x : x \text{ is integer and } -1 \leqslant x \leqslant 3\}$

c $M = \{x : x \text{ is integer and } -3 \leqslant x \leqslant 4\}$
    $N = \{x : x \text{ is integer and } -1 \leqslant x \leqslant 2\}$

d $M = \{x : x \text{ is integer and } -3 \leqslant x \leqslant 0\}$
    $N = \{x : x \text{ is integer and } 1 \leqslant x \leqslant 4\}$

Lines, regions and spaces

6

If **all** points over part of a number line are required, then x is allowed to have non-integer values. This diagram shows the sets $P = \{x : -3 < x < 2\}$ and $Q = \{x : 1 < x < 5\}$.
Notice that the end values of both sets are **not** included in the set, and this is shown by using empty dots.
Write in symbols   **a** $P \cup Q$ **b** $P \cap Q$.

7 For each pair of sets P and Q, draw a number line from -6 to 6.
Draw both sets on it and write in symbols $P \cup Q$ and $P \cap Q$.
    a $P = \{x : -4 < x < 2\}$ and $Q = \{x : 0 < x < 4\}$
    b $P = \{x : -1 < x < 3\}$ and $Q = \{x : 1 < x < 5\}$
    c $P = \{x : -3 < x < -1\}$ and $Q = \{x : -2 < x < 1\}$
    d $P = \{x : -5 < x < 1\}$ and $Q = \{x : -2 < x < 2\}$
    e $P = \{x : 0 < x < 5\}$ and $Q = \{x : 2 < x < 3\}$

8 This diagram shows the sets $A = \{x : 1 \leqslant x \leqslant 4\}$
                and $B = \{x : x \geqslant 3\}$.
Notice that solid dots are used on the diagram so the end values *are* included in the set.
Write $A \cap B$ in symbols.

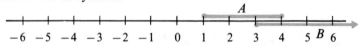

9 For each pair of sets A and B, draw both sets on a number line labelled from -6 to 6 and write in symbols the intersection $A \cap B$.
    a $A = \{x : x \geqslant 2\}$ and $B = \{x : x \leqslant 4\}$
    b $A = \{x : x \geqslant -3\}$ and $B = \{x : x \leqslant 2\}$
    c $A = \{x : x \geqslant 1\}$ and $B = \{x : -2 < x < 3\}$
    d $A = \{x : -3 < x < \frac{1}{2}\}$ and $B = \{x : x > 0\}$
    e $A = \{x : 0 < x < 2\frac{1}{2}\}$ and $B = \{x : x < 1\}$

10   **a**

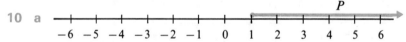

This diagram shows $P = \{x : x \geqslant 1\}$.
Write P', the complement of P, in symbols.
    b   If $A = \{x : x \geqslant 4\}$, find A'.
    c   If $B = \{x : x \geqslant -2\}$, find B'.
    d   If $C = \{x : x \leqslant 3\}$, find C'.
    e   If $D = \{x : x < 0\}$, find D'.

11   **a**

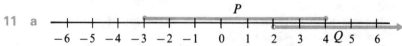

This diagram shows the sets $P = \{x : -3 \leqslant x \leqslant 4\}$ and $Q = \{x : x > 2\}$.
Write in symbols   (i) Q' (ii) $P \cap Q'$.
    b   If $E = \{x : 1 < x < 5\}$ and $F = \{x : x > 3\}$, find $E \cap F'$.
    c   If $G = \{x : -2 < x < 3\}$ and $H = \{x : x < 1\}$, find $G \cap H'$.
    d   If $R = \{x : x \geqslant 4\}$ and $S = \{x : x \leqslant 1\}$, find $(R \cup S)'$.
    e   If $T = \{x : x > 0\}$ and $V = \{x : x < -2\}$, find $(T \cup V)'$.

Lines, regions and spaces

12 a

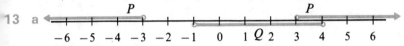

This diagram shows $P = \{x : x^2 < 4\}$ and $Q = \{x : x > 0\}$.
Write $P \cap Q$ in symbols.

b If $A = \{x : x^2 < 9\}$ and $B = \{x : x > 1\}$, find $A \cap B$.

c If $C = \{x : x^2 < 16\}$ and $B = \{x : x < 2\}$, find $C \cap D$.

d If $G = \{x : x^2 < 25\}$ and $H = \{x : 4 < x < 6\}$, find $G \cap H$.

e If $I = \{x : x^2 < 1\}$ and $J = \{x : 0 < x < 3\}$, find $I \cap J$.

13 a

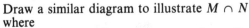

This diagram shows $P = \{x : x^2 > 9\}$ and $Q = \{x : -1 < x < 4\}$.
Write $P \cap Q$ in symbols.

b If $K = \{x : x^2 > 4\}$ and $L = \{x : 0 < x < 5\}$, find $K \cap L$.

c If $M = \{x : x^2 > 9\}$ and $N = \{x : -4 < x < -1\}$, find $M \cap N$.

d If $N = \{x : x^2 > 16\}$, find N'.

e If $P = \{x : x^2 > \frac{1}{4}\}$, find P'.

Part 2 Points in regions

1 This diagram shows a set of points P which
can be written as
$P = \{(x, y) : x$ and y are integer and $x \geq 1\}$.
For each of the following sets of points,
draw and label both axes from -1 to 5 and
mark the points of the required set.

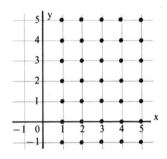

a $Q = \{(x, y) : x$ and y are integer and $x \geq 4\}$

b $R = \{(x, y) : x$ and y are integer and $y \geq 3\}$

c $S = \{(x, y) : x$ and y are integer and $x \geq 2\}$

d $T = \{(x, y) : x$ and y are integer and $y \leq 2\}$

2 This diagram shows two sets of points
$P = \{(x, y) : x$ and y are integer and $x \geq 2\}$
using dots and
$Q = \{(x, y) : x$ and y are integer and $y \geq 3\}$
using rings.

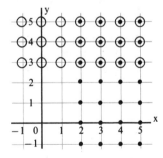

The intersection of these two sets can be
written as
$P \cap Q = \{(x, y) : x$ and y integer, $x \geq 2, y \geq 3\}$.

Draw a similar diagram to illustrate $M \cap N$
where
$M = \{(x, y) : x$ and y are integer and $x \geq 3\}$
and
$N = \{(x, y) : x$ and y are integer and $y \geq 4\}$.
For each pair of sets, draw and label both axes from -1 to 5 and mark the
points of both sets using dots and rings. In each case, take only *integer* values
of x and y.

a $M = \{(x, y) : x \geq 2\}$ and $N = \{(x, y) : y \geq 3\}$

Lines, regions and spaces

b $M = \{(x, y) : x \geqslant 3\}$ and $N = \{(x, y) : y \leqslant 2\}$
c $M = \{(x, y) : x \geqslant 4\}$ and $N = \{(x, y) : y \leqslant 3\}$
d $M = \{(x, y) : x \leqslant 2\}$ and $N = \{(x, y) : y \leqslant 1\}$

4   This diagram shows the set of points
$P = \{(x, y) : x$ and y are integer, $2 \leqslant x \leqslant 4, 1 \leqslant y \leqslant 3\}$.
Draw similar diagrams to illustrate these
sets, taking only *integer* values for x and y.
a $Q = \{(x, y) : 1 \leqslant x \leqslant 4, 2 \leqslant y \leqslant 3\}$
b $R = \{(x, y) : 3 \leqslant x \leqslant 5, 1 \leqslant y \leqslant 2\}$
c $S = \{(x, y) : 0 \leqslant x \leqslant 3, 2 \leqslant y \leqslant 5\}$
d $T = \{(x, y) : 2 \leqslant x \leqslant 3, 0 \leqslant y \leqslant 4\}$

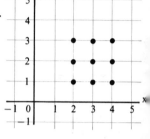

5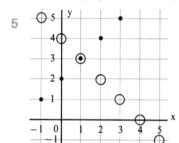

This diagram shows two sets of points
$P = \{(x, y) : x$ is integer and $y = x + 2\}$ using dots
and
$Q = \{(x, y) : x$ is integer and $x + y = 4\}$ using rings

Which point on the diagram is the
only member of $P \cap Q$?

6   Draw similar diagrams with both axes labelled from -1 to 5 to illustrate these
pairs of sets P and Q and in each case give their intersection $P \cap Q$.
Take only *integer* values of x.
a $P = \{(x, y) : y = x + 1\}$ and $Q = \{(x, y) : x + y = 3\}$
b $P = \{(x, y) : y = x + 3\}$ and $Q = \{(x, y) : x + y = 5\}$
c $P = \{(x, y) : y = x - 1\}$ and $Q = \{(x, y) : x + y = 4\}$
d $P = \{(x, y) : y = 2x - 1\}$ and $Q = \{(x, y) : y = x + 2\}$
e $P = \{(x, y) : y = 2x + 1\}$ and $Q = \{(x, y) : y = x + 1\}$

7   This diagram shows three sets of points.
$L = \{(x, y) : x$ is integer and $y = x + 1\}$
$M = \{(x, y) : x$ is integer and $y < x + 1\}$
$N = \{(x, y) : x$ is integer and $y > x + 1\}$
Which of the sets L, M and N are shown on
the diagram using
a   rings   b   dots   c   crosses?

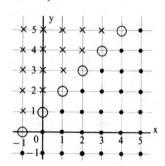

8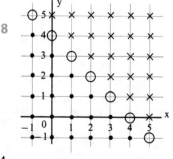

This diagram shows three sets of points.
$A = \{(x, y) : x$ is integer and $x + y = 4\}$
$B = \{(x, y) : x$ is integer and $x + y > 4\}$
$C = \{(x, y) : x$ is integer and $x + y < 4\}$

Which of the sets A, B or C are shown on
the diagram using
a   rings   b   dots   c   crosses?

Lines, regions and spaces

9 Draw and label similar diagrams to illustrate these sets.
Take only *integer* values of x and y.

a $E = \{(x, y) : y = x + 2\}$ b $K = \{(x, y) : y = x - 1\}$
    $F = \{(x, y) : y > x + 2\}$ $L = \{(x, y) : y < x - 1\}$
    $G = \{(x, y) : y < x + 2\}$ $M = \{(x, y) : y > x - 1\}$

c $H = \{(x, y) : x + y = 3\}$
    $I = \{(x, y) : x + y > 3\}$
    $J = \{(x, y) : x + y < 3\}$

0 When x and y can take a range of **all** values,
not just integers, then the set of points can
be shown on a diagram by shading a region.
This diagram shows the two sets
$P = \{(x, y) : x \geqslant 3\}$ and
$Q = \{(x, y) : y \leqslant 2\}$.
Draw similar diagrams to illustrate these
pairs of sets.

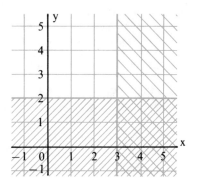

a $A = \{(x, y) : x \geqslant 2\}$ and $B = \{(x, y) : y \leqslant 4\}$

b $C = \{(x, y) : x \geqslant 4\}$ and $D = \{(x, y) : y \geqslant 3\}$

c $E = \{(x, y) : x \geqslant 3\}$ and $F = \{(x, y) : y \leqslant 1\}$

d $G = \{(x, y) : x \leqslant 4\}$ and $H = \{(x, y) : y \leqslant 0\}$

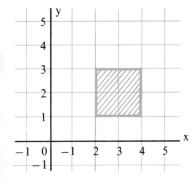

This diagram shows the set of points
$P = \{(x, y) : 2 \leqslant x \leqslant 4, 1 \leqslant y \leqslant 3\}$.
Draw similar diagrams to illustrate these
sets of points and for each set state the area
of the region.

a $P = \{(x, y) : 1 \leqslant x \leqslant 3, 2 \leqslant y \leqslant 3\}$

b $P = \{(x, y) : 3 \leqslant x \leqslant 4, 1 \leqslant y \leqslant 3\}$

c $P = \{(x, y) : 0 \leqslant x \leqslant 2, 3 \leqslant y \leqslant 5\}$

d $P = \{(x, y) : 2 \leqslant x \leqslant 5, 0 \leqslant y \leqslant 3\}$

e $P = \{(x, y) : -1 \leqslant x \leqslant 1, 2 \leqslant y \leqslant 4\}$

f $P = \{(x, y) : 1 \leqslant x \leqslant 4, -1 \leqslant y \leqslant 3\}$

This diagram shows three sets of points.
$L = \{(x, y) : y = x + 1\}$
$M = \{(x, y) : y > x + 1\}$
$N = \{(x, y) : y < x + 1\}$
Draw similar diagrams to illustrate these
sets and label each set with its letter.

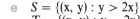

a $A = \{(x, y) : y < x + 2\}$
    $B = \{(x, y) : y = x + 2\}$
    $C = \{(x, y) : y > x + 2\}$

b $P = \{(x, y) : y < x - 2\}$
    $Q = \{(x, y) : y = x - 2\}$
    $R = \{(x, y) : y > x - 2\}$

c $L = \{(x, y) : x + y < 3\}$ d $E = \{(x, y) : x + y < 4\}$ e $S = \{(x, y) : y > 2x\}$
    $M = \{(x, y) : x + y = 3\}$ $F = \{(x, y) : x + y = 4\}$ $T = \{(x, y) : y = 2x\}$
    $N = \{(x, y) : x + y > 3\}$ $G = \{(x, y) : x + y > 4\}$ $U = \{(x, y) : y < 2x\}$

Lines, regions and spaces

In these problems label both axes from -1 to 8.

13 On a diagram, show the sets A and B by two different kinds of shading, where
$A = \{(x, y) : y \geqslant x + 1\}$ and $B = \{(x, y) : x + y \geqslant 6\}$.
Label that part of the diagram which gives $A \cap B$.

14 On a diagram, show the sets C and D by two different kinds of shading, where
$C = \{(x, y) : y \leqslant 2x\}$ and $D = \{(x, y) : y \leqslant x + 1\}$.
Label that part of the diagram which gives $C \cap D$.

15 On a diagram, show the sets R, S and T by different shadings, where
$R = \{(x, y) : x \geqslant 2\}$
$S = \{(x, y) : y \leqslant 6\}$
$T = \{(x, y) : y \leqslant x - 1\}$.
Label that part of your diagram which gives $R \cap S \cap T$.

16 Given that $L = \{(x, y) : x \geqslant 2\}$
$M = \{(x, y) : x + y \leqslant 7\}$
$N = \{(x, y) : y \geqslant x + 1\}$
shade the set $L \cap M \cap N$ on a diagram and
a calculate the area it occupies
b find the point in $L \cap M \cap N$ which has the largest value of x.

17 Given that $P = \{(x, y) : y \leqslant \frac{1}{2}x + 5\}$
$Q = \{(x, y) : y \geqslant 2x - 1\}$
$R = \{(x, y) : x + y \geqslant 5\}$
shade the set $P \cap Q \cap R$ on a diagram and
a calculate the area it occupies
b find that point in $P \cap Q \cap R$ which has the least value of y.

18 Given that $S = \{(x, y) : y \geqslant x\}$
$T = \{(x, y) : y \leqslant \frac{1}{2}x + 4\}$
$L = \{(x, y) : x + y = 7\}$
indicate $S \cap T \cap L$ on a diagram and find the member of $S \cap T \cap L$ which has
a the least x-value   b the greatest y-value.

19 Indicate on a diagram the two sets M and N where $M = \{(x, y) : y = 2x + 1\}$
and $N = \{(x, y) : x + y = 7\}$.
Find the one and only member of the set $M \cap N$.

20 Given that $A = \{(x, y) : x \geqslant 3\}$
$B = \{(x, y) : y \leqslant x + 2\}$
and $C = \{(x, y) : y \leqslant 7 - \frac{1}{2}x\}$,
shade the set $(A \cup B) \cap C$ on a diagram and find that member of it with the greatest y-value.

21 On a diagram with the x-axis labelled from -3 to 3, indicate the two sets A and B, where $A = \{(x, y) : y = x^2\}$ and $B = \{(x, y) : x + y = 6\}$.
Find all the members of $A \cap B$.

22 Given that $R = \{(x, y) : y \geqslant x^2 + 1\}$
$L = \{(x, y) : y = 3x - 1\}$,
indicate $R \cap L$ on a diagram and find the member of $R \cap L$ which has
a the least x-value   b the greatest x-value.

Lines, regions and spaces

Part 3   Points in space

1   The set of points
$P = \{(x, y, z) : 1 \leqslant x \leqslant 2, 2 \leqslant y \leqslant 4, 0 \leqslant z \leqslant 3\}$
is shown on this diagram, where x, y and z
take *integer* values only.

Write in symbols the sets of points shown in
these diagrams, where x, y and z take integer
values only.

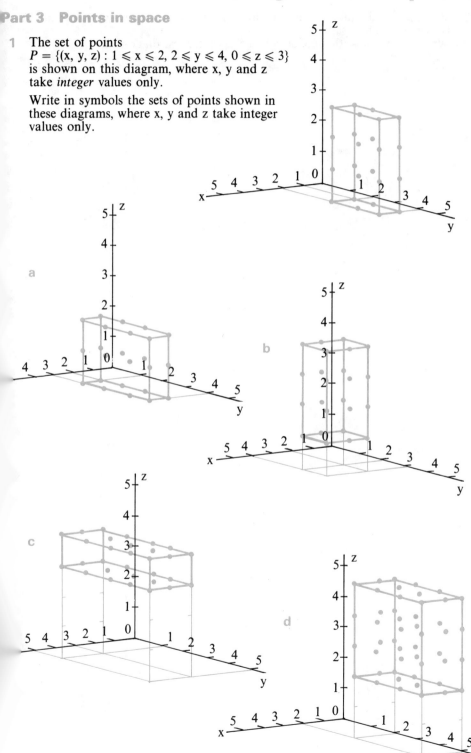

Lines, regions and spaces

2 When x, y and z take *all*, not just integer, values then the set of points can be
   shown as a solid space.
   Write, in symbols, the sets of points shown in these diagrams.

a

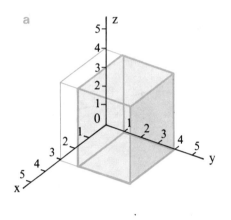

b

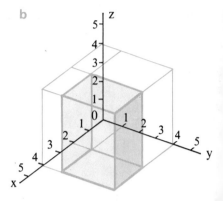

c

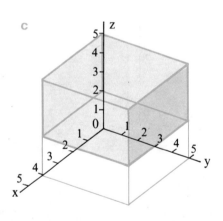

d

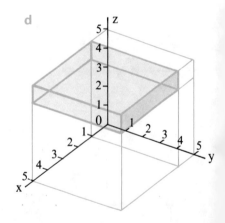

e

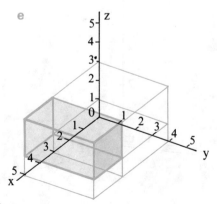

f

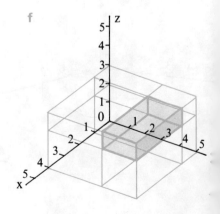

Sets of numbers

Introduction

1 One set X of numbers can be mapped onto another set Y using a relation.
Copy each of these diagrams and draw arrows to map set X onto set Y.

a

X	Y
1	6
2	7
3	8
4	9

$x \longrightarrow x + 5$

b

X	Y
2	0
4	2
6	4
8	6

$x \longrightarrow x - 2$

c

X	Y
1	2
3	6
5	10
7	14

$x \longrightarrow 2x$

2 Copy each of these diagrams and complete each set Y for the given relation.

a

X	Y
1	
2	
3	
4	

$x \longrightarrow 3x$

b

X	Y
0	
1	
2	
3	

$x \longrightarrow 2x + 1$

c

X	Y
5	
10	
15	
20	

$x \longrightarrow 3x - 2$

3 Suggest a relation for each of these mapping diagrams.

a

X	Y
1	5
2	6
3	7
4	8

b

X	Y
1	0
2	1
3	2
4	3

c

X	Y
0	0
1	3
2	6
3	9

d

X	Y
1	3
2	5
3	7
4	9

e

X	Y
1	1
2	3
3	5
4	7

f

X	Y
1	5
2	8
3	11
4	14

Part 1 Patterns in shapes

diagram 1   diagram 2   diagram 3

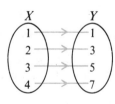

a This set of triangles can be made using
matches. Copy and complete the
mapping diagram by counting and by
spotting the pattern.

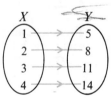

Diagram number	Number of matches
1	
2	
3	
4	
5	
10	
20	
x	

69

Sets of numbers

   b Describe the pattern in words.
   c Complete the last row in the diagram by writing the relation.

2 Use the same table for this set of squares.

diagram 1   diagram 2   diagram 3

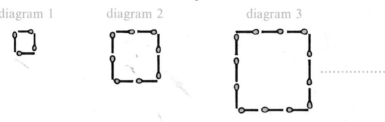

3 Use the same table for this set of L-shapes.

diagram 1   diagram 2   diagram 3

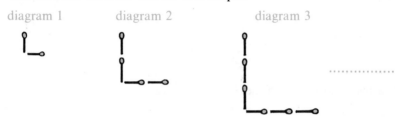

4 diagram 1   diagram 2   diagram 3

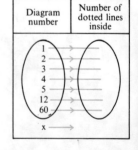

The diagrams in this set grow by adding one
square each time.
   a Count the number of dotted lines inside
      the rectangles and complete the mapping
      diagram by spotting the pattern.
   b Describe the pattern in words.
   c Complete the last row by writing the
      relation.

Diagram number	Number of dotted lines inside
1 →	
2 →	
3 →	
4 →	
5 →	
12 →	
60 →	
x →	

5 diagram 1   diagram 2   diagram 3

These zigzag diagrams can be made with
matches and they grow by adding one extra
match each time.
   a Count the number of matches used and
      complete the mapping diagram.
   b Describe the mapping in words.
   c Complete the last row by writing the
      relation.

Diagram number	Number of matches
1 →	
2 →	
3 →	
4 →	
5 →	
15 →	
70 →	
x →	

Sets of numbers

6 These diagrams grow by adding a black
   vertical line joined by a coloured cross.
   Copy and complete the mapping and
   include the relation.
   Describe the relation in words.

   diagram 1   diagram 2   diagram 3

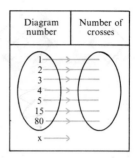

Diagram number	Number of crosses
1 →	
2 →	
3 →	
4 →	
5 →	
15 →	
80 →	
x →	

7 Each coloured dot sprouts two branches,
   produces two more coloured dots and then
   dies.
   Copy and complete the mapping and
   include the relation.
   Describe the relation in words.

   diagram 0 diagram 1 diagram 2 diagram 3

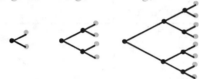

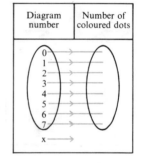

Diagram number	Number of coloured dots
0 →	
1 →	
2 →	
3 →	
4 →	
5 →	
6 →	
7 →	
x →	

Here are many sets of diagrams, each one growing into another.
Each mapping diagram has been simplified into a table.
Copy and complete each table.
Describe each relation in words (e.g. "double and add 3").

1   2   3

Diagram number	1	2	3	4	5	6	10	20	x
Number of matches									

1   2   3

Diagram number	1	2	3	4	5	6	10	20	x
Number of dots									

1   2   3

Diagram number	1	2	3	4	5	6	10	20	x
Number of dots									

71

Sets of numbers

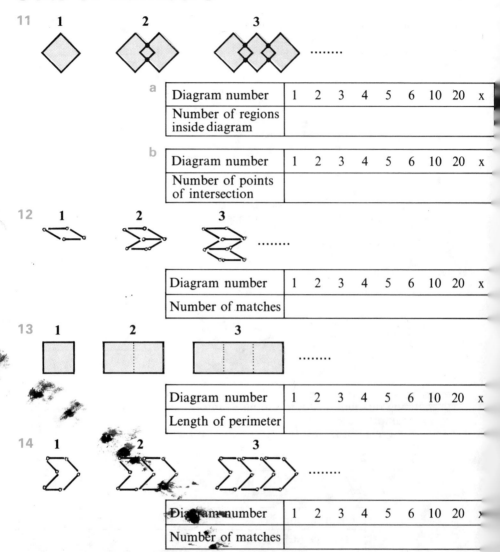

11

a

Diagram number	1	2	3	4	5	6	10	20	x
Number of regions inside diagram									

b

Diagram number	1	2	3	4	5	6	10	20	x
Number of points of intersection									

12

Diagram number	1	2	3	4	5	6	10	20	x
Number of matches									

13

Diagram number	1	2	3	4	5	6	10	20	x
Length of perimeter									

14

Diagram number	1	2	3	4	5	6	10	20	x
Number of matches									

15 Construct your own table for the number of dots in these diagrams and continue the pattern to find the relation.

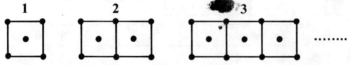

16 Construct your own table for the number of matches and continue the pattern to find the relation.

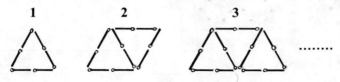

Sets of numbers

17 Construct your own table for the length of the perimeter of these shapes and find the relation.

1   **2**   **3**

  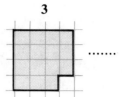

....

18 Construct your own table for the number of matches and find the relation.

1   **2**   **3**

  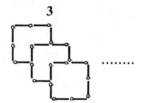

....

9 Construct your own tables for the number of   **a** dots   **b** chords   **c** regions   in these diagrams. Find the relation in each case.

1   **2**   **3**   **4**

 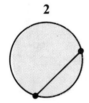 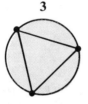 

......

)   **a**   Two people shake hands once. If there are 3 people in the group and each person shakes hands once with each other person, how many handshakes will there be?

   b   If there are 4 people in the group, how many handshakes will there be?

   c   If there are 5 people in the group, how many handshakes will there be?

   d   Copy this table and enter your results.

Can you follow the pattern of your results to complete the table?

Number of people p	2	3	4	5	6	7	8	9	10
Number of handshakes h									

   e   Can you find the relation connecting the number of handshakes with the number of people in the group?

rt 2   Sequences and difference tables

A **sequence** is a set of numbers which follow a given rule or pattern. Can you find the missing numbers in each of these sequences?

a	1	4	7	10	13	16	19	... ...
b	1	5	9	13	17	21	25	... ...
c	1	2	4	8	16	32	...	...
d	1	3	9	27	81	...	...	
e	1	$\frac{1}{2}$	$\frac{1}{4}$	$\frac{1}{8}$	$\frac{1}{16}$	...	...	
f	1	0.1	0.01	0.001	...	...		

Sets of numbers

g	28	24	20	16	12	8	...	...
h	8	5	2	−1	−4	−7	...	...
i	−20	−14	−8	−2	4	10	...	...
j	$1\frac{1}{8}$	$2\frac{1}{4}$	$4\frac{1}{2}$	9	...	...		

2 Find the missing numbers in these sequences.

a	6	10	14	...	22	26	...
b	17	15	...	11	...	7	5
c	$\frac{1}{2}$	2	8	32	...	...	2048
d	81	27	9	3	...	$\frac{1}{3}$	...
e	5	$3\frac{1}{2}$	2	$\frac{1}{2}$	...	...	−4
f	−9	...	5	12	19	...	33
g	16	...	6	1	−4	−9	...
h	...	64	16	4	1	...	$\frac{1}{16}$

3 The patterns in these sequences are more difficult. Can you find the missing numbers?

a	1	3	6	10	15	21	...	...
b	1	3	7	13	21	31	...	...
c	1	4	10	19	31	46	...	...
d	2	3	5	8	12	17	...	...
e	100	90	81	73	66	60	...	...
f	40	39	37	34	30	25	...	...
g	60	58	54	48	40	30	...	...
h	1	4	9	16	25	36	...	...
i	2	5	10	17	26	37	...	...
j	0	3	8	15	24	35	...	...
k	11	−14	19	−26	35	−46	...	...

4 When patterns in sequences are too difficult to pick out, the method here might help you.
Consider finding the next two numbers in this sequence.

5	15	29	47	69	95	...	...

a Copy this table, where each number in the two new rows is the difference between the two numbers above it, as the arrows indicate. Find the numbers for the shaded squares and enter them in your table.

Sequence	5	15	29	47	69	95	...	...
1st differences		10	14				...	...
2nd differences			4	4			...	...

b What do you notice about the row of 2nd differences?
Fill the gaps in this row, and work upwards through the gaps in the table find the two missing numbers in the sequence.

5 Copy and complete these tables to find the next two numbers in the given sequences.

a

Sequence	1	3	9	19	33	51	...	...
1st differences								
2nd differences								

Sets of numbers

b

Sequence	2	5	14	29	50	77	...	...
1st differences								
2nd differences								

c

Sequence	0	6	16	30	48	70	...	...
1st differences								
2nd differences								

d

Sequence	1	13	33	61	97	141	...	...
1st differences								
2nd differences								

e

Sequence	5	9	15	23	33	45	...	...
1st differences								
2nd differences								

f

Sequence	4	6	10	16	24	34	...	...
1st differences								
2nd differences								

6 With some sequences, you will need to go beyond the second differences before a row has constant entries. Copy and complete these tables to find the next two numbers in the sequences.

a

Sequence	4	5	12	31	68	129	...	...
1st differences								
2nd differences								
3rd differences								

b

Sequence	0	2	10	30	68	130	...	...
1st differences								
2nd differences								
3rd differences								

c

Sequence	0	3	18	55	124	235	...	...
1st differences								
2nd differences								
3rd differences								

d

Sequence	0	0	14	79	232	510	...	...
1st differences								
2nd differences								
3rd differences								

Sets of numbers

7 Use this method to find the missing numbers in these sequences. You will need
   to construct your own tables of differences.

a	0	6	24	60	120	210	...	...
b	3	12	33	72	135	228	...	...
c	11	28	57	104	175	276	...	...
d	2	12	36	80	150	252	...	...	...
e	0	4	18	48	100	180	294	...	...
f	2	18	84	260	630	1302	2408	...	...
g	0	8	54	192	500	1080	2058	...	...
h	0	12	72	240	600	1260	2352	...	...
i	1	15	79	253	621	1291	2395	...	...
j	0	16	162	768	2500	6480	14406	...	...
k	9	10	91	522	1885	5194	12015	...	...
l	224	1750	4928	7028	7840	7994	8000	8008	... ...

8 Not all sequences will give constant differences as above.
   See what happens when you work out the differences for these three sequences
   and see if you can find some other similar ones of your own.

a	**Powers of two**	1	2	4	8	16	32	64	128	... ...
b	**Powers of three**	1	3	9	27	81	243	729	2187	... ...
c	**Fibonacci numbers**	1	1	2	3	5	8	13	21	... ...

Part 3 More patterns and shapes

Some shapes give numerical patterns which are more difficult to pick out than the
patterns in **Part 1**. Difference tables can be used to continue the sequences.
For each set of diagrams, copy the table and fill in the shaded entries by looking at
the diagrams.
Then complete the difference table, find the next numbers in the sequence and check
your answers by drawing the next diagrams.

1 diagram 1   diagram 2   diagram 3   diagram 4

Diagram number	1	2	3	4	5	6
Number of short lines	4	12	▓	▓		
1st differences						
2nd differences						

2 diagram 1   diagram 2   diagram 3   diagram 4

Diagram number	1	2	3	4	5	6
Number of short lines	4	10	▓	▓		
1st differences						
2nd differences						

76

Sets of numbers

3   diagram 1   diagram 2   diagram 3   diagram 4

  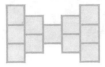 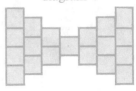

Diagram number	1	2	3	4	5	6
Number of squares	1					
1st differences						
2nd differences						

4   diagram 1   diagram 2   diagram 3   diagram 4

  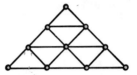

Diagram number	1	2	3	4	5	6
Number of dots	1					
1st differences						
2nd differences						

5   diagram 1   diagram 2   diagram 3   diagram 4

Diagram number	1	2	3	4	5	6
Number of short lines						
1st differences						
2nd differences						

Some patterns can arise from three-dimensional sets of objects.
Checking your answers here is more difficult unless you have some equipment.

6   diagram 1   diagram 2   diagram 3   diagram 4

Diagram number	1	2	3	4	5	6
Number of small spheres						
1st differences						
2nd differences						

Sets of numbers

7 diagram 1   diagram 2   diagram 3   diagram 4

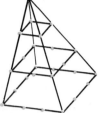

Diagram number	1	2	3	4	5	6
Number of small spheres						
1st differences						
2nd differences						

8 diagram 1   diagram 2   diagram 3   diagram 4

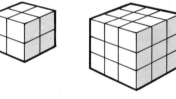
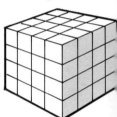

Diagram number	1	2	3	4	5	6
Number of small cubes						
1st differences						
2nd differences						
3rd differences						

9 diagram 1   diagram 2   diagram 3   diagram 4

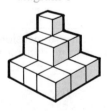

Diagram number	1	2	3	4	5	6
Number of small cubes						
1st differences						
2nd differences						
3rd differences						

Sets of numbers

For these next diagrams, the rows of differences are not given.
Add enough rows to your own tables for the number pattern to become clear.

10 diagram 1   diagram 2   diagram 3   diagram 4

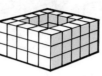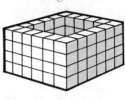

Diagram number	1	2	3	4	5	6
Number of small cubes round the sides						

11 diagram 1   diagram 2   diagram 3   diagram 4

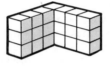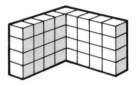

Diagram number	1	2	3	4	5	6	7	8
Number of small cubes								

2 diagram 1   diagram 2   diagram 3   diagram 4

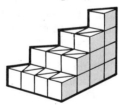

Diagram number	1	2	3	4	5	6	7	8
Number of small triangular prisms								

diagram 1   diagram 2   diagram 3   diagram 4

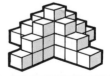

Diagram number	1	2	3	4	5	6	7	8
Number of small cubes								

Sets of numbers

14   diagram 1   diagram 2   diagram 3   diagram 4

   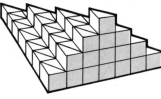

Diagram number	1	2	3	4	5	6	7	8
Number of small triangular prisms								

Part 4 Famous patterns

1 a   This is a game for two players.
        Make a triangular arrangement of ten coins as shown here.
        Take turns to remove *from any row* as many coins as you like (*not necessarily all of them*).
        The winner is the player who takes the *last* coin.

    b   Another game can be played with the same rules *except* the winner this time is the player who makes *his opponent* take the last coin.

    c   A more complicated game can be played with an extra row of five coins beneath the four rows shown here.

2   This set of diagrams shows dots arranged in triangles.
    The numbers of dots in the sequence are the *triangular numbers*.

    a   Copy the table and draw your own diagrams to complete it up to the tenth triangular number.

1st   **2nd**   **3rd**   **4th**

Diagram number	1	2	3	4	1
Number of dots or triangular number	1	3	6		

    b   By breaking each triangle into separate rows, we can write
$$1 = 1$$
$$3 = 1 + 2$$
$$6 = 1 + 2 + 3$$
$$10 = \ldots$$
$$\vdots$$

        Copy these and continue the pattern up to the tenth triangular number.

Sets of numbers

c We can make a staircase from each triangular number as shown here.

Neighbouring pairs of triangular numbers can be joined together to make square numbers.

Breaking each triangular number into its rows, we can write:

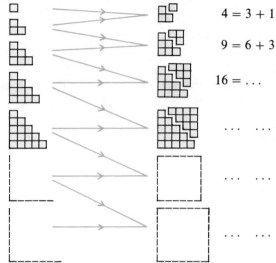

$4 = 3 + 1$ $4 = 1 + 2 + 1$

$9 = 6 + 3$ $9 = 1 + 2 + 3 + 2 + 1$

$16 = \ldots$ $16 = \ldots$

Copy and complete this diagram.

d Can you *quickly* find the sum of these numbers *without* adding them together? Look first at the pattern of the numbers in part **c**.
(i) $1 + 2 + 3 + 4 + 5 + 6 + 7 + 6 + 5 + 4 + 3 + 2 + 1$
(ii) $1 + 2 + 3 + 4 + 5 + 6 + 7 + 8 + 7 + 6 + 5 + 4 + 3 + 2 + 1$
(iii) $1 + 2 + 3 + 4 + 5 + 6 + 7 + 8 + 9 + 8 + 7 + 6 + 5 + 4 + 3 + 2 + 1$
(iv) $1 + 2 + 3 + 4 + 5 + 6 + 7 + 8 + 9 + 10 + 11 + 12$
$\qquad\qquad + 11 + 10 + 9 + 8 + 7 + 6 + 5 + 4 + 3 + 2 + 1$

a If a ball is placed at the entrance at the top of this maze, it will reach *one* of the four exits G, H, I or J, after turning at several junctions.
How many different routes can it take to reach each of the lettered junctions and exits?
Copy the maze and write your answers in place of the letters (or just write them in the triangular pattern of the letters).
What is the connection between your answers for
(i) E, B and C   (ii) H, D and E?

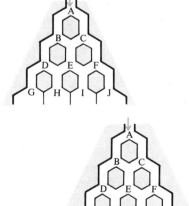

b This maze has an extra row of junctions. Repeat the instructions of part **a** to find the number of different routes to each lettered junction and exit.
What connection is there between your answers for
(i) I, E and F   (ii) L, G and H   (iii) M, H and I?

81

Sets of numbers

c Repeat with these two larger
mazes.
Do the same connections still
hold?

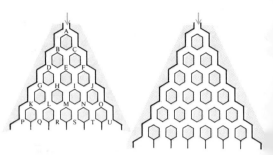

4 This pattern of numbers is known as **Pascal's Triangle**. Blaise Pascal, born in
1623, was a French mathematician and theologian. When 19 years old, he
invented the first adding
machine to help his father who
was a tax inspector. He was also
the first to develop the
mathematical ideas of
probability. However, he suffered
illness for most of his life and
died in 1662 before he was 40
years old.

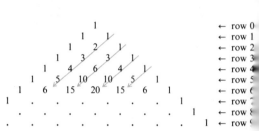

← row 0
← row 1
← row 2
← row 3
← row 4
← row 5
← row 6
← row 7
← row 8
← row 9

a Copy the triangle of numbers shown here and extend it three more rows
by following the pattern.

b (i) Add together the numbers along each of the coloured arrows.
Copy and complete.
$1 + 2 + 3 + 4 + 5 = \ldots$ $1 + 3 + 6 + 10 = \ldots$
$1 + 4 + 10 = \ldots$ $1 + 5 = \ldots$
Can you see your answers on the next row of the triangle?

(ii) Use this method to find the answers to these next additions, by using the
triangle and *without* doing any calculations.
$1 + 2 + 3 + 4 + 5 + 6 + 7 = \ldots$
$1 + 3 + 6 + 10 + 15 + 21 + 28 = \ldots$
$1 + 5 + 15 + 35 + 70 = \ldots$
$1 + 6 + 21 + 56 = \ldots$
$1 + 4 + 10 + 20 + 35 = \ldots$

c Add together all the numbers in each row of the triangle and enter your
totals in a copy of this table.
Can you see a pattern in your totals? Continue this pattern to complete the
table.

Row number	0	1	2	3	4	5	6	7	8	9	10	11	12	n
Total of numbers	1	2												

d Use a calculator to find the values of 11^2 and 11^3 and 11^4.
Do you see a connection with Pascal's Triangle?
Does the connection still hold for 11^5 and 11^6?

e Work out these powers of $x + y$ by multiplying brackets together.
Use each answer to help you with the next stage.
$(x + y)^2 = (x + y)(x + y) = \ldots$
$(x + y)^3 = (x + y)(x + y)^2 = \ldots$
$(x + y)^4 = (x + y)(x + y)^3 = \ldots$
Do you see a connection with Pascal's Triangle?
Can you expand $(x + y)^5$ and $(x + y)^6$ *without* doing any more calculations?

Sets of numbers

f   Do you see any connection between your answers for parts **d** and **e**?
What values of x and y make this connection obvious?
What is the reason why the pattern appears to break down for 11^5 and 11^6?

5   a   A male bee or drone hatches from an unfertilised egg, so it has a mother but
no father. A female bee (a worker or a queen) hatches from a fertilised egg,
so it has both a mother and a father.
This diagram shows the family tree of a particular male bee, going back for
seven generations. M stands for a male and F for a female.

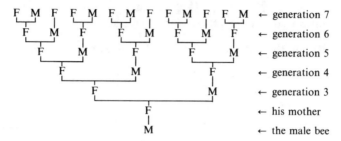

Copy and complete this table.

Generation number	1	2	3	4	5	6	7
Number of bees in that generation	1	1	2				

b   As plants grow, a new shoot branches out at
the point where a leaf forms on the stem.
This diagram shows such a plant.
Copy and complete this table.

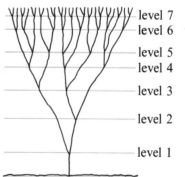

Level number	1	2	3	4	5	6	7
Number of new branches formed at that level							

c   This sequence of numbers is
named after an Italian mathematician
Leonardo Fibonacci who lived from about
1170 to 1250. Born in Pisa, he· learned about the "new Indian numerals"
from his father and then travelled to Egypt, Syria and Greece to meet local
scholars. He was the first distinguished Christian mathematician of Western
Europe.
Can you see how the number pattern is formed? Investigate adding pairs
of numbers together to find the pattern.
Check the numbers you have found and then carry on to write the first
fifteen numbers of the **Fibonacci sequence**.

d   Here are *three* consecutive numbers, x, y and z, of the sequence.

$$\begin{array}{ccc} x & y & z \\ 5 & 8 & 13 \end{array}$$

Multiply the *outer* pair, xz, and square the *middle* number, y^2.
Write any other three consecutive numbers from the sequence and
calculate xz and y^2.
Repeat several times for other consecutive numbers.
What do you notice?

Sets of numbers

e   Here are *four* consecutive numbers, w, x, y and z, of the sequence.

$$\begin{array}{cccc} w & x & y & z \\ 3 & 5 & 8 & 13 \end{array}$$

Multiply the *outer* pair wz and multiply the *inner* pair xy.
Write down any other four consecutive numbers and calculate wz and xy.
Repeat several times for other numbers.
What do you notice?

f   Write each adjacent pair of numbers in the sequence as a *fraction*.
Change these fractions to decimals, perhaps using a calculator .

$$\tfrac{1}{1} \quad \tfrac{2}{1} \quad \tfrac{3}{2} \quad \tfrac{5}{3} \quad \tfrac{8}{5} \quad \tfrac{13}{8} \quad \tfrac{21}{13} \quad \tfrac{34}{21} \quad \ldots \quad \text{etc.}$$

What do you notice about your answers?

g   Calculate the value of $\dfrac{1 + \sqrt{5}}{2}$ and compare it with your answers.

6

P   Q   R   S

a   Here are four rectangles. Ask every member of your class which one they
would choose to use for a picture frame or as a sheet of writing paper for a
letter. Measure the length l and width w of the most popular choice and
calculate the ratio $\dfrac{l}{w}$. Do you recognise the answer?

b   The architects of Ancient Greece were concerned with proportions when
constructing their buildings. This drawing shows the front of the Parthenon
now in ruins, which was built in Athens between 447 and 438 B.C.
Measure the length l and the overall height h and calculate the ratio $\dfrac{l}{h}$.
Do you recognise your answer?

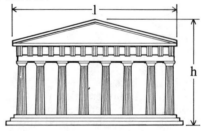

c   Some artists are aware of the need for pleasing proportions when painting
picture. The central feature
in this sketch divides the
picture both horizontally
and vertically.
Use a ruler to measure the
four lettered lengths, and
calculate the two ratios

$$\frac{h_1}{h_2} \quad \text{and} \quad \frac{v_1}{v_2}.$$

Do you recognise the
answers?

Sets of numbers

7 This diagram shows part of a piano keyboard.
   a How many keys (both
      black and white) are there
      between the two arrows? This range of notes is called a *chromatic scale*.

   b How many *white* keys are there between the same arrows? This is called a
      major scale.

   c How many black keys are there between the arrows? This is called a
      pentatonic scale.

   d Do you recognise your three answers? This does not *prove* a connection
      between musical scales and the Fibonacci series, but the musical patterns are
      still mathematically interesting.

8 Copy this diagram *twice* and make two
   number squares; *firstly* by adding the
   numbers given and *secondly* by multiplying
   the numbers.

   a **The addition square**
      (i) Choose a 2 × 2 square anywhere
           within the addition square;
           for example

	5	6
	6	7

      Add the two numbers on each diagonal.
      Repeat for other 2 × 2 squares. What do you notice?
      (ii) Choose a 3 × 3 square within the addition square.
           Again, *add* all the numbers on each diagonal.
           Repeat for other 3 × 3 squares. What do you notice?
      (iii) Choose other sizes of squares and investigate additions along the
            diagonals.
      (iv) Would you have the same result if you had a *rectangle* of numbers and
           added pairs of opposite corners?

   b **The multiplication square**
      (i) Choose a 2 × 2 square anywhere within the multiplication square and
           multiply the two numbers on each diagonal.
           Repeat for other 2 × 2 squares. What do you notice?
      (ii) Choose several 3 × 3 squares; *multiply* the three numbers on each
           diagonal (using a calculator).
      (iii) Investigate other sizes of squares and also investigate rectangles where
            you multiply pairs of opposite corners.

   Another familiar number square runs from 1 to 100.
   a Choose various 2 × 2 squares as before, and
      investigate multiplying the numbers in opposite
      corners.
   b Choose various 3 × 3 squares and multiply as before.
   c Increase the size of your squares step by step and
      investigate the multiplications.
      Copy and complete this table.

ze of square	2 × 2	3 × 3	4 × 4	5 × 5	6 × 6	7 × 7	8 × 8	9 × 9	10×10	n × n
fference of products opposite corners										

Sets of numbers

d Investigate various rectangles, again multiplying opposite corners. Can you build up a pattern to predict your results?

e The whole investigation can be repeated in (for example) a 9×9 number square labelled from 1 to 81.
What patterns can you find and what predictions can you make?

Part 5 Patterns with a calculator

1 Find the answers to each of these sets of calculations.
Notice the patterns in the calculations and in your answers.
Follow the pattern to write the next few calculations in each set and predict their answers.
Check your predictions using a calculator.

a
3×37
6×37
9×37
12×37

b
1×9
21×9
321×9
4321×9

c
3×9
33×9
333×9
3333×9

d
$143 \times 7 \times 2$
$143 \times 7 \times 3$
$143 \times 7 \times 4$

e
6×7
66×67
666×66

f
$1 \times 8 + 2$
$2 \times 8 + 4$
$3 \times 8 + 6$
$4 \times 8 + 8$

g
$1 \times 8 + 1$
$12 \times 8 + 2$
$123 \times 8 + 3$
$1234 \times 8 + 4$

h
11×9
21×9
31×9
41×9

i
$0 \times 9 + 1$
$1 \times 9 + 2$
$12 \times 9 + 3$
$123 \times 9 + 4$

j
$9 \times 9 + 7$
$98 \times 9 + 6$
$987 \times 9 + 5$

k
1×1
11×11
111×111

l
15873×7
15873×14
15873×21
15873×28

m
$\sqrt{1}$
$\sqrt{1 + 3}$
$\sqrt{1 + 3 + 5}$
$\sqrt{1 + 3 + 5 + 7}$

n
$12345679 \times 9 \times 1$
$12345679 \times 9 \times 2$
$12345679 \times 9 \times 3$

o
6×6
66×66
666×666

p
4^2
34^2
334^2

q
$\sqrt{(1 \times 2 \times 3 \times 4) + 1}$

$\sqrt{(2 \times 3 \times 4 \times 5) + 1}$

$\sqrt{(3 \times 4 \times 5 \times 6) + 1}$

r
$\dfrac{1}{1}$

$\dfrac{3 + 5}{2}$

$\dfrac{7 + 9 + 11}{3}$

$\dfrac{13 + 15 + 17 + 19}{4}$

s
$\dfrac{1 \times 1}{1}$

$\dfrac{22 \times 22}{1 + 2 + 1}$

$\dfrac{333 \times 333}{1 + 2 + 3 + 2 + 1}$

2 Calculate $37037 \times n$ for $3 \leqslant n \leqslant 27$ and see what patterns you get.

Sets of numbers

3 A numerical **palindrome** is a number which reads the same forwards or backwards (e.g. 76267).

   a Enter any number into your calculator.

   b Add to it the number which uses the same digits as the first number but in *reverse* order.

   c Is your answer a palindrome?

   d If not, add the number formed by reversing that which you see.

   e Repeat **c** and **d** until you get a palindrome.

   f Can you find any number for which this procedure does *not* give a palindrome?

4 Use your calculator to estimate the values of these four series.
The series in **a** was discovered by the Englishman John Wallis (1616–1703) and the one in **b** by the German Gottfried Wilhelm von Leibnitz (1646–1716).

   a $2\left\{\dfrac{2}{1} \times \dfrac{2}{3} \times \dfrac{4}{3} \times \dfrac{4}{5} \times \dfrac{6}{5} \times \dfrac{6}{7} \times \dfrac{8}{7} \times \dfrac{8}{9} \times \ldots \right\}$

   b $4\left\{1 - \dfrac{1}{3} + \dfrac{1}{5} - \dfrac{1}{7} + \dfrac{1}{9} - \dfrac{1}{11} + \dfrac{1}{13} - \ldots \right\}$

   c $\sqrt{12}\left\{1 - \dfrac{1}{3 \times 3} + \dfrac{1}{3^2 \times 5} - \dfrac{1}{3^3 \times 7} + \dfrac{1}{3^4 \times 9} - \ldots \right\}$

   d $1 + \dfrac{1}{1} + \dfrac{1}{1 \times 2} + \dfrac{1}{1 \times 2 \times 3} + \dfrac{1}{1 \times 2 \times 3 \times 4} + \ldots$

   e Do you recognise any of your answers?

5 Can you use four 4's with the symbols of the basic operations to make all numbers from 1 to 100?
For example, $15 = 4 \times 4 - \dfrac{4}{4}$ and $66 = 4 \times 4 \times 4 + \sqrt{4}$.

Other topics

Sets and switches

Loci

Envelopes

Linkages

Gears and belts

Sets and switches

1 *Switches*

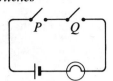

Venn diagram

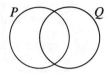

Statement

a If 0 stands for *"switch open"* and *"no flow"* and 1 stands for *"switch closed"* and *"current flows"*, copy and complete this table.

	P	Q	current
a	0	0	
b	0	1	
c	1	0	
d	1	1	

b If 0 stands for *"outside the set"* and 1 stands for *"inside the set"*, copy this diagram and label the regions **a, b, c** and **d** to correspond to the table. Shade the region which corresponds to the current flowing.

c Copy and complete the following: "The statement *'Current flows only when* **both** *switch P* **and** *switch Q are* ...', is equivalent to the region $P \cap Q$ on the Venn diagram."

2 *Switches*

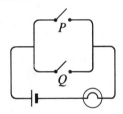

Venn diagram

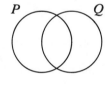

Statement

a Taking 0 and 1 as above, copy and complete this table.

	P	Q	current
a	0	0	
b	0	1	
c	1	0	
d	1	1	

b Taking 0 and 1 as above, copy this diagram, label its regions **a** to **d,** and shade those regions which correspond to the current flowing.

c Copy and complete the following: "The statement *'Current flows when* **either...or... or both** *are closed'*, is equivalent to the region $P \cup Q$ on the Venn diagram."

a Copy and complete this table for the switching circuit shown.

Circuit 1

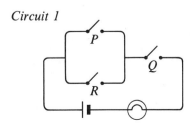

	P	Q	R	current
a	0	0	0	
b	0	0	1	
c	0	1	0	
d	0	1	1	
e	1	0	0	
f	1	0	1	
g	1	1	0	
h	1	1	1	

Sets and switches

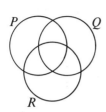

b Copy the Venn diagram. Label corresponding regions of the diagram **a** to **h** and shade those regions which represent when current flows.

c Which one of these four sets represents all the shaded parts of the diagram?
(i) $P \cap Q \cap R$
(ii) $P \cup (Q \cap R)$
(iii) $P \cup Q \cup R$
(iv) $(P \cup R) \cap Q$

4 Use the same table and Venn diagram for these three circuits. Copy and complete both the table and the diagram. Decide which of the sets in part **c** above matches with these three circuits.

a *Circuit 2*   b *Circuit 3*   c *Circuit 4*

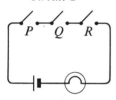
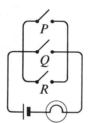
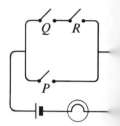

5 Some switches have more than one arm. The coloured lines on these circuits show those arms which are linked together so that they open and close together Use the same table and Venn diagram as in question **3** and copy and complete them for these two circuits.
Which *two* of these four sets represent the shaded parts of your diagram?
(i) $(P \cap Q) \cup R$ (ii) $(Q \cup R) \cap P$ (iii) $(P \cup Q) \cap R$ (iv) $(Q \cap R) \cup$.
Which circuits in questions **3** or **4** are equivalent to the two circuits here?

a   b

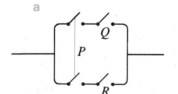
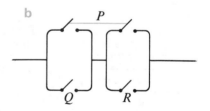

6 a Use the same table and Venn diagram as before. Copy and complete them both for this circuit. Look at the shading on your diagram and choose the simplest way of describing it in symbols.

b What does your answer tell you about how this switching circuit could be simplified?

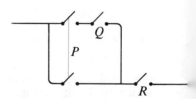

This is a simple example of how a circuit can be translated into mathematical symbols. The symbols are then simplified and translated bac into a circuit of a simpler design. This method is particularly useful in the design of computer circuits and the algebra used is called **Boolean algebra**, after George Boole (1815–1864), the English mathematician who first developed these ideas.

c Do you recognise the patterns of the 0's and 1's in the tables you have use What type of numbers do they remind you of?

7 Use the same table and Venn diagram of question **3** for each of these circuits.
   Then answer these questions.

   a From the shading on your diagrams, which one of the circuits is
   equivalent to circuit (i)?

   b Which circuit in questions **3** or **4** is also equivalent to circuit (i)?

   c Which other two circuits are equivalent to circuit (ii)?

   d Which circuit in questions **3** or **4** is also equivalent to circuit (ii)?

   e Which of these circuits can be simplified so that it uses only *two* switches?
   Draw the equivalent simplified circuit.

(i)   (ii)   (iii)

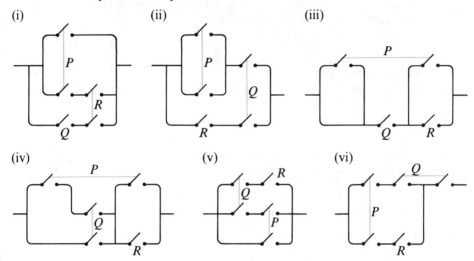

(iv)   (v)   (vi)

3 Some "double switches" are made so that as one arm P closes, the other arm P'
opens. On the Venn diagram, P' is the *complement* (or outside) of P.
Copy and complete this table and Venn diagram for this circuit. Does the
shading on your Venn diagram suggest a simpler equivalent circuit?

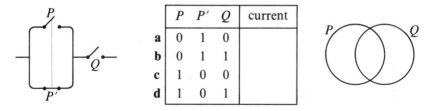

	P	P'	Q	current
a	0	1	0	
b	0	1	1	
c	1	0	0	
d	1	0	1	

Use the table of question **3** with extra columns for P' and R' as required and
the same Venn diagram for these two circuits.

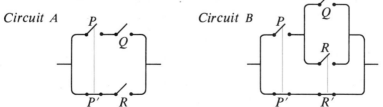

Is either of these circuits equivalent to any of the circuits in questions **3** or **4**?

Loci

Part 1

A **locus** is a set of points which satisfy a given condition. If a point is allowed to move in a certain way, then the positions it can take form the locus.

To find the loci in this exercise, you will need some equipment – a sharp pencil, compasses, scissors, cotton or thin string, drawing pins and thick card.

1 a Fix one end of a long piece of cotton to the bottom edge of a cylinder and hold it on a sheet of paper as shown. Tighten the cotton with a pencil point X in a loop at the other end and draw the locus of X as the cotton winds round the cylinder. A curve such as this is called an **involute**. Can you give this curve a more common name?

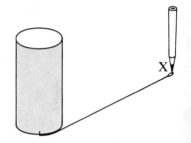

   b Repeat with the cotton fixed to the base of a cuboid. Be sure to make the length of cotton long enough to wrap round the cuboid.

2 a Fix two drawing pins P_1 and P_2 on a sheet of paper 8 cm apart. Make a loop with 18 to 20 cm of thin string. Draw the loop tight with a pencil point X and keep it tight as you draw the locus of X. What is the name of the curve you draw? This is an easy way of marking out a flower bed of this shape in a garden.

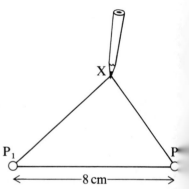

   b Keep the loop the same size but move the pins symmetrically together by 1 cm each so that they are 6 cm apart. Draw the new locus of X. Repeat with the pins 4 cm and then 2 cm apart, and finally with the pins together

   Describe in words what happens.

   c On a new sheet of paper, fix the pins 8 cm apart as before. Make a loop with 30 cm of string. Draw the locus of X. Now, keep the pins in the same place, but make the loop smaller by about 2 cm and draw the new locus of X. Keep reducing the loop by about 2 cm and draw the locus of X each time, until the loop is too small. Describe what happens.

3 a A simple see-saw can be made with a cylinder and a straight ruler. Fix the circular end of the cylinder on a sheet of paper and place the midpoint of the ruler so that it touches the circle. Mark a point X, roll the ruler both clockwise and anticlockwise around the circle *without* sliding, marking the position of X several times. Draw the locus of X to give you another type of **spiral**.

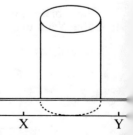

   b Repeat with point Y on the other side of the midpoint. Repeat with X and Y at different distances from the midpoint.

Loci

4 a Cut out of card or thick paper a right-angled triangle with sides of 10 cm, 10 cm and 14.1 cm.
Mark two points P and Q 8 cm apart on a sheet of paper.
Place the triangle so that its 10 cm sides pass through P and Q; mark the position of corner X on the paper.
Repeat for different positions of the triangle and so find the locus of X as the triangle "slips" between the points P and Q.

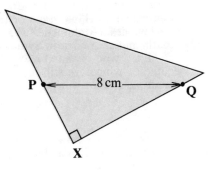

b Repeat this exercise with an equilateral triangle of side 10 cm. How does this locus differ from that in part **a**?

5 Trace this ellipse onto a sheet of paper. Trace and cut out this right-angled triangle (or cut out a bigger one, or use a set square). Position the triangle over the ellipse so that the two shorter sides are tangents to the ellipse.
Mark the position of corner X on the paper.
Move the triangle, keeping the same sides as tangents; mark X in its new position.
Repeat until you can draw the locus of X.
Describe the locus in words.

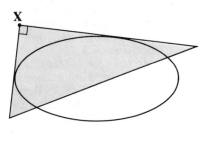

6 Trace this ellipse, cut it out and make a hole at its centre X. Draw two perpendicular lines on paper and position the ellipse so that they are tangents to it as shown. Mark the position of X on the paper. Move the ellipse, keeping the two lines as tangents, marking the position of X as you move. Draw the locus of X and describe it.

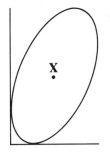

7 a A ladder is leaning against a wall and a man is at the top of the ladder. If the bottom starts to slide along the ground away from the wall, describe in words the locus of the upper end E *without* drawing a diagram.

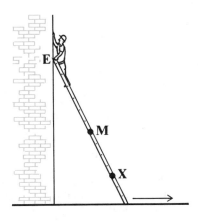

b To find the locus of the midpoint M, draw two perpendicular lines 10 cm long on paper and draw a line L 8 cm long on tracing paper to represent the ladder. Place the line L so that its ends are on the two perpendicular lines and mark the position of M. Repeat with line L in different positions, marking the position of M each time. Draw the locus of M and describe it in words.

c Now consider any other point X on the ladder. Mark it on the tracing paper. Repeat the instruction of part **b** to draw the locus of X. Describe it in words.

Loci

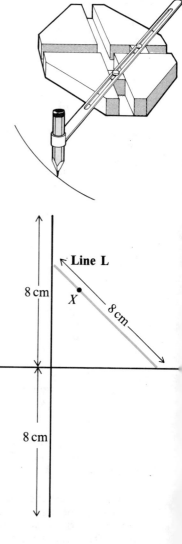

8 The ideas developed in **7** are used in this instrument to be found in drawing offices and called an **ellipsograph** or the **trammel of Archimedes**. (Archimedes was a Greek mathematician born in Syracuse, Sicily in 287 B.C., who invented many machines, some of which are still in use today.) An example is shown here.

a You can see how it works by drawing two perpendicular lines 16 cm long bisecting each other.
Draw an 8 cm line L on tracing paper and mark the point X 2 cm from one end. Position L with its ends on the two perpendicular lines and mark the position of X.
Move line L so that its ends slide on the perpendicular lines and mark the new position of X. Repeat several times and so draw the locus of X. This should be an **ellipse.**

b By altering the position of X on line L you can alter the shape of the ellipse. Where should X be for a **circle** to be drawn?

c Would you say this statement is *true* or *false*?

$$\{circles\} \subset \{ellipses\}$$

9 Draw a circle of radius 8 cm on a sheet of paper. Draw and cut out a second circle of radius 4 cm and draw any diameter PQ. Place the smaller circle inside the larger one as shown and mark the positions of P and Q on the sheet of paper.
Roll the smaller circle around the inside of the bigger one, marking the positions of P and Q as you go, and so draw their loci. Describe these two loci in words.
As PQ was *any* diameter, this means *all* points on the smaller circumference have this type of locus. This result should surprise you; indeed, this motion is similar to that in **8** and has been used to make a different type of ellipsograph using two cogs.

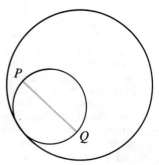

10 There are other ways of obtaining ellipses and other curves without using the ideas of a locus.

a

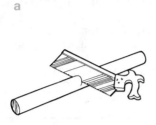

b

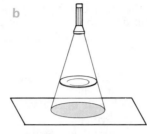

c

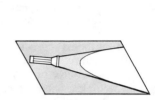

When you saw on the slant through a wooden cylinder such as a broom handle can you imagine what shape the area of cross-section will be?

Hold a torch above a table and place a circular plate in the beam to cause a shadow on the table. When the plate is horizontal, what shape is the shadow? As you rotate the plate about a horizontal axis, what shape does the shadow take? Is the shadow ever a straight line?

Hold a torch a few centimetres above the floor in a dimly-lit room. Notice the edge of the illuminated area. This edge is *not* an ellipse. Can you name the curve?

Tie a small button or washer to one end X of a piece of cotton XY 8 cm long. Draw a line AB and lay the cotton perpendicular to it with Y on the line. Mark the position of X.

Move Y along the line AB without touching the cotton except at Y. Mark the position of X for various positions of Y (the diagram shows the cotton in the position $X'Y'$). Hence, draw the locus of X.

The name of this curve is the **tractrix**, a word taken from the Latin "tractum" meaning "dragged", which also gives us other words such as *tractor* and *extraction*.

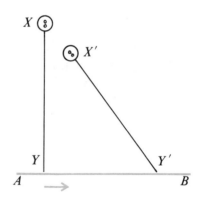

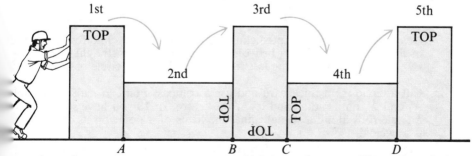

a A workman wants to move a crate which is too heavy to lift; so he rolls it over four times as shown.
Rolling about A takes it from the first to the second position.
Rolling about B takes it from the second to the third position, etc.

Loci

To find the locus of the letter O in the word TOP, draw a straight line and use a rectangle 6 cm by 3 cm cut from thick card, write the word TOP and make a hole through the letter O for your pencil point, rotate the rectangle as described above and draw the locus as you go.

b You could repeat this with a crate of *triangular* cross-section.
How many times will the workman have to roll it before it is upright again?

13 In mathematics, a **roulette** is the locus of a point on a curve which rolls on a fixed curve. One of the simplest roulettes to draw is for a point X on the circumference of a circle which rolls on a fixed straight line.

a Stick a sheet of paper to a ruler as shown and place a circular coin or a circle of thick card on the ruler. Mark point X on both circle and paper.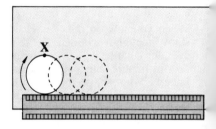
Roll the circle *slowly and carefully* along the ruler (without slipping), marking the position of X on the paper as you go. Continue until the circle has made *at least* one full revolution.
Draw the locus of the point X to get a curve which is called a **cycloid**.

b If X is the head of a nail stuck into a car tyre, the locus of the head as the car moves is a cycloid. Can you think of other objects which would have this locus?

c Draw a cycloid on squared paper for one full turn of each circle given in this table. Find
  (i) the length of the cycloid, using a piece of cotton
  (ii) the area of the circle, by calculation to 3 significant figures
  (iii) the area between the cycloid and the straight line, by *either* counting squares *or* using the trapezium rule *or* any other method.
Copy this table and enter your results.

Radius of circle, cm	Diameter of circle, cm	Length of the cycloid, cm	Area of circle, cm^2	Area between cycloid and straight line, cm
3				
4				
5				
6				
r				

Can you see any way of predicting the length of the cycloid for one full turn of the circle and the area between the cycloid and the straight line?
Can you now complete the last row of the table for a circle of radius r?

14 a Cut a circle from thick card and use a compass point to make three holes X_1 and X_2 on a radius and X_3 at the centre. In **13** you have seen that when a circle rolls along a straight line, the locus of a point on its circumference is a cycloid.
Repeat the instructions of **13a** for the point X_1 with your pencil through the hole.
Similarly, find the loci of points X_2 and X_3.
This family of curves is called the **trochoids.** Can you describe the trochoid for X_3 in words?

b   If point X_1 represents the valve
on the wheel of a bicycle, what could
X_2 and X_3 represent?

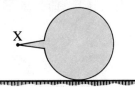

5 a   The final locus of this type is when the point
X is *outside* the circle.
Cut a circle with a spike from thick card. Roll
it along a straight line drawn on paper (or use
a ruler as before), marking the positions of X
as you go. Draw the locus of X.

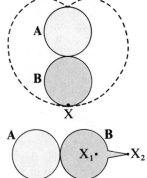

b   When an express train is travelling at speed, which parts of the train are
moving *backwards* in the opposite direction to all the passengers?

6 Curves called **epicycloids** are formed when one circle rolls round the *outside* of
another circle.

a   Circles A and B have the same radius (of, say,
4 cm); A is drawn on paper and B is cut out
of thick card. Mark the position of X, and
then roll B around A, marking the position of
X as you go.
See if you can develop the locus of X as
shown. This curve is called a **cardioid,** from the
Greek "kardia" meaning "heart", and the
sharp point on the curve is called a **cusp.**

b   Repeat with a point X_1 which lies *inside*
circle B.

c   Repeat with a point X_2 which is *outside* circle
B (on a spike as in **15**).

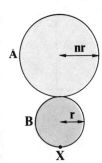

Draw the locus of point X as in **16a**, but choose
different sizes for circle B.

a   If B has a radius r and A has a radius nr, let
n = 2, 3, 4 and 5. What do you notice about
the value of n and the number of cusps on
each locus? (When n = 2, the curve produced
is called a **nephroid**, from the Greek
"nephros" meaning "kidney".)

b   If n has a *fractional* value, what difference
does it make to the locus and the number of
cusps?

Curves called **hypocycloids** are formed when one circle rolls round the *inside* of
another circle.

a   If circle B has a radius r and circle A has a
radius nr, draw circle A on paper, cut circle B
out of thick card and draw the locus of point
X for
(i)   n = 2 and describe the shape of the
locus
(ii) n = 3 which produces a curve called a
deltoid
(iii) n = 4 which produces a curve called an
astroid
(iv) n = 5
(v)   n having a *fractional* value.

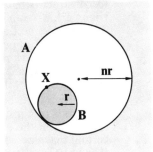

Loci

b

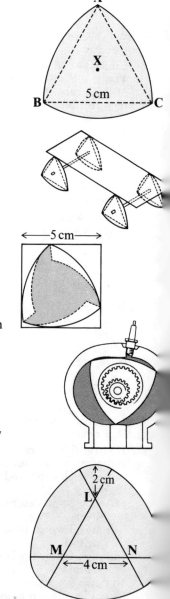

Investigate the locus when *X* is *inside* circle *B*, and then when *X* is *outside* circle *B*.

These investigations are useful in the design of gears and this diagram shows the arrangement inside the 3-speed gear of a bicycle.

If you have a toy known as *Spirograph*, these loc and many more can be drawn very quickly using cogs.

19 The *circle* is the only curve of constant *radius*, and so the best wheel mounted on an axle will be circular. But the circle is *not* the only curve of constant *width*. There are an infinite number of such curves, all of which can be used as *rollers*.

a Draw an equilateral triangle *ABC* of side 5 cm on thick card. Draw an arc of a circle on each side using the opposite corner as centre. Cut the shape out. Draw two parallel lines 5 cm apart and roll the shape between them. Watch the width across the shape as you do it.
Find the centre of the triangle *X*, make a small hole and draw the locus of *X* as the shape rolls *without slipping* along one of the lines.
How does this locus differ from the locus of the centre of a *circular* roller? Why would these shapes not be used as wheels?

b Mount four of the shapes, in pairs as shown, on wooden rods. Place a flat sheet of card on them and roll it along. It will move evenly in spite of the rollers looking as if they are "bumping" along.

c Draw a square of side 5 cm and see if you can rotate the shape inside the square. The dotted lines show the basic shape of a drill which is used for cutting *square* holes.
The same shape is also important in the design of the rotary car-engine (known as a Wankel engine) which uses a rotating shape instead of the usual pistons.

d Another curve of constant width which is easy to construct is based on the equilateral triangle *LMN* of side 4 cm shown here.
The three longest arcs have radii of 6 cm and centres at the opposite corners. The three shorter arcs have radii of 2 cm and centres at the near corners. You can try any of the above exercises with this shape too.

e Which two British coins are *not* circular? Are they coins of constant width? Constant width is essential if these coins are to be used in certain machines. In what type of machine is it essential to have coins of constant width?

Part 2

1 a Draw and label both axes from 0 to 10.
Label the points $A(0, 5)$ and $B(10, 5)$.
Which *one* of the three points (4, 8), (5, 8), (6, 8) is the same distance from
A as it is from B? Label this point X.
If X now moves so it is *always* as far from A as it is from B, mark four
other possible positions of X and draw the line on which *all* possible
positions lie.

b Draw and label both axes from 0 to 10.
Label the points $M(1, 6)$ and $N(5, 2)$. Find any point equidistant from M
and N and label it X.
If X now moves so that it is *always* equidistant from M and N, draw the
line on which it moves.

c   A boy wants to pass through an opening in
an electrified fence.
Make a sketch of the path he should take so
that he is always as far from one gate post as
he is from the other.

d Construct the points P, Q and X these
distances apart. X now moves so that
$PX = QX$ at all times. Use a ruler to find
several positions of X and so draw its locus.
Give a name to the line you have drawn.
How could you have used your compasses to
help you?

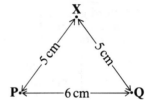

a Draw and label both axes from 0 to 10.
Draw a line joining points (5, 10) and (5, 0) and a second line joining points
(0, 5) and (10, 5).
Which *one* of these three points (7, 8), (8, 8), (9, 8) is the same distance from
one of these lines as it is from the other? Label the point X. If X now moves
so it is always equidistant from these two lines, mark other possible
positions of X and draw the line on which all possible positions lie.

b Draw and label both axes from 0 to 10.
Draw the line joining points (8, 0) and (0, 8) and a second line joining
points (8, 10) and (0, 2). Find any point which is equidistant from these two
lines and label it X.
If X moves so that it is *always* equidistant from these two lines, draw the
path on which it moves.

c 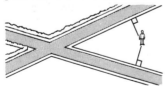 Two straight roads cross at an angle as
shown. A boy stands in a field so he is as far
from one road as he is from the other.
Make a sketch of the route he must take so
that he is *always* the same distance from each
road.

Use a protractor to draw the lines L and M at
an angle of 60°. Use a ruler to help you mark
a point X which is equidistant from both
lines. Let X move so that it is *always*
equidistant from the two lines. Mark some
possible positions and so draw the locus of X.
Give a name to the line you have drawn.
How could you have used your compasses to
help you?

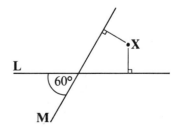

Loci

3 A goat is tethered to a stake O by a rope
   3 metres long. Describe in words the locus of
   a the furthest point which the goat can reach
   b the locus of *all* the points which it can reach.
   Notice that a locus can be not only a curve or
   line, but also an area and, in three dimensions,
   even a volume.

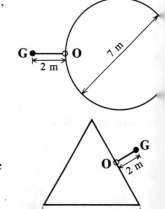

4 Another goat G is held by a 2-metre rope OG
   where the end O can slide along a 4-metre wire
   XY with X and Y fixed. This is called a *running-
   lead.*
   Use a scale of 1 cm = 1 m and
   a draw accurately using a ruler and compasses
      the locus of the furthest point which it can
      reach
   b shade the locus of *all* points which it can
      reach.

5 A third goat G is also held by a 2-metre rope OG,
   where the end O can now slide along a fixed
   horizontal circular wire of diameter 7 metres. The
   goat can graze both inside and outside the circle.
   Use a scale of 1 cm = 1 m and
   a draw accurately the locus of the furthest point
      which it can reach
   b shade the locus of *all* points which it can
      reach.

6 Another goat G, also held by a 2-metre rope OG,
   has the end O allowed to slide along the 8-metre
   sides of a fixed horizontal equilateral triangle. The
   goat can graze both inside and outside the
   triangle.
   Using the same scale, construct the same two loci
   as before.

7 Each of these three diagrams shows a wooden block of different cross-section
   A piece of string is tied to one corner as shown.
   Draw each diagram accurately and use compasses to help you construct the
   locus of the end E of the string as it is wound clockwise around each block.
   string is kept tight at all times.

   a A square of   b A rectangle   c An equilateral
      side 2 cm   2 cm by 3 cm   triangle of side 3

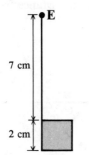

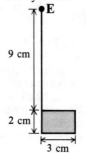

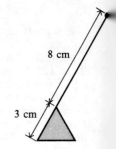

Loci

8   A heavy metal ball *B* is tied by a horizontal piece
    of string 6 cm long to a fixed point *O*. A peg *P* is
    fixed 4 cm vertically below *O*. After ball *B* is let
    fall, the string collides with the peg *P* and wraps
    round it as the ball rotates a full turn about *P*.
    Draw this diagram and construct the locus of *B*.

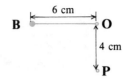

9   Draw a circle of radius 4 cm and label a fixed
    point *A* on its circumference. Point *P* is a variable
    point on the circumference and *M* is the
    midpoint of the chord *AP*.
    Draw the chord *AP* for different positions of *P*
    and mark the midpoint *M* each time. Hence,
    draw the locus of *M* as *P* moves around the
    whole circumference. Describe the locus in words.

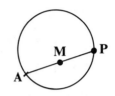

10 Draw a circle of radius 5 cm and in it draw any
    chord which is 8 cm long. Label the midpoint *M*
    of the chord.
    Draw several possible positions of the chord
    which is always 8 cm long and mark the
    midpoint *M* each time. Draw the locus of *M* as
    the chord moves around the circle. Describe it in
    words.

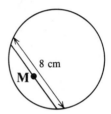

    Draw a circle of radius 4 cm and any diameter
    AB. Draw any chord which is at right-angles to
    AB. Mark the points *Q* one quarter of the way
    along the chord from each end.
    Now let the chord move across the circle, always
    at right angles to *AB*. Draw several positions and
    mark the points *Q* each time. Draw the locus of
    Q and describe it in words.

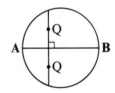

a   Use a ruler and compasses to
    copy this diagram where the
    spacing between the lines is
    the same as for the circles.
    Label the lines and circles
    with numbers as shown.
    Mark the points of
    intersection of lines and
    circles with the same
    number. Join these points
    with a smooth curve and give
    the curve a name.

b   Experiment with the lines
    spaced further apart than the
    circles, and again with the
    lines nearer together than the
    circles.

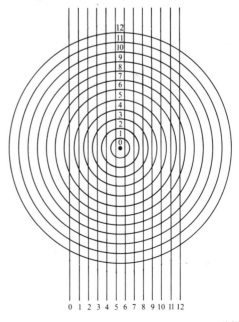

Loci

13

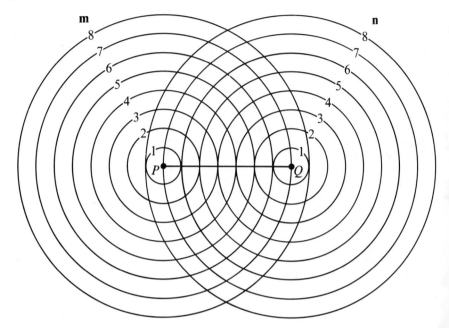

Trace this diagram, or draw it for yourself. The centre points P and Q are $3\frac{1}{2}$ cm apart and the radii of the circles increase in $\frac{1}{2}$ cm steps from $\frac{1}{2}$ cm to 4 cm. Each circle centred on P has an m-value from 1 to 8 and each circle centred on Q has an n-value from 1 to 8.

a   Mark in colour the points of intersection of the two sets of circles where the m and n-values are related by $m+n = 8$.
    If m and n are allowed to have fractional values, draw a smooth curve on which the points of intersection lie.

b   Repeat with $m+n = 10$ and draw another smooth curve.
    What is the name of these curves?

14

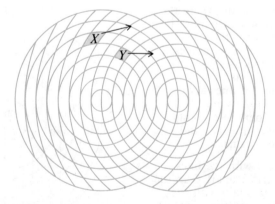

This diagram can be drawn by following the instructions for problem **13** and then continuing to increase the radii beyond 4 cm, still in $\frac{1}{2}$ cm steps, but now only drawing the *arcs* of circles *inside* the diagram.

a   Shade space X and then shade *every other* space, working in the direction the arrow until you arrive back at X. You should have shaded an elliptical pattern.

b Repeat with space Y to get another elliptical pattern. Then continue until the whole diagram has *every other* space shaded. Does the final pattern remind you of the ripples moving out from two stones dropped into still water at the same time? Scientists call this effect an *interference pattern*.

5 Stick a piece of paper around the outside of a cylindrical tin and use your compasses to draw a curve on the paper as shown here. Open the paper out.
This curve is *not* an ellipse. Some people call it an **oval**.

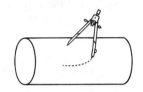

6 Draw a circle of radius 6 cm and divide it into 24 equal sectors using angles of 15°.

a Copy and complete this table where $x = \dfrac{\theta}{60}$.

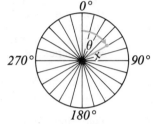

θ	0	15	30	45	60	75	90	...	360
x									

b Plot a point on each radius for each pair of values in the table and so find the locus of the point which moves so that its distance x cm from the centre of the circle depends on the angle θ as in the table.
What is the name of this locus?

a The fixed point P is 4 cm from the fixed line L. A variable point X moves so that it is always as far from P as it is from L. Three possible positions are shown.
Draw the diagram accurately and add more possible positions of X. Hence draw the locus of X as a smooth curve. Can you give a name to the curve?

b Take the same fixed point P and the same fixed line L. Now find the locus of point X so that it is always *twice* as far from L as it is from P.
What name can you give to the curve you get?

The shaded vertical rectangle is to be moved sideways by rotating it four times, about each of its corners in turn. First it is rotated clockwise through 90° about C_1 until it lies horizontal; another quarter turn about the next corner has it vertical again but upside down. Two more rotations of 90° about its other two corners bring it back upright.

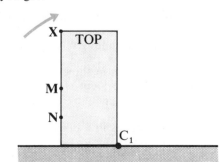

Draw a diagram of these various positions using a rectangle 4 cm by 2 cm, and use compasses to draw the locus of the corner X. Also draw the loci of the midpoint M and of the point N.
Through what sideways distance has your rectangle finally been translated?

Loci

19 The shaded isosceles triangle is "rolled" along the line in three stages, about the centres C_1, C_2 and lastly C_3, until it is upright again.
Draw the diagram accurately and use compasses to draw the locus of corner X.
Also draw the loci of midpoint M and point N.

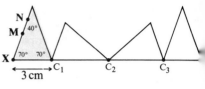

20 a A child's bicycle has wheels of radius 30 cm and it approaches a step 30 cm high. Draw an accurate diagram of the wheel (scale 1 cm = 10 cm) and the step as shown, then draw the wheel in several different positions. Hence construct the locus of the centre C as the wheel approaches the step, climbs over it and rolls on.

b Repeat this for the same wheel rolling up a step only 20 cm high.

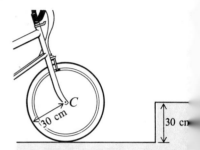

21 a Two guard dogs are tied to points A and B 6 metres apart. A young child X wishes to pass between them so he is always the same distance from each dog. Draw a diagram and show the path he should take.

b If the same child wishes to pass between the two dogs so that he is always twice as far from A as he is from B, draw the path he should take.

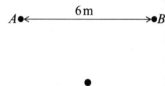

c

If there is now a third guard dog C so that A, B and C are the corners of an equilateral triangle, draw the safest path for the child to take as he passes throu the triangle.

The following questions are multiple-choice questions. Choose the *one* correct answ in each case.

22 A point moves in a plane so that it is always the same distance from a fixed point. Its locus is
a a straight line   b a sphere   c a circle   d two straight lin

23 A point moves in three dimensions so that it is always the same distance from fixed point. Its locus is
a a straight line   b a sphere   c a circle   d two straight lir

24 A point moves in a plane so that it is always the same distance from a fixed line. Its locus is
a a straight line   b a cylinder   c a cuboid   d two straight li

25 A point moves in three dimensions so that it is always the same distance fro fixed line. Its locus is
a a straight line   b a cylinder   c a cuboid   d two straight li

26 A point P moves in a plane so that angle $APB = 90°$ where A and B are two fixed points. The locus of P is

  a   a straight line   b   a cylinder   c   a circle   d   a sphere.

27 A point moves in three dimensions so that angle $APB = 90°$ where A and B are two fixed points. The locus of P is

  a   a straight line   b   a cylinder   c   a circle   d   a sphere.

28 A point P moves in a plane so that angle $APB = 60°$ where A and B are two fixed points. The locus of P is

  a   a circle   b   a straight line   c   the arcs of two circles   d   two straight lines.

29 Triangle LPM has a certain area. Point P moves so that this area stays constant. The locus of P is

  a   a circle   b   a straight line   c   the arcs of two circles   d   two straight lines.

30 A point P moves in a plane so that it is always 1 cm from the circumference of a circle of radius 3 cm. The locus of P is

  a   a circle   b   a straight line   c   two circles   d   a doughnut or torus.

31 For each part of this problem, draw a new diagram of this triangle ABC. Take as the Universal set $\mathscr{E}$ all points inside this triangle.

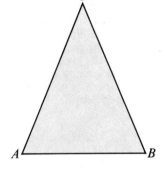

  a   Indicate the set of points equidistant from A and B.

  b   Shade the set of points which are nearer to A than to B.

  c   Use compasses to indicate the set of points which are as far from A as B is from A.

  d   Shade the set of points which are nearer to A than B is to A.

  e   Shade the set of points which are further from A than B is from A.

  f   Indicate the set of points which are as far from side AC as from side AB.

  g   Shade the set of points which are nearer to side AC than to side AB.

For each part of this problem, draw a new diagram of the square $PQRS$. Take as the Universal set $\mathscr{E}$ all points inside this square.

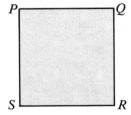

Indicate the set of points which are as far from

  a P as from R b P as from S

  c P as Q is from P d   side PQ as from side SR

  e   side PQ as from side PS.

Shade the set of points which are

  f   nearer to P than to S g   further from P than from R

  h   further from P than S is from P i   nearer to side PS than to side QR

  j   nearer to side PS than to side PQ.

Envelopes

An **envelope** is a curve which has, as its tangents, a set of straight lines drawn according to certain rules.

Part 1 Paper folding

1 a Draw and cut out a circle of radius 8 cm.
Mark a point P inside the circle, not too close
to either the centre or the circumference.
Fold the circle so that the circumference falls
on P as shown. Crease the paper, open it out
and mark the crease in pencil.
Repeat many times.
What is the name of the curve which appears
as the envelope?

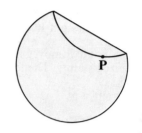

b Repeat with P at the centre of the circle.
What curve do you get now?

c Repeat with P on the circumference of the
circle. Do you get a curve at all? Which single
point has the envelope been reduced to?

d Draw the circle of radius 8 cm on a large
sheet of paper but do *not* cut it out. Mark a
point P *outside* the circle (on the edge of the
paper will be easiest). Fold as before so that P
lies on the circumference. Notice that the
envelope is in two separate parts – such a
curve is called a **hyperbola**.

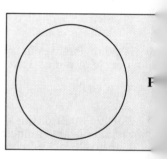

2 Draw a line L and mark a point P about 3 cm
from the line.
Fold the paper so that P lies on L, crease it and
mark the crease in pencil.
Repeat many times.
What is the name of the curve which appears as
the envelope?

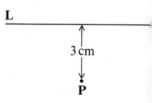

Part 2 Using a set-square

The size of the circles which you draw in these exercises will depend on the size of
your set-square. A radius of about 5 cm should give a satisfactory result.

1 Draw a circle and mark a point P inside it.
Position the set-square with the right angle L on
the circumference of the circle and the side LM
passing through P.
Draw the line LN and repeat for many positions
of L.
Name the curve which appears as the envelope.

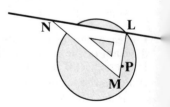

2

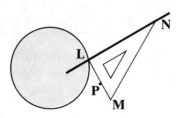

Repeat exercise **1** but with point P outside the
circle.
This envelope appears in two separate parts.
Can you name the curve?

Envelopes

3 Draw a straight line *AB* and mark point *P* about
2 cm off the line.
Position the set square with the right angle *L* on
the line and the side *LM* passing through *P*.
Draw the line *LN* and repeat several times.
What is the name of the curve which appears as
the envelope?

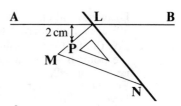

Part 3   Using a ruler and a pair of compasses

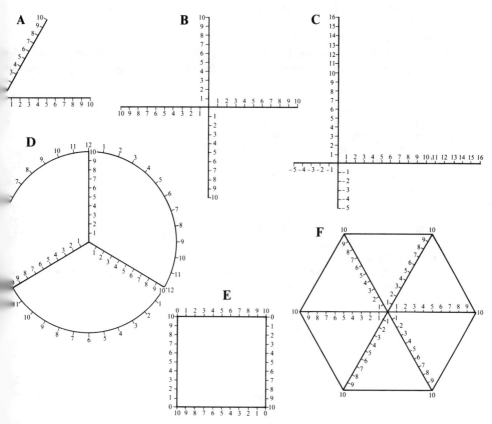

a Select one or several of these diagrams. Draw and label the lines as shown.
Draw straight lines in colour which join pairs of points totalling 11
(e.g. 1 + 10, 2 + 9, ...).
The envelope from diagram **B** is called an **astroid**, from the Latin "astra"
meaning "star". What is the name of the envelope from diagram **C**?

b *Curve-stitching* is the name used when these envelopes are made on card or
cloth with a needle and different coloured cottons. Loose ends can be
secured using sticky tape or glue on the back of the card or cloth.

c *Pin-and-thread* is a much more time-consuming activity. Small panel pins are
nailed into a sheet of hardboard and coloured cottons stretched tightly
between them.

You can use these patterns or others of your own invention to design more
elaborate pictures.

Envelopes

2 a Draw several circles of radius 5 cm and mark points on the circumference 30° apart, numbering them from 1 to 12.

b For the first circle, join each point n to the point n + 2 by a straight line, i.e. n → n + 2.
For values greater than 12, count on beyond 12 round the circle.

c Use your other circles for n → n + 3
n → n + 4
n → n + 5.
If n is allowed to take fractional values, what curves do all these envelopes produce?

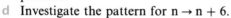

d Investigate the pattern for n → n + 6.

e If you draw the envelope for n → n + 7, which other envelope is it identical

f Attractive patterns can be found by combining two or more of these envelop on the same diagram. Try some for yourself.

3 a Draw a circle of radius 5 cm and mark points on the circumference 10° apart, numbering them from 1 to 36 as shown. Each point n is joined by a straight line to the point 2n, i.e. n → 2n.
For values greater than 36, keep counting round the circle, e.g. 37 is point 1, 38 is point 2.
The name of the curve whose envelope you draw is the **cardioid**, or heart-shape.
Draw and label a second circle and join point n to point 3n, i.e. n → 3n.
The name of the curve for this envelope is the **nephroid** or kidney-shape.

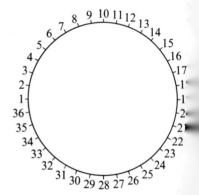

4 Draw a circle of radius 4 cm and on a diameter *LM* mark points ½ cm apart. Working from *L* to *M*, take each point, draw a chord perpendicular to *LM*, and with this chord as diameter, draw a circle. This diagram shows two such circles with centres P_1 and P_2.
What is the name of the curve which appears?

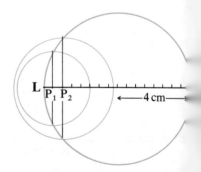

5 Draw a circle of radius 2 cm and mark twelve points on the circumference 30° apart. Select one of these points and label it *X*. Take each of the other eleven points as the centre of a circle which is drawn to pass through *X*.
This diagram shows two such circles with centres P_1 and P_2.
What is the name of the curve which appears?

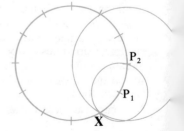

Envelopes

6   Draw a circle of radius 3 cm and mark 18 points on the circumference 20° apart. Join two points to give a diameter *LM*.
Take each of the other 16 points as the centre of a circle which is drawn so that *LM* just touches it. Two such circles are shown here with centres P_1 and P_2.
What is the name of the shape which appears?

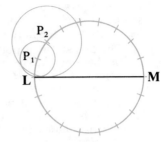

7   a   Draw two lines 6 cm long at 90° to each other and bisecting each other as shown.
    b   Draw three lines 6 cm long at 60° to each other and bisecting each other as shown.
Mark points on all the lines at $\frac{1}{2}$ cm intervals and, taking each point as centre, draw circles all of radius 3 cm. Name the two shapes whose envelopes you draw.

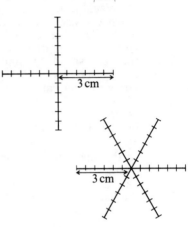

8   This curve is a hyperbola with *C* as its centre. Points are marked along both parts of the curve.
Copy it onto a large sheet of paper and, taking each point on the curve as the centre of a circle, draw circles to pass through point *C*.
The envelope you draw is for a curve called the **lemniscate of Bernoulli**, named after a famous mathematician.

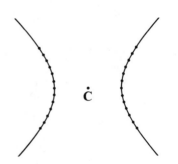

9   Draw this mapping diagram onto squared paper and draw arrows so that $x \to \dfrac{1}{x}$.

For example, $2 \to \frac{1}{2}$
             $-4 \to -\frac{1}{4}$
             $\frac{2}{3} \to \frac{3}{2}$

Draw as many arrows as you need to form an envelope.
What is the name of the curve for this envelope?

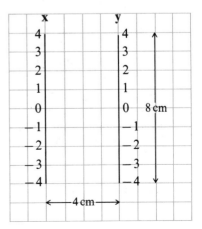

Envelopes

10 **Curves of pursuit** are developed by imagining a dog chasing a hare on various shapes of track. The dog always runs directly towards the hare, but has to alter its direction as the hare moves along the track.

a The dog starts at point D_1 when it sees the hare at H_1. The dog starts running along the line $D_1 H_1$ as the hare runs along the line $H_1 Z$.
When the dog reaches D_2, the hare has reached H_2, so the dog alters direction and runs along the line $D_2 H_2$.
On reaching D_3 it sees that the hare has reached H_3 so it alters direction onto the line $D_3 H_3$, and so on.
Notice that the dog and hare both have the same speed, so that
$H_1 H_2 = D_1 D_2 = H_2 H_3 = D_2 D_3$ etc.
Draw the diagram with
$D_1 H_1 = H_1 Z = 10$ cm and
$H_1 H_2 = 1$ cm. Complete it up to the point where the hare reaches its hole at Z.

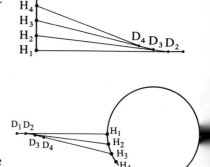

b In this diagram, the hare runs on a circular track. The dog at D_1 sees the hare at H and runs to D_2, by which time the hare has reached H_2. The dog alters direction, and so on as before.

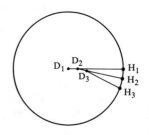

Again, note that $D_1 D_2 = H_1 H_2 = D_2 D_3 = H_2 H_3$ etc. Draw the diagram with a circle of radius 5 cm and $D_1 H_1 = 10$ cm, and construct the curve of pursuit with $H_1 H_2 = 1$ cm. Does the dog ever catch the hare?

c Again the hare follows a circular track, but now the dog starts at the centre D_1, when it sees the hare at H_1.
(i) This diagram shows
$D_1 D_2 = H_1 H_2 = D_2 D_3 = H_2 H_3$,
etc., so the dog and the hare have the same speed. Draw a circle of radius 6 cm, take $H_1 H_2 = 1$ cm, and draw the curve of pursuit. Does the dog catch the hare?

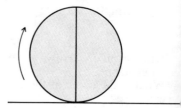

(ii) You can make it more difficult for the dog by halving his speed. Draw a circle of radius 6 cm, take $H_1 H_2 = 1$ cm and $D_1 D_2 = \frac{1}{2}$ cm, and draw the new curve of pursuit. Does the dog catch the hare now?

d Invent your own curves of pursuit. The hare might run on a triangular or square track. The dog might run slower or faster than the hare.

11 Draw a circle of radius 2 cm on tracing paper, cut it out and draw a diameter on it. Roll the circle a full turn on a straight line, starting with the diameter at right angles to the line.
Draw the diameter in many positions to construct an envelope.
Can you give a name to the curve obtained?

Linkages

The practical work of this chapter requires some basic equipment which can be *either* commercial plastic strips and clips *or* lengths of thick card with holes 2 cm apart with drawing pins and paper fasteners. A piece of chipboard or thick cardboard can be used as a base to hold the linkages.

1 Pin one end *A* of any strip and turn the strip about *A* with a sharp pencil in hole *B*. Describe the locus of *B*.
Put the pencil in another hole, draw its locus and describe it.

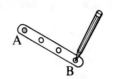

2 Make this linkage from a pair of 6-hole strips and a pair of 4-hole strips. Fix points *A* and *B*.
  a What is the name of the shape you have made?
  b Put the pencil in any hole of *CD*, draw its locus as the linkage moves and describe it.
  c Put the pencil in another hole of *CD*. Draw and describe its locus.
  d Does *DC* always stay parallel to *AB*?

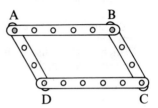

3 Add two pieces of elastic (small elastic bands would do) as diagonals *AC* and *BD*.
  a What is the greatest possible length of diagonal *AC*?
  b As *AC* gets longer, what happens to *BD*?
  c What is special about the point where the two elastic bands cross each other?
  d What name describes the shape of the linkage when *AC* = *BD*?

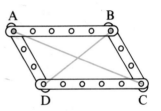

4 Make this linkage from one 4-hole strip and four 6-hole strips, with *A* and *B* fixed.
  a Draw the loci of *J* and *K*.
  b Draw the loci of *L* and *M*.
  c Describe these loci.
  d Which strips always stay parallel to *AB*?

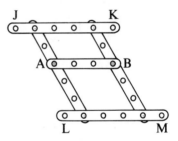

The **parallelogram linkage** is used in the construction of several objects where parallel motion is required. Here are some objects with the linkage *ABCD* in colour. Which of them use a parallelogram linkage and which do not?

a playground swing

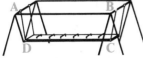

b sewing box

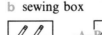

c pruning shears

d lorry windscreen wipers

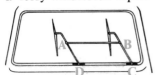

e automatic door closer

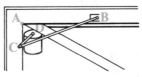

f car suspension

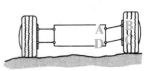

Linkages

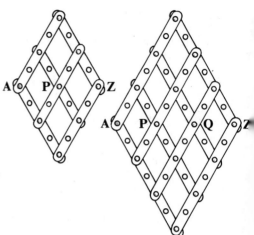

6 Make these two **rhombic linkages**: one uses six 5-hole strips and the other uses eight 7-hole strips.
  For each linkage, fix corner A only and move corner Z on the straight line AZ.

  a Describe the loci of points P and Q.

  b How many different sizes of angle does each linkage have in any one position?

7 Here are some more applications of linkages.
  Which of these use a rhombic linkage and which do not?

  a lazy tongs

  b clothes drier

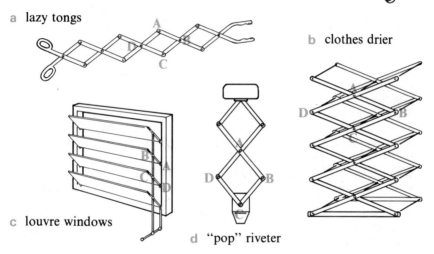

  c louvre windows

  d "pop" riveter

8 Make this **quadrilateral linkage** using one 3-hole, one 4-hole, one 6-hole and one 7-hole strip.
  Fix A and B.

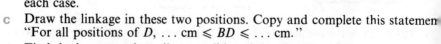

  a Use a pencil to draw the loci of C and D.

  b Find the positions of the linkage where D is
    (i) at its nearest to B
    (ii) at its furthest from B.
    Measure the distance BD in each case.

  c Draw the linkage in these two positions. Copy and complete this statement
    "For all positions of D, ... cm $\leqslant BD \leqslant$ ... cm."

  d Find the largest and smallest possible values of angle ABC.

  e Describe in words the motion of the link BC as D makes one complete revolution about A.

  f Replace AD by a 4-hole strip, then a 5-hole strip, then a 6-hole strip, ...
    Can D always make a complete revolution about A?

9 An extension of the quadrilateral linkage of **8** is where two of the links cross over each other. Make this linkage from 2, 3, 7 and 8-hole strips. Fix *A* and *B*. Draw the loci of *C* and *D* and also the mid point of *CD*

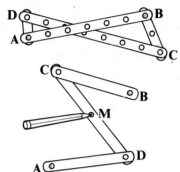

10 A special case of the crossed-quadrilateral occurs when $AB = CD$, $AD = BC$ and $AB = \sqrt{2}AD$ where *A* and *B* are fixed. The locus of the midpoint *M* of *CD* is a curve called the *lemniscate of Bernoulli*.

11 Here are more applications of linkages. Decide which of them are based on the quadrilateral linkage of **8**, the crossed-quadrilateral of **9**, or neither of these.

a rocking horse

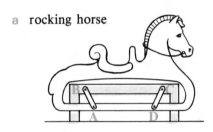

b car bonnet

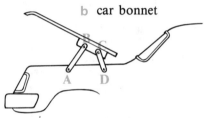

e treadle sewing machine.

d piano lid

c pedal bin

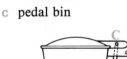

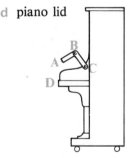

a Make this linkage from a 5-hole, a 6-hole and a 7-hole strip. Is it possible for *C* to move if *A* and *B* are fixed?

b In order to use a triangular linkage, one side has to vary in length so that the opposite corner can move. Remove the 7-hole strip *AB* and fix *A*. Let *B* move on the straight line *AB*. What is the nearest distance to *A*? What is its furthest distance from *A*? Copy and complete this statement:
   "For all positions of *B*,
   ... cm $\leqslant AB \leqslant$ ... cm."

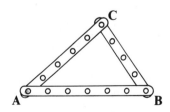

c What is the locus of *C* as *B* moves?

Linkages

13 Here are several applications of **triangular linkages**.
In each case, one side of the triangle can vary its length.
Name the variable side in each diagram.

a car jack

b crank and piston

c deck chair

d car foot-pump

e garage trolley-jack

14 The linkages in this chapter so far have been based on the parallelogram, the rhombus, the quadrilateral and crossed-quadrilateral, and the variable-based triangle.
Here are more applications. Decide which type of linkage is used in each one.

a letter balance

b car's steering mechanism

c trellis fencing

d car suspension

e venetian blinds

f child's pushchair

g angle poise lamp

h car jack

i tip-up lorry

j man riding a bicycle

k adjustable lamp holder

l up-and-over garage door

m mole wrench

n nut-cracker

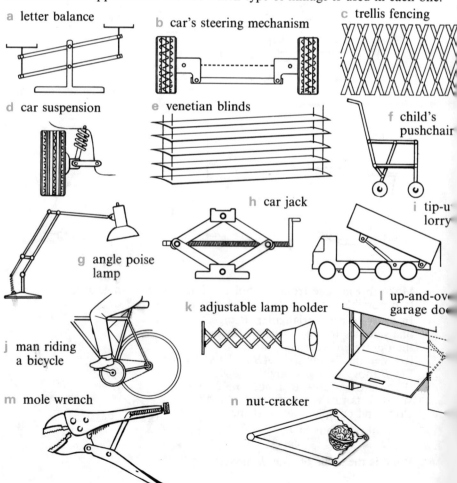

Linkages

5 Historically, the early engineers of the Industrial Revolution had to solve the problem of how to produce straight-line motion using linkages. The earliest attempts were only approximations.

a James Watt, the inventor of the steam engine, also invented this crossed-quadrilateral linkage in 1784. Use two 8-hole strips and one 3-hole strip.
Draw the locus of the midpoint M of CD when A and B are fixed.
How is the locus affected if AD and BC are made longer?

b Tchebycheff invented a different crossed-quadrilateral linkage in 1850. AD and BC are both 5-hole strips; AB is a 4-hole and CD a 2-hole strip. With AB fixed, draw the locus of the midpoint M of CD.

c Roberts in 1860 invented this linkage which includes an isosceles triangular plate CDM where $AC = CM = MD = BD$ and $CD = \frac{1}{2}AB$.
Fix A and B and draw the locus of M.

d In 1864 a French army officer called Peaucellier was the first to invent a linkage which gives exact straight-line motion. The five short strips are all the same length and the two longer ones are also equal.
Construct the linkage, fix A and B and draw the loci of C and D.

A **pantograph** is a linkage used for making enlargements of a drawing.

Four rods are joined as shown such that $ABCD$ is a parallelogram with $OA = AD$ and $DC = CE$.

Point O is fixed; at point D there is a metal pointer; and at point E there is a pen or pencil.

As the pointer at D traces over the object shape, the pen at E draws an enlarged image of length scale factor $\dfrac{OB}{OA}$.

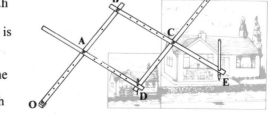

Interchanging D and E produces an image smaller than the object.
By moving points A and C along the rods, different scale factors can be obtained.
See if you can make a pantograph out of your strips.

Gears and belts

Part 1 Two gear wheels

Gear trains are used in many kinds of machines to increase or decrease a rotational speed.

In which of these machines and instruments are gears used?

a	egg-whisk	b	clock	c	clarinet
d	windmill	e	up-and-over garage door	f	hand drill
g	angle poise lamp	h	food mixer	i	car transmission
j	doorbell	k	winch	l	airgun

Find the speed in revolutions per minute (rpm) and the direction of rotation (either clockwise or anticlockwise) of each lettered cog in these diagrams.

Set your answers out in a table as shown.

The number printed inside the rim of each cog gives the number of teeth on the cog.

Cog	Speed, rpm	Direction
A		
B		
C		

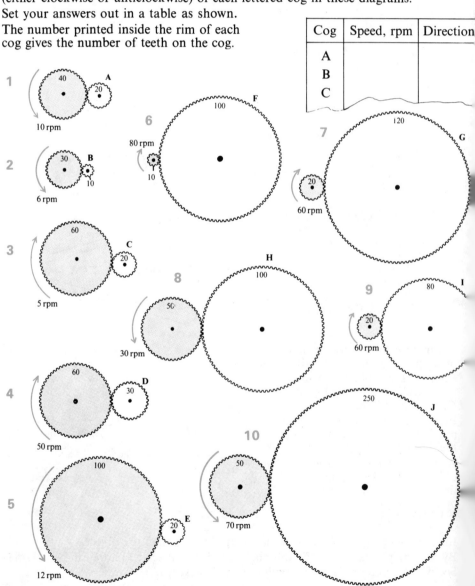

Gears and belts

11 The *transmission factor* (or gear ratio) is the number of full turns made by the
second cog (or *follower*) when the first cog (or *driver*) makes just one full turn.
If the directions of rotation of the driver and follower are the same, then the
transmission factor is *positive*.
In all the diagrams here in **Part 1,** the directions of rotation are different, so all
the transmission factors are *negative*.
Write the transmission factor (or gear ratio) for each diagram in **1** to **10**.

Part 2 Gear trains

These gear trains have intermediate gears.
Find the speed in rpm and the direction of rotation of each lettered cog in these
diagrams.

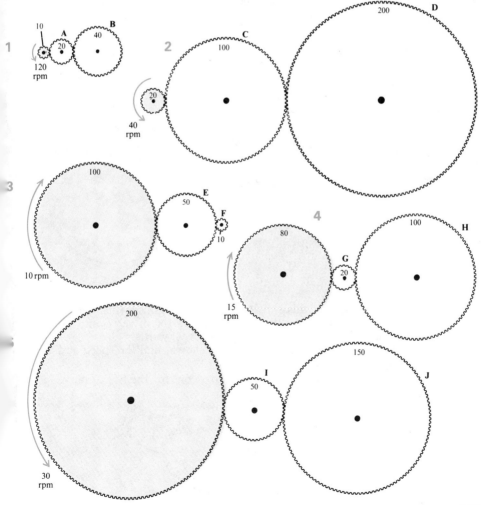

Gears and belts

6

7

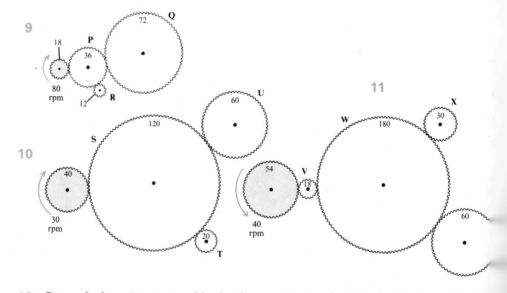

8 Find the transmission factor across the whole gear train in each of the diagrams **1** to **7** above.

The next three gear trains divide so that there is more than one *follower* for each *driver*. Find the speed in rpm and the direction of rotation for each lettered cog.

9

11

10

12 Some clockwork toys use this simple reversing mechanism (inside the *shaded* outline) which introduces an extra cog X between the driver D and the followe F. This then allows the toy to go forwards or backwards.

    a If the driver D has a speed of 60 rpm as shown, find the speed and directio of the follower F in each case.

    b Which diagram shows the position of the cogs for the toy to move
       (i) forwards   (ii) backwards?

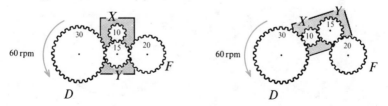

Gears and belts

Part 3 Sharing an axle

One disadvantage of the gear trains in **Part 2** is that they can become long and bulky. Also, to get a very high (or very low) gear would need very large (or very small) cogs. These disadvantages can be overcome by having more than one cog on the same axle. Find the speed in rpm and the direction of rotation of each lettered cog in these diagrams.

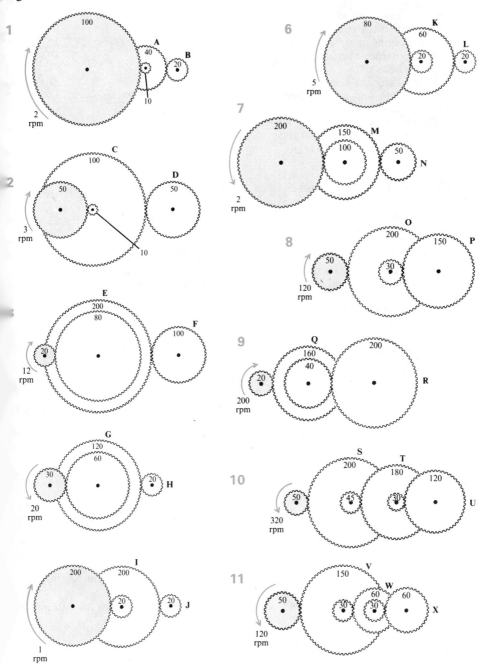

119

Gears and belts

Part 4 Sprockets and chains

Two wheels geared together rotate in *opposite* directions. One way to make them rotate in the *same* direction is to introduce a third cog between them as in **Parts 2** and **3**. Another way is to introduce a chain which has the advantage of allowing the two wheels to be some distance apart.

1 A bicycle has a large driving wheel or **crank wheel** C connected to the pedals.
A chain connects it to the follower or **free wheel** F on the bicycle's back axle.
This diagram has a crank wheel C with 48 teeth and a free wheel F with 12 teeth.
If the cyclist wants the rear wheel to rotate at 120 rpm, how fast will he have to turn the crank wheel?

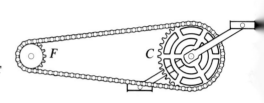

2 This second bicycle has three choices of gears on the free wheel, F, G and H. The crank wheel C has 48 teeth and the free wheel has 12 teeth on F, 16 teeth on G and 24 teeth on H.

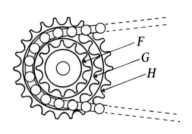

   a If the cyclist pedals the crank wheel C at a speed of 60 rpm, what will be the speed of the rear wheel for each of the three choices of gear?

   b Which is the best choice of gear wheel for cycling
   (i) uphill   (ii) downhill?

   c If the rear wheel has a diameter of 64 cm, how far forward does the bicycle move when it rotates just once?
   If the cyclist pedals at 60 rpm with gear G engaged, how far forward does he go   (i) every second   (ii) every hour?
   What is his forward speed in km/h (to 3 significant figures)?

Part 5 Pulleys and belts

Another common method of transmitting power from one axle to another is by means of pulleys connected by a belt. Electric motors are often used to rotate the driving pulley which in turn rotates the driven pulley or follower. One disadvantage is that the connecting belt can stretch and slip.

1 In which of these machines do you think there might be a belt connecting rotating pulleys?
   a a fan and dynamo of a car engine
   b a conveyor belt from an automatic packing machine
   c a domestic hair dryer
   d a sewing machine
   e a household washing-machine
   f an electric doorbell

Gears and belts

2 a An electric motor rotates a driving pulley of diameter 24 cm which is connected by a belt to a following pulley of diameter 8 cm.
If the motor turns at a speed of 50 rpm, find the speed of the output shaft.

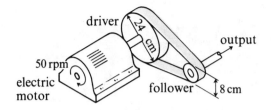

Find the speed of the follower *F* in each of these systems where the speed of the driver *D* is given.

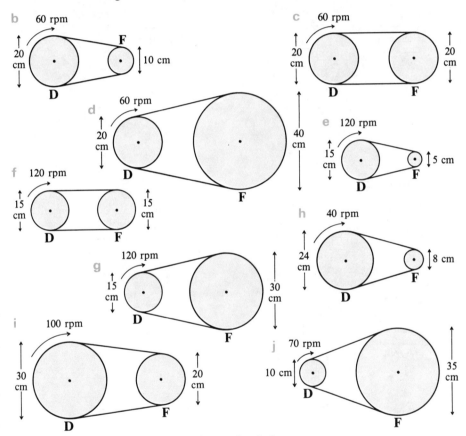

k Find the *transmission factor* for each of these systems.

3 This electric motor drives three belt selectors A, B and C on its axis. (Your school workshop might have a lathe which works in this way.)
Each of the diagrams on the next page shows the pulley wheel diameters in centimetres.
Find the three speeds of each output shaft when the belt is in the positions A, B and C.

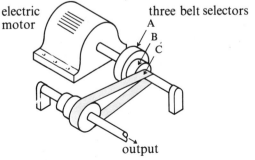

Gears and belts

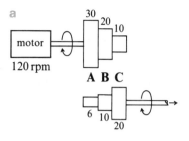

a

motor

120 rpm

30 20 10

A B C

6 10 20

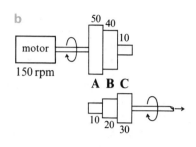

b

motor

150 rpm

50 40 10

A B C

10 20 30

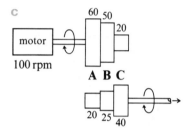

c

motor

100 rpm

60 50 20

A B C

20 25 40

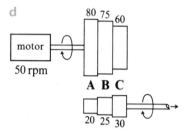

d

motor

50 rpm

80 75 60

A B C

20 25 30

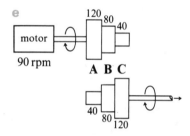

e

motor

90 rpm

120 80 40

A B C

40 80 120

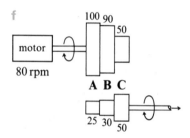

f

motor

80 rpm

100 90 50

A B C

25 30 50

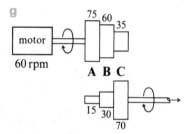

g

motor

60 rpm

75 60 35

A B C

15 30 70

4   This diagram shows an electric motor driving *four* belt selectors. Calculate the four possible speeds of the output shaft.

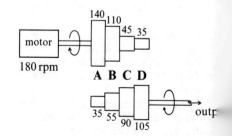

motor

180 rpm

140 110 45 35

A B C D

35 55 90 105

output

5   Design a system of your own so that your three output speeds are 30 rpm, 60 r and 90 rpm when the speed of the electric motor is 60 rpm. Draw a diagram of

Gears and belts

6 An engine or electric motor can be used to rotate more than one output shaft
by using more than one belt. In addition, the direction of rotation for any
output shaft can be changed by putting a twist in the belt connected to it.

Find the speed in rpm and the direction
of rotation for each of the lettered
pulleys in the following systems.
Enter your answers in a table like the
one shown here.

The numbers printed on the diagrams
inside the rims of the pulleys give their
diameters in centimetres.

Pulley	Speed, rpm	Direction
A		
B		
C		

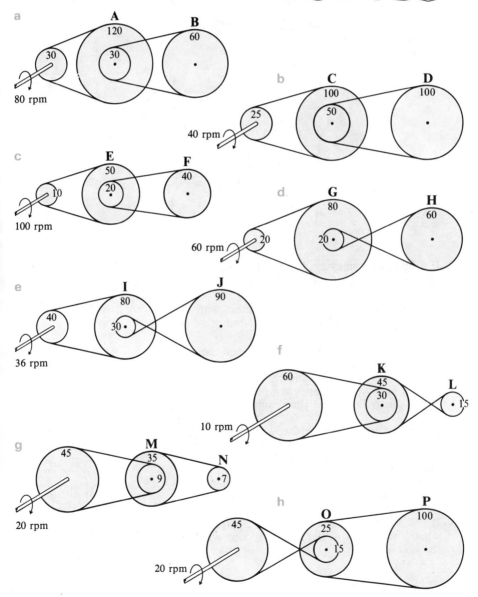

Gears and belts

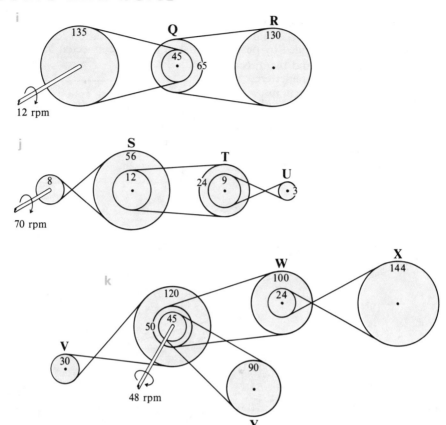

7 If a belt has a sideways twist in it as shown in this diagram, it forms a Möbius strip. This is done for two reasons.

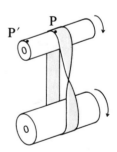

   a Which side of the belt is in contact with the two pulleys? Which side of the belt takes the most wear?

   b If the pulleys are badly aligned and the belt at point P is slowly moving sideways towards P' nearer the edge of the pulley, what happens when P returns to this pulley "next time round"?

8 A car has been manufactured so that instead of a gearbox, the wheels are powered by the engine through a belt connecting two conical pulleys.

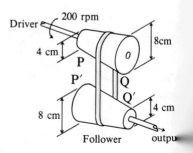

The speed of the engine can then stay fairly constant while the gear changes by moving the belt along the two cones.

If the *driving* cone has a speed of 200 rpm, what is the speed of the *following* cone when the belt is

   a at the end PP'

   b at the end QQ'?

Probability

Simulation

An experiment which is set up to try to copy the main features of a real situation is called a **simulation**. The experiment tries to *model* actual events.

1 The collector's problem

A boy's mother buys packets of tea, each of which has one picture card inside. The boy needs six different cards to make a complete set. How many packets of tea should he ask his mother to buy in order to collect all six cards?

The simulation

Let the scores 1 to 6 on an ordinary dice represent the six different cards. Rolling a particular score represents (or *simulates*) collecting that particular card.

Roll the dice again and again until each score from 1 to 6 has been rolled at least once. Count the number of rolls you have to make before this happens. Repeat several times and enter your results in a copy of this table.

Trial number	Scores on dice (i.e. cards collected)	Number of throws required
1 2 3 ⋮		

How many packets would you advise the boy to buy?

2 The birthday cake

Six coins are hidden inside a birthday cake which is then divided equally amongst six children. How many children will on average get

a no coins

b more than one coin?

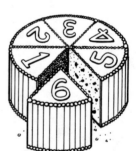

The simulation

Let the scores 1 to 6 on an ordinary dice represent the six pieces of cake. Draw a circle divided into six equal sectors and label them 1 to 6. Take six coins, roll the dice six times and place the coins on those sectors of your circle corresponding to the six scores you get.

Count a the empty sectors

b the sectors with more than one coin.

Enter your results in the first column of a copy of this table.

	Trial number						
	1	2	3	4	...	Total	Average
Number of sectors with no coins							
Number of sectors with more than 1 coin							

Repeat several times and complete the *total* and *average* columns in your table How many children would you expect on average to get

a no coins

b more than one coin?

Simulation

3 Christmas tree lights

My Christmas tree lights need 10 bulbs and the
set is so old that I cannot buy any spare bulbs.
I do have two spare bulbs now, but when three
bulbs fail, the lights will be useless.
If the chance of any particular bulb failing during
the Christmas period is $\frac{1}{36}$, how many years can I
expect the set of lights to last?

The simulation

Place 10 coins in a row in front of you to represent the 10 bulbs, and have two
other coins in your pocket to represent the two spare bulbs.
For the first Christmas, test the first of the 10 bulbs by throwing two dice. If
you get a "double six", then that bulb has failed and remove that coin
completely; otherwise the bulb is good and the coin stays. Test all 10 coins in
the same way. This represents one year's use.
Before the second Christmas, use your spares to make up the set of 10 coins. If
you *can* make a set of 10, test all of them in the same way for the second
Christmas.
Continue to make up the set of 10 after each Christmas, if you have enough
spares. If you run out of spares, then the lights are useless and the experiment is
over. Record how many years they lasted.
Repeat the whole experiment several times and compare your results. Find the
average number of years that the lights were used.

In a nuclear reactor

This diagram represents a nuclear reactor in which
an atomic pile P is surrounded by shielding
$ABCDEF$. This shielding is supposed to absorb
neutrons emitted from the pile P so that they do
not escape from the shielding.
How effective is this shielding? Is it thick enough?

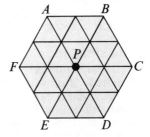

The simulation

Assume that a neutron starting from P moves one unit along the grid of the
diagram every second. If it is still inside $ABCDEF$ after 5 seconds, then it has so
little energy left that it is absorbed and does not
escape. If it reaches the edge $ABCDEF$ within 5
seconds, then it escapes.
Place a small coin on P to represent the neutron.
Throw a dice five times, moving the neutron each
time in the direction given by the arrows on this
diagram. Record whether the neutron escapes or
is absorbed.

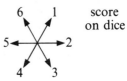

Repeat many times. Combine your results with others if possible.
a What fraction of your neutrons escaped from the reactor?
b How can you alter the simulation to make the shielding thicker?
c What would happen if the neutrons were more energetic and could survive
for more than 5 seconds?

Up for the Cup

You decide to hire a minibus to take friends to the Cup Final. You will drive
and you need to have 10 passengers. You have organised this before several
times and have discovered that one passenger in six lets you down and fails to
take his place in the minibus.
How many people should you invite to be passengers?

Simulation

The simulation

Roll a dice to represent a passenger deciding whether to turn up or not. If you roll a 1, he does not come; if you roll any other score, he does come. Write a cross (×) if he does not, or a tick (✓) if he does.

Repeat several times until you have 10 ticks.

Enter your results in the first column of a copy of this table.

Repeat several times and find the average number of people invited.

	Trial number				
	1	2	3	4	...
Number of ticks					
Number of crosses					
Total number of people invited					

a   Do you think this average number is a reasonable number of people to invite? What could be the consequence of asking this number of people?

b   What do you think *is* a reasonable number of people to ask? Give your reasons.

6 Radioactive decay

In a given time interval, a small number of radioactive atoms in a substance become non-radioactive (i.e. they *decay*); but most atoms stay radioactive. This decay reduces the total number of radioactive atoms and so the rate of decay decreases with time.

How long does it take for *all* the atoms to decay?

How long does it take for *half* the initial number of atoms to decay? (This is called the *half-life*.)

The simulation

Put a large number (over a hundred) of drawing pins in a beaker, shake them and pour them out onto a flat surface. Pins landing point *downwards* represent atoms which decay in 1 unit of time, and those with points *upwards* represent atoms still radioactive.

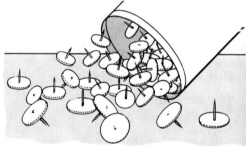

Remove all pins which point downwards and count them. Calculate or count the number which point upwards. Enter your results in the first column of a copy of this table.

Repeat for a second unit of time and again remove pins which point downwards. Count them and enter your results in the table.

Repeat until no radioactive atoms are left.

	Units of time				
	1	2	3	4	...
Number of atoms decayed					
Number of atoms still radioactive					

a   Draw a graph of your results on axes similar to these drawn here.

b   How long did it take for *all* the radioactive atoms to decay?

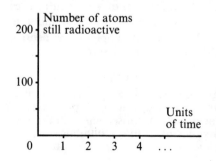

Simulation

c How long did it take for *half* the initial number to decay? This is the *half-life*.

d Repeat the whole experiment several times, or combine your results with your friends and find the average values for each unit of time. Draw a graph of these average values.

e 100 grams of a substance contains about 100 000 000 000 000 000 000 000 (that is 10^{23}) atoms. Is it more sensible to ask how long it takes for *all* of these to decay or for *half* of them to decay? Give your reasons.

7 The spread of disease

This map shows the area near a harbour H where flying insects carrying disease have accidentally been brought ashore with a ship's cargo. The insects cannot survive over the sea or on highland (shown shaded), and it is most likely to spread in the direction of the prevailing wind towards the south-east. How quickly does it spread and infect the area?

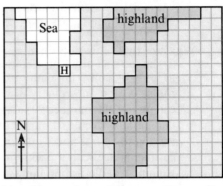

The simulation

Throw two dice, add the scores and use this table to find which square next to the harbour H is infected; label this square 1.

Repeat to find the next square infected; label this square 2. Remember that many throws will be wasted when the chosen square is sea, highland or already infected. In these cases, the infection does not spread.

How far has the infection spread after you have numbered 20 or 30 squares?

How does the geography of the area and the prevailing wind affect the spread?

Sum of scores on the two dice

	2	3
12	present square	4 or 5
11	9 or 10	6, 7 or 8

Prevailing wind

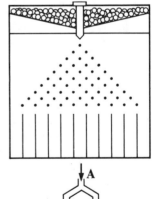

The quincunx

This early pin-table was invented by the English explorer and scientist Sir Francis Galton (1822–1911). When the balls are released they fall through the pins and collect in the slots underneath. What will be the distribution in the slots when all the balls have fallen through?

The simulation

The route through this pattern of hexagons is a simplified version of the quincunx. Imagine a ball entering at A. Toss a coin and let a *head* represent the ball turning to your *right* and a *tail* to your *left*. Repeat this four times to find which slot V, W, X, Y or Z the ball enters.

Repeat many times for many balls until a pattern in the distribution builds up. You may want to combine your results with your friends. Compare your results with problem **3b** on page 81.

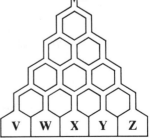

Experimental probability

Introduction

1 Which of these statements show that the speaker is aware of probabilities?
- a "I expect the bus will be late again today."
- b "It looks as though it will be sunny this afternoon."
- c "That loaf of bread cost 52 pence."
- d "You'll be lucky to find him at home today."
- e "It's quite likely to be busy in town this morning."
- f "You need your hair cutting."
- g "She'll probably not bother to go."

2 Which of these situations involve probabilities which you can investigate
   (i) by looking at all possibilities without the need to do any experiment
or (ii) only by collecting data or doing an experiment?
- a rolling a 6 on an ordinary dice
- b calling out the number 99 in a game of bingo
- c finding out which first names are most likely to be given to new-born babies
- d waiting for a bus and wondering how late it is likely to be
- e cutting an ace with a pack of cards
- f winning a raffle having bought ten tickets

Part 1 Experiments

1 Draw a hexagonal spinner on card and use a matchstick pushed through point O which is off-centre.
- a Can you predict the results of several spins or do you need to experiment to find out which are the most likely and least likely scores?
- b Spin the hexagon 50 times.
   Copy this table and record your results.

Score	1	2	3	4	· 5	6	
Tally							Totals
Frequency							50
Experimental probability							

- c Draw a bar chart of your experimental probabilities on axes as shown here.
- d Answer these questions.
   (i) Which score occurred most often?
   (ii) Which score had the highest probability?
   (iii) Which score occurred least often?
   (iv) Which score had the lowest probability?
   (v) What is the total of all six probabilities?
   (vi) If the experiment was repeated for 150 trials, how often would you expect to get a score of
   (a) 3 (b) 5?

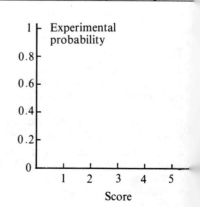

Experimental probability

2 a Would the manufacturer of letters for a printing set or for sheets of transfers be sensible to make the same number of letters for each letter of the alphabet?
Can you predict how likely it is that a particular letter will be needed or do you need an experiment to decide?

b Take a book and count and record 500 letters.
Copy this table and enter your results.

Letter	A	B	C	D	E	F	Y	Z	
Tally									Totals
Frequency									
Experimental probability									

c Draw a bar chart of your results and answer these questions.
  (i) Which was your most common letter and what was its experimental probability?
  (ii) Which were your ten most common letters? Write them in order.
  (iii) If the manufacturer is to make 6000 transfers of letters in a pack for sale in shops, how many of each vowel would you recommend there to be in each pack?
  (iv) Another firm makes crossword games using 50 letters for each game. How many of each vowel would you recommend there be in each game?
  (v) Can you use your results to decode this message?
  FGMXUM ZRXLWMSZ XJDLML XJZF DWNOF. W GWXX QMMF FOMQ JF MXMUMD RAXRAP KV FOM MDL RB FOM QJWD SRJL WDFR FOM FRGD.

a Messages, notes and letters sent to people are often sorted and arranged using pigeon-holes labelled with initials of surnames. Should each letter of the alphabet have the same size of pigeon-hole? Can you predict how likely certain initials will be or do you need to do an experiment to find out?

b Take a telephone directory.
Find the number of pages given to names starting with each letter of the alphabet.
Use the same table as in experiment **2** (without its tally row) to record your results, but use a calculator to write the experimental probabilities to three significant figures.

c Draw a bar chart of your results and answer these questions.
  (i) Which was the most common initial in your experiment?
  (ii) If 10 000 people in the area of the directory went to a football match, how many in the crowd would you expect to have surnames beginning with (a) H (b) C (c) M?
  (iii) What differences would you expect between telephone directories for Scotland, Northern Ireland and England?

How likely do you think it is that two pupils in the same class at school have identical birthdays?
Ask your own class and other classes about their birthdays.
Will the *size* of the class be important? If you think so, what can you do about it?
Estimate the probability of two people having the same birthday in a class size of your choice.

Experimental probability

Part 2 Problems

1 Simon is interested in cars. He went to a car park and recorded the countries in which 100 cars were made.

Origin	British	French	Swedish	German	Japanese	Others	Total
Frequency	42	13	11	7	20	7	100

If a car leaves the car park, what is the probability that it is made in
a Britain   b Sweden   c Germany   d either France or Japan?
If there are 300 cars altogether in the car park, how many would you expect to be made in   e Britain   f Sweden   g Germany?

2 A shop has a display of 60 styles of shoes.

Style	Sandals	Lace-ups	High-heels	Sling-backs	Slip-ons	Total
Frequency	8	12	13	8	19	60

If an assistant picks up a box of shoes at random, what is the probability of her having a pair of
a sandals   b slip-ons   c lace-ups   d either sandals or lace-ups
e any style except sling-backs?
If there are 1800 boxes of shoes in the store behind the shop, how many boxes would you expect to contain
f sandals   g lace-ups   h high-heels?

3 Mrs Staines stands at a bus-stop looking at the timetable. She sees that during the next hour, five different services call at the stop with these frequencies.

Service	City Centre	Fartown	Bywell	Monksby	Netherton	Total
Frequency	10	6	1	3	5	25

What is the probability that the next bus arriving at the stop is going to
a Fartown   b Netherton   c either Bywell or Monksby
d any service except the City Centre?
e If Mrs Staines wants to go to the City Centre every day from Monday to Friday and she does not want to plan when she arrives at the bus-stop, how many times might she expect to catch the first bus which comes?

4 Lesley Culpin collects the first 100 seashells she sees on the beach and counts the different types.

Type	Winkles	Limpets	Mussels	Scallops	Whelks	Total
Frequency	35	28	24	6	7	100

If she goes on the same beach the next day, what is the probability that the first shell she sees is
a a limpet   b a mussel   c a scallop   d either a winkle or a whelk

Experimental probability

e not a limpet   f not a mussel?

If she collects another 500 shells, how many might she expect to be

g winkles   h scallops   i either mussels or whelks?

5

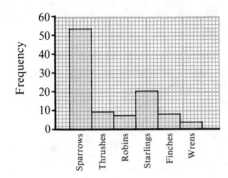

Tim noted the different species of bird which land in the garden, and this bar chart shows the results for the first 100 birds which land.

Copy and complete this frequency table.

Species	Sparrows	Thrushes	Robins	Starlings	Finches	Wrens	Total
Frequency							

What is the probability of the next bird to land being

a a sparrow   b a thrush   c a bird whose name begins with S

d not a starling   e not a wren?

If 25 birds are seen at breakfast-time tomorrow, how many might be expected to be

f starlings   g finches?

6 This bar chart shows the number of different types of dog which live in a village.

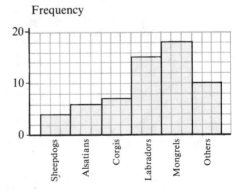

Copy and complete this frequency table.

Type	Sheepdogs	Alsatians	Corgis	Labradors	Mongrels	Others	Total
Frequency							

If a visitor sees a dog in the village, what is the probability that it is

a a sheepdog   b a corgi   c a mongrel   d not a mongrel

e either a Labrador or an Alsatian   f either a sheepdog or an Alsatian?

The dog warden catches 20 stray dogs in one week. How many might be expected to be

g mongrels   h Labradors   i Alsatians?

Experimental probability

Part 3 In the long run

Experimental probability depends on the number of trials which are done in the experiment. The experiments in this exercise illustrate what happens *in the long run*.

1   When a coin is tossed, let a *success* be a head
and a *failure* be a tail.
You will need a copy of this diagram.

   a   Toss a coin 24 times.
Start at the top of your diagram and draw a line, moving down to the *right* for a success and down to the *left* for a failure.
After 24 tosses, your path will have reached the bottom of the diagram.

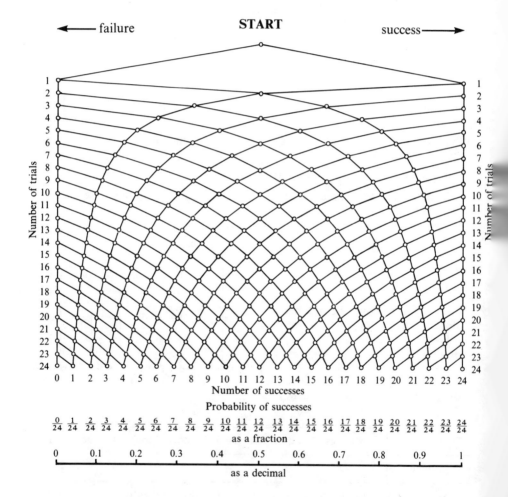

   b   Using different colours, you can do this experiment several times, drawing your results on the same diagram.
Do your paths seem to settle down or "home-in" to a particular position?
If the diagram continued for 50 or 100 tosses, would you expect the paths continue to settle down? What would you say the experimental probability of getting a head is *in the long run*?

Experimental probability

2 In a certain children's game, a player starts by
throwing a 5 or a 6 on one dice.
Let a *success* be a score of 5 or 6
and a *failure* be any other score.

  a Throw a dice 24 times.
    Use another copy of the diagram and draw
    your path from the start to the bottom of the
    diagram.
  b Repeat the same experiment using different
    colours to record your results on the same
    diagram.
  c Do your results seem to be settling down to a
    particular position?
    What would you say the experimental
    probability of getting a 5 or 6 is *in the
    long run*?

3 Either use a regular octagon with a matchstick as
a spinner or use an octahedron as a dice with
faces numbered from 1 to 8.
Let a *success* be a score of 1, 3 or 6
and a *failure* be any other score.
Use another copy of the diagram to record
the results of an experiment of 24 spins or rolls.
Repeat the experiment several times, recording your
results on the same diagram. What would you say
the experimental probability of a score of 1, 3 or
6 is *in the long run*?

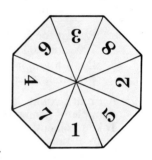

4 Take a well-shuffled pack of 52 playing-cards and cut them.
Let a *success* be a diamond
and a *failure* be any other suit.

  a Cut the pack ten times, copy this table and record your results. Write the
    experimental probabilities as decimals.

	Number of times the pack is cut						
	10	20	30	40	50	100	200
Number of diamonds							
Experimental probability of cutting a diamond							

  b Repeat a further 10 times, making 20 cuts in all.
    Enter your results for the 20 cuts.
    Repeat for 40 cuts and 50 cuts.
    Combine with other peoples' results to enter results for 100 cuts and
    200 cuts.

  c Draw a graph of the
    experimental probabilities on
    axes as shown. Do they seem
    to be settling down to a
    certain value as the number
    of cuts increases?
    Estimate this value.

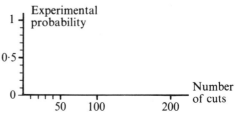

Experimental probability

5 Shake one drawing pin in your hand and gently
drop it on a table.
Let a *success* be a pin pointing *upwards*
and a *failure* be a pin pointing *downwards*.

a Drop the pin ten times, copy this table and
enter your results. Write the experimental
probability as a decimal.

	Number of times the pin is dropped						
	10	20	30	40	50	100	200
Number of times it points upwards							
Experimental probability of the point being upwards							

b Repeat for 20, 30, 40 and 50 times. Combine with others to get results for
100 and 200 drops of a pin.

c Draw a graph on similar axes to those in **4**. Do the experimental
probabilities seem to be settling down to a certain value? Estimate this value

6 A French count, le Comte de Bouffon, in 1777 was the first to introduce an
example of geometrical probability. His experiment is as follows.
Take ten identical needles or matches (preferably without their heads) and drop
them at random on a sheet of paper which has been ruled with straight parallel
lines, with the distance between adjacent lines equal to the length of the needles
or matches.
Count the number of needles or matches which
cross (or touch) any of the lines.
Repeat 10 times, so that altogether you have
made 100 drops.

Copy this table, enter your results in the first
column and use a calculator to work out the

value of $\frac{2}{p}$.

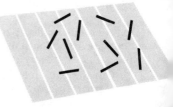

Number of drops, N	100	200	300	400	500
Number of needles crossing the lines, n					
Experimental probability of crossing a line, $p = \frac{n}{N}$					
$\frac{2}{p}$					

Repeat another 100 times, making 200 drops in all; enter your results in the
second column.

Either keep repeating the experiment yourself *or* combine your results with
other pupils and extend the table as shown.

Draw a graph of p against N and a second graph of $\frac{2}{p}$ against N.

Estimate the values to which p and $\frac{2}{p}$ seem to be settling down.

Do you recognise the limiting value of $\frac{2}{p}$?

Theoretical probability

Part 1   Equally likely outcomes

Because a set of objects might have the same shape and the same size (i.e. be **congruent**) or because an object has a certain symmetry, it is often reasonable to suppose that certain outcomes of an action are *equally likely* to happen.
In which of the following trials do you think the given outcomes are *equally likely* to occur?

Trial		**Outcomes**
1	tossing a coin	either a head or a tail
2	cutting a pack of cards	either a black card or a red card
3	rolling a dice	either an even score or an odd score
4	throwing a dart at random at a dart board	either a score of 20 or a bull's eye
5	throwing a dart at random at a dart board	any one of the sectors between 1 and 20
6	cutting a pack of cards	either an ace or a picture card or any other card
7	cutting a pack of cards	any one of the four suits
8	opening a telephone directory at random	surnames beginning with either a vowel or a consonant
9	switching on a television at random	either a programme or advertisements
0	looking at a clock at random	the time either *past* the hour or *to* the hour
1	choosing a shoe at random	either a right shoe or a left shoe
2	taking a glove from a drawer	either a right-hand glove or a left-hand glove
3	opening a book at random	having a page either at the start of a chapter or in the middle of a chapter
4	rolling one dice	a score either greater than 4 or less than 4
5	pressing a random key on a typewriter	either a letter or a number
6	picking up a book at random	the pages either upside-down or the right way up
7	looking at the electricity meter	either an odd or an even number of units on the dial.
8	opening a tin of food without a label on	a tin of either fruit or vegetables
9	letting your watch run down until it stops	the minute hand between either 12 and 5 or 5 and 12
	buying a raffle ticket	either winning or not winning a prize

e idea of outcomes being *equally likely* allows us to *model* a situation without ving to do any experiment. In these next two exercises, you are asked to *compare* a bability model with experimental results.

Theoretical probability

21 a **The model** If a dice is fair, each score is equally likely to occur. If the dice is rolled 60 times, what will the expected frequencies be for each score?

The experiment Ten pupils are each given one fair dice. The pupils each roll their dice 60 times and record their results separately in a table.

Do this for yourself and record your own results in a copy of this table.

Score	1	2	3	4	5	6	
Tally							Totals
Observed frequency							60
Expected frequency							60

b If all ten pupils combine their results, construct a similar table to show the results of the 600 trials.

c Comment on the two sets of results.

22 a **The model** If a pack of 52 playing-cards is well shuffled and cut at random, each suit is equally likely to be picked.

If the pack is cut 12 times, what will be the expected frequencies of each suit?

The experiment Ten pupils cut a well-shuffled pack, each recording their results in a separate table.

Do this for yourself and record your own results in a copy of this table.

Suit	Spades	Clubs	Hearts	Diamonds	
Tally					Totals
Observed frequency					
Expected frequency					

b If the ten pupils combine their results, construct a similar table to show the results of 120 cuts.

c Comment on the two sets of results.

Part 2 Theoretical probability

If an experiment can result at random in several equally likely outcomes, then the probability of a *desirable* event is given by:

$$P \text{ (desirable event)} = \frac{\text{the number of desirable outcomes}}{\text{the total number of possible outcomes}}$$

1 Find the theoretical probabilities of each of these events, cancelling any fractions where possible.

Rolling one fair dice:

a a score of 2

b a score of 3

c a score of 6

d an even score

e an odd score

f a score less than 3

g a score more than 3

h a score less than or equal to 4

i a score greater than 6

j either an odd or an even score

Theoretical probability

Cutting a pack of 52 cards:

k any red card
m any spade
o any ace
q any picture card
s a black six
u the Jack of Hearts
w either a Jack or a King
y either a black or a red card

l any black card
n any heart
p any King
r any six
t a red nine
v the King of Diamonds
x either a King or an ace
z a joker

2 What is the probability of
a tossing "Heads" with a coin
c being born on a Monday
e being born a girl?

b tossing "Tails" with a coin
d having a birthday in December

3 A raffle sells two hundred tickets. You buy four tickets. What is the probability that you will win the raffle?

4 Five horses run in a race. You choose one horse at random. What is the probability that you choose the winner?

5 You apply for a job. There are twenty applicants and nothing to choose between them. What is the probability that you will get the job?

6 A box holds six eggs; one of them is bad. What is the probability that you choose the bad egg?

7 Your watch has a second hand on it. If you look at it quickly, what is the probability that it is pointing between the 3 and the 6?

8 You live in a town of 25 000 people. A travelling salesman will visit every tenth house. What is the probability that he calls at your house?

9 A mail-order firm sends a brochure to every fifth person in a town of 42 000 people. What is the probability that your house will receive a brochure?

10 Because of an electricity strike, your house will be without electricity for any eight hours on one particular day. You switch the kettle on at 5 p.m. What is the probability that it will work?

A shop has 300 bars of chocolate which are not selling well. The shopkeeper decides to give one bar away free to every fourth customer. What is the probability of your being given a free bar when you make a purchase?

Half of the twenty people in an office are women. What is the probability of the next person to leave the room being a man?

A crate of apples has 10 bad apples and 90 good apples. Without looking, you choose an apple. What is the probability that it is a bad one?

You buy a bag of sweets. There are 12 blue sweets and 8 red ones. What is the probability of choosing a red one at random from the bag?

There are 24 girls in the same class as 8 boys. A teacher chooses one pupil at random. What is the probability that a boy is chosen?

Theoretical probability

16 Another class has 20 boys and 12 girls. The teacher collects in all the exercise books. What is the probability that the book on the top of the pile belongs to a girl?

17 A car-park contains 12 British cars, 6 Japanese cars, 4 French cars and 8 other cars. What is the probability that the next car to leave the car-park is Japanese?

18 Mrs Kitchener has a larder with 15 jars of jam, 12 jars of marmalade, 8 jars of lemon curd and 5 jars of honey. What is the probability that her young son takes a jar of honey at random?

19 A new member of a committee is chosen by lot from 6 men and 4 women. What is the probability that the new member will be a woman?

20 A raffle is held after tickets of various colours have been sold. If 450 blue, 275 red, 125 green and 50 yellow tickets are sold, what is the probability that the winning ticket is green?

21

This number line from 0 to 1 represents all probabilities. Pair each capital letter A to H with the probabilities of these events.
(i) the sun rising tomorrow
(ii) anyone swimming across the Atlantic Ocean
(iii) winning the football pools
(iv) scoring a 6 with a fair dice
(v) a child being born a boy
(vi) cutting a club with a pack of cards
(vii) going to bed before midnight tonight
(viii) choosing an even number at random from this set {2, 3, 4, 5, 6, 8, 10, 12}

22 Draw your own number line of probabilities from 0 to 1.
Label it with capital letters A to H to represent the probabilities of events which
A are utterly impossible
B are absolutely certain
C will happen as likely as not
D will most likely happen
E are very unlikely to happen
F are almost bound to happen
G are fairly likely to happen
H are quite likely not to happen.

23 This circular board at a fairground is divided into 12 sectors and it spins about its axis.
For 20 pence, you throw a dart at it as it spins. If you hit a WIN, you are given 50 pence; if you hit a LOSE, you get nothing; if you hit a RETURN, you get your 20 pence back.
Find the probability of hitting
a a WIN   b a LOSE   c a RETURN.
d You pay for 6 darts, win once and have your money returned twice. Are you "in pocket" at the end, and if so, by how much?

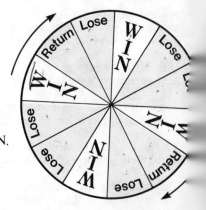

Theoretical probability

24 You address the front of an envelope without checking that it is the right way up. What is the probability that the address is written the right way up?

25 What is the probability of putting a slide in a slide projector correctly at the first attempt without looking?

Part 3 More problems

1 A multiple-choice question in a test gives five alternatives of which only one is correct. If you make a guess, what is the probability of choosing
   a the right answer
   b a wrong answer?

2 A children's book of 20 double pages has 17 pages with pictures on them. If a child opens the book at random, what is the probability of opening
   a at a picture
   b not at a picture?

3 Farmer Brown goes to market once every week but on no particular day. What is the probability of him going to market
   a tomorrow
   b not tomorrow?

4 If the probability of it raining tomorrow is $\frac{1}{5}$, what is the probability of it being dry tomorrow?

5 If the probability of getting up late in a morning is $\frac{2}{7}$, what is the probability of being up on time?

6 If the probability of breaking the yolk when I crack open an egg is $\frac{2}{9}$, what is the probability of cracking an egg without breaking the yolk?

7 The probability that Mr Knapp is late for work is $\frac{2}{5}$. Over a period of 30 working days, how many times would you expect him to be
   a late
   b on time?

8 The probability of the first bus to arrive at the stop being full is $\frac{3}{10}$. If I catch a bus to work every day for 40 days, how many times will I expect the first bus
   a to be full
   b to have an empty seat?

9 A biologist finds that in 50 square metres of field there are 8 foxgloves growing.
   a What is the probability that there will be a foxglove in the next square metre he looks at?
   b How many foxgloves can he expect in 1000 m^2?

10 Mrs Jones buys 16 apples and finds that 6 are bruised.
   a What is the probability of getting a bruised apple?
   b If the next person in the queue buys 40 apples, how many bruised ones can they expect to get?

Theoretical probability

11 Jane Penman is writing a 6000 word essay. In her first 400 words she uses the word "the" 25 times.
   a What is the probability that her next word is "the"?
   b How many times might she expect to use "the" in her essay?

12 A bag holds some toffees and some mints. The probability of taking out a toffee is $\frac{1}{3}$. If there are 15 sweets in the bag, find
   a how many toffees there are
   b how many mints there are.

13 A tin holds 8 chocolate biscuits and 28 plain ones.
   a What is the probability that, without looking, you take a chocolate one?
   b What is the probability that, after eating a chocolate biscuit, the next one you take is also chocolate?

14 There are six white and two coloured handkerchieves in a pile.
   a What is the probability that, without looking, you choose a coloured one?
   b What is the probability that, having removed a coloured one, you take a second one which is also coloured?

15 A fridge holds 10 cans of orange squash and 6 cans of lemonade.
   a What is the probability that, without looking, you take out a can of lemonade?
   b What is the probability that after drinking a lemonade, the next one you take out is an orange?

16 You have 8 copper and 2 silver coins in your pocket.
   a What is the probability of taking out a copper coin at random?
   b What is the probability of taking out a second copper coin if
      (i) you do not replace the first copper one
      (ii) you do replace the first copper one?

17 a To decide who starts a card game, Andrew and Brian cut the pack of 52 playing-cards. Andrew cuts first, gets a King and replaces his cards in th pack. What is the probability of Brian
      (i) cutting an ace
      (ii) cutting a King
      (iii) cutting lower than a King?
   b To decide their next game, Andrew takes the top card of the pack, finds it a King but does not return it. Brian then takes the next card from the pack What is the probability of Brian's card
      (i) being an ace
      (ii) being a King
      (iii) being lower than a King?
   c Which of these two methods gives Brian the fairer chance of starting?

18 There are five fuses in a box and one of them has blown. You inspect the fuse
   a What is the probability of taking out the blown fuse first?
   b If your first choice gives a good fuse, what is the probability of your secon choice being the blown one?
   c If your first two choices give good fuses, what is the probability of your third choice being the blown one?

Theoretical probability

d If your first four choices give good fuses, what is the probability of your last choice being the blown one?

A bag holds six yellow cubes and four red cubes. You take two cubes out in turn without looking. What is the probability of your second cube being yellow if
a you replaced the first cube
b you did not replace the first cube which was red
c you did not replace the first cube which was yellow?

a Write all the different ways in which the three letters T, R and A can be arranged.
b If the three letters are written down at random, what is the probability that
   (i) they will spell TAR
   (ii) they will spell a word
   (iii) they will be in alphabetical order?

Mother M, father F and daughter D sit down at random on a bench.
a How many different ways can they be arranged?
b What is the probability that
   (i) the daughter will be in the middle
   (ii) the two females will be sitting next to each other
   (iii) the father will be at one end
   (iv) they will be sitting in order of age?

a Write all the different three-figure numbers which can be formed from the digits 3, 2 and 5 if none are repeated.
b What is the probability of selecting one of these numbers at random and getting
   (i) a number greater than 500
   (ii) a number less than 200
   (iii) a number greater than 200
   (iv) an even number
   (v) a multiple of 25?

a Write all the different arrangements of the four letters H, S, P and O.
b If one of these arrangements is selected at random, what is the probability
   that   (i) it is in alphabetical order
           (ii) it makes a word
           (iii) the letter O is in one of the middle positions
           (iv) the letters S and H are not together?

An electrical goods shop sold the following goods during one week.

	Kettles	Irons	Lamps	Radios	Televisions	Other items
umber f items	25	17	43	6	15	44

a What is the total number of items sold?
b What is the probability that the first customer the following week buys
   (i) a television
   (ii) a kettle
   (iii) either an iron or a lamp?

143

Theoretical probability

25 A shop sells screws in plastic packets. A batch of 100 packets contained some defective screws as shown in this table.

Number of defective screws per packet	0	1	2	3	4	5	6	Total
Number of packets	21	34	23	10	6	4	2	100

If you buy one of these packets at random, what is the probability of getting a packet with

a no defective screws
b 3 defective screws
c more than 3 defective screws
d less than 2 defective screws?

If the shop ordered another 500 packets, how many packets might it expect to get with

e no defective screws in them
f 5 defective screws in them
g 5 or 6 defective screws in them?

26 During one month a garage sells 30 new cars and a record is kept of the number of visits each car has to make to the garage to have faults put right.

Number of visits	0	1	2	3	4	5	6	7	Total
Number of cars	6	12	5	1	1	2	2	1	30

If you bought a car from this garage, what would be the probability that you would bring it back

a twice
b not at all
c more than 3 times
d at least once?

If the following month, the garage sold another 20 cars, how many cars would they expect to be brought back

e not at all
f more than 3 times?

27 An English exam is taken by 1000 candidates who have to answer just one question out of a choice of five. Their choices are listed in this table.

Question	1	2	3	4	5	Total
Number of candidates	356	250	82	100	212	1000

What is the probability that when the examiner marks the first paper it will be

a question 1
b question 2
c question 3 or 5
d not question 4?

If another 200 candidates take the same exam,

e how many answers to question 4 can be expected
f how many answers to question 2 can be expected?

28 A firm has 200 applicants for a job and the interviewer places each applicant in one of five categories as shown in this table.

	Over qualified	Well qualified	Poorly qualified	Unqualified	Unsuitabl
Number of applicants	18	80	62	28	12

If he replies to each applicant, what is the probability that his next reply will b to someone who is

a well-qualified
b either well or over-qualified

Theoretical probability

c   either unqualified or unsuitable?

Some months later a similar post is advertised and the firm has 120 applicants. How many of these applicants might the firm expect to be

d   well-qualified   e   either unqualified or unsuitable

f   either poorly qualified or unqualified?

29   This Venn diagram shows how many pupils take French or biology (or both subjects or neither) in a particular class in school.

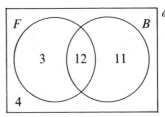

$\mathscr{E}$ = {all pupils in the class}
F = {those who study French}
B = {those who study biology}

a   What is the total number of pupils in this class?

b   If a pupil is chosen at random, what is the probability that the pupil studies
   (i)   both French and biology
   (ii) French
   (iii) either French or biology (or both)
   (iv) French but not biology?

30   This Venn diagram shows how many members of a youth club enjoy playing football and tennis.

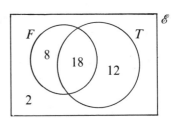

$\mathscr{E}$ = {all members of the club}
F = {those who enjoy football}
T = {those who enjoy tennis}

a   How many members has this youth club?

b   If a secretary for the club is elected, what is the probability that he/she will
   (i)   enjoy tennis but not football
   (ii) enjoy tennis
   (iii) enjoy either football or tennis but not both
   (iv) not enjoy tennis
   (v)   enjoy either both games or neither game?

In a certain part of Britain, farmers keep cattle, sheep, pigs or no livestock at all. This Venn diagram gives the numbers of farms according to the stock they rear.

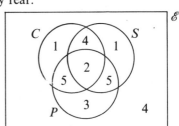

$\mathscr{E}$ = {all farms in the area}
C = {those rearing cattle}
S = {those rearing sheep}
P = {those rearing pigs}

a   How many farms are in this area?

b   If a farm is chosen at random, what is the probability that it rears
   (i)   all three types of livestock
   (ii) both cattle and pigs
   (iii) pigs
   (iv) only pigs

145

Theoretical probability

      (v) both cattle and pigs but not sheep
      (vi) just one type of beast
     (vii) no beasts at all?

  c If a pig-rearing farm is chosen at random, what is the probability that it
      (i) also rears cattle but not sheep
     (ii) also rears cattle
    (iii) rears just pigs?

32 In a bag are 10 building blocks, all the same size, but some are red and some
    are blue. You take one block out, note the colour, then replace it; this is
    repeated 100 times with 38 blue results and 62 red results.
    How many blue and how many red blocks do you suspect there are in the bag?

33 I can count 20 coins in my pocket, but I bring only one out at a time, look at
    it, then put it back in my pocket. I repeat this 100 times and count 73 copper
    coins and 27 silver coins.
    How many copper and how many silver coins should I suspect there are in my
    pocket?

Two successive events

Part 1

To calculate the theoretical probabilities of an event, a list of all possible outcomes is required. Such a list is called the **possibility space** and each outcome is assumed to be *equally likely* to happen.
Possibility spaces when *two* events occur can be found by using diagrams as shown below.

1 A family have four children, Alan, Barry, Colin and Diane. Two children are chosen at random to go on a shopping errand.

   a Copy and complete this diagram using the children's initials to find the possibility space of all possible pairs of children.

   b How many possible pairs are there?

   c What is the probability of having a pair
      (i) with Barry in it
      (ii) of one boy and one girl
      (iii) of two boys
      (iv) with Alan in it but not Barry?

   d If the children run 60 errands during the month, how many times might Diane expect to go?

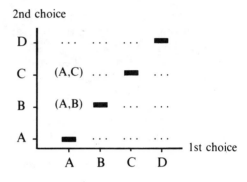

2 A firm has five vans labelled A to E and there are always three of them out on jobs, leaving two behind at the warehouse.

   a Copy and complete this diagram to find all the different possible pairs of vans left behind.

   b How many possible pairs are there?

   c What is the probability of having two vans at the warehouse when
      (i) one of them is van A
      (ii) one is either A or B (but not both together)
      (iii) neither of them is van E?

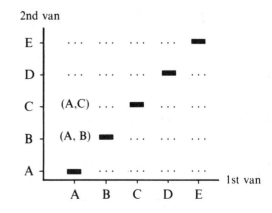

   d The daughter of the driver of van E calls at the warehouse every day to see her father on her way home from school. How many times in 40 school days might she expect to be disappointed and not see him?

3 a You toss a coin and throw a dice. Using the letters H and T for heads and tails, write all possible results by copying and completing the diagram.

   b How many possible pairs of results are there?

Two successive events

c What is the probability of having
(i) a head with an even score
(ii) a tail with an odd score
(iii) a head with a score greater than 4
(iv) a tail with a score less than 5?

d If this experiment is repeated 60 times, how many times would you expect to have a head with an even score?

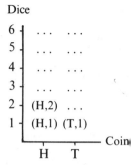

4 a You toss two coins, one after the other. Copy and complete this diagram to list all possible results.

b How many possibilities are there?

c What is the probability of having
(i) two heads
(ii) two tails
(iii) one head and one tail in either order
(iv) both coins showing the same result?

d If you tossed two coins 100 times, how many times would you expect to get two heads?

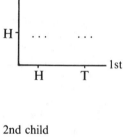

5 a Some families have two children. Copy and complete this table to find the probability of a two-children family having
(i) two boys
(ii) two girls
(iii) a boy and a girl in either order
(iv) a boy and a girl with the girl older than the boy.

b If a housing estate has 80 two-children families, how many of them would you expect to have two girls?

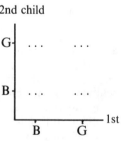

6 a You roll two dice, one after the other. Copy and complete this diagram find the possibility space.

b How many different results are possible?

c What is the probability of rolling
(i) a double four
(ii) a double six
(iii) two even scores
(iv) two odd scores
(v) a six on the first dice and an even score on the second dice
(vi) a total score of 2
(vii) a total score of 3
(viii) a total score of 4
(ix) scores which differ by 1
(x) scores which differ by 2?

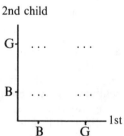

d If you rolled two dice 144 times, how many times would you expect any double score?

Two successive events

Part 2   Comparing experiment and theory

This exercise compares theoretical and experimental results to see how good a model the theory is providing of actual situations.

1   Tossing two coins

Experiment

Each pupil in your class is to toss two coins 20 times and note the results. Combine the results for all the class and complete this table.

Theory

Use your diagram from **Part 1** question **4** to find the probabilities and so complete the row of expected or theoretical frequencies in the table.

Outcome	Two heads	One head, one tail (in either order)	Two tails	Totals
Observed or experimental frequencies				
Expected or theoretical frequencies				

2   Two-child families

Experiment

Ask the pupils in your class if they come from a two-children family. If they do, ask if they have a brother or sister. If possible, repeat with pupils in other classes.

Theory

Use your diagram from **Part 1** question **5** to find the probabilities and so complete the row of expected or theoretical frequencies in the table.

Outcome	Two boys	One boy, one girl (in either order)	Two girls	Totals
Observed or experimental frequencies				
Expected or theoretical frequencies				

3   Rolling two dice

Experiment

Each pupil in your class is to roll two dice, add the scores together, note the total and repeat 36 times. Combine the results for all the class and copy and complete this table.

Theory

Use your diagram from **Part 1** question **6** to find the probabilities and so complete the row of expected frequencies in the table.

Total score	2	3	4	5	6	7	8	9	10	11	12	Totals
Observed frequencies												
Expected frequencies												

Which total score is
a   most likely in theory   b   most common in practice
c   least likely in theory   d   least common in practice?

Draw bar charts to illustrate your results.
Comment on any differences between theoretical and experimental results.
How might the experiments be altered to reduce these differences?

Tree diagrams

The diagrams used in the last chapter are of no use when three or more events occur. The possibility space which lists all possible outcomes can now be found using a **tree diagram**.

Part 1 Equally likely branches

1 Tossing three coins
   a Three coins are tossed, one after the other.
      Copy and complete this tree diagram to show all the possible outcomes.

1st coin	2nd coin	3rd coin	Outcomes
	H	H	HHH
H		...	...
	T	...	...
		...	...
	...	...	...
T		...	...
	...	...	...
		...	...

   b Copy and complete this table to show the probability of each possible outcome. The order in which H and T occur is not important in the table.

Outcome	3 heads	2 heads & 1 tail	1 head & 2 tails	3 tails	Totals
Frequency					
Probability					

   c Use the results in your table to answer these questions.
      If you toss three coins 160 times, how many times would you expect to get
      (i)   three heads
      (ii) two heads and one tail
      (iii) two tails and one head
      (iv) three tails?

2 A three-children family
   Some families have three children in them.
   a Copy and complete this tree diagram to show all the possible ways of listing children in a three-children family.
      Use B for boy and G for girl.

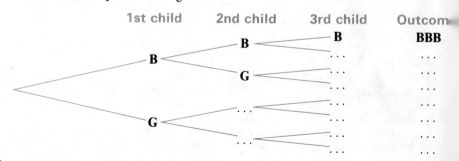

150

Tree diagrams

b   Copy and complete this table to show the probabilities of the different outcomes. The order in which B and G occur is not important in the table.

Outcome	3 boys	2 boys & 1 girl	1 boy & 2 girls	3 girls	Totals
Frequency					
Probability					

c   Use your results in the table to answer these questions.
    If 40 three-children families live on an estate, how many of them would you expect to have   (i)   3 boys
                          (ii) 2 boys and 1 girl
                          (iii) 1 boy and 2 girls
                          (iv) 3 girls?

3   A four-children family

Some families have four children in them.
a   Copy and complete this tree diagram to show all the possible ways of listing children in a four- children family.
    Use B for boy and G for girl.

| 1st child | 2nd child | 3rd child | 4th child | Outcomes |

b   Copy and complete this table to show the different probabilities.

Outcome	4 boys	3 boys & 1 girl	2 boys & 2 girls	1 boy & 3 girls	4 girls	Totals
Frequency						
Probability						

c   Use the results in your table to answer these questions.
    If in a small town there are 48 families with four children, how many of these families would you expect to have   (i)   4 boys
                          (ii) 3 boys and 1 girl
                          (iii) 2 boys and 2 girls
                          (iv) 1 boy and 3 girls
                          (v)   4 girls?

Tree diagrams

4 **Triangular spinners**

The triangular spinner shown here is equally likely
to give a score of 1, 2 or 3.
It is spun three times.

a Copy and complete this tree diagram to show all the
possible combinations of the three scores. Complete
the possibility space and the total score column.

1st spin	2nd spin	3rd spin	Outcomes	Total score
		1	1 1 1	3
	1	2	1 1 2	4
		3	...	...
1	2	...	...	...
		...	...	...
	3	...	...	...
		...	...	...
	...	...	...	...
2	...	...	...	...
	...	...	...	...
...	...	...	...	...
	...	...	...	...

b Copy and complete this table to show the probabilities of all the possible
total scores.

Total score	3	4	5	6	7	8	9	Tot.
Frequency								
Probability								

c Use the results in your table to answer these questions.
If the spinner is spun 270 times, how many times would you expect a tot.
score of (i) 3 (ii) 4 (iii) 6 (iv) 9?

Tree diagrams

5 Rolling two dice

Two ordinary dice are rolled, one after the other.

a Copy and complete this tree diagram to show all the possible outcomes and total scores.

1st dice	2nd dice	Outcomes	Total score
	1	1, 1	2
	2	1, 2	3
	3	1, 3	4
1	4	1, 4	5
	5	1, 5	6
	6	1, 6	7
	1	2, 1	3
	2	2, 2	...
2	3	2, 3	...
	4	...	...
	5	...	...
	6	...	...
	1	...	...
	2	...	...
3	...	...	...
	...	...	...
	...	...	...
	...	...	...
	...	...	...
	...	...	...
4	...	...	...
	...	...	...
	...	...	...
	...	...	...
	...	...	...
	...	...	...
...	...	...	...
	...	...	...
	...	...	...
	...	...	...
	...	...	...
	...	...	...
...	...	...	...
	...	...	...
	...	...	...
	...	...	...

153

Tree diagrams

b Copy and complete this table to show the probabilities of the different total scores.

Total score	2	3	4	5	6	7	8	9	10	11	12	Totals
Frequency												
Probability												

c If you roll two dice 180 times, how many times would you expect a total
score of (i) 2 (iv) 11
(ii) 4 (v) 12?
(iii) 7

6 An experiment to test the theoretical results for rolling two dice will need the help of all the pupils in your class.
Give two dice to as many pairs of pupils as possible. As one throws the dice, the other can record the total score.
Combine the results of all the class, copy this table and enter the results in the last row.

Total score	2	3	4	5	6	7	8	9	10	11	12	Totals
Probability												
Expected frequency												
Observed frequency												

Enter the probabilities from your tree diagram in **5** above and use a calculator to work out the expected frequencies.
Which total score was *expected* to occur most often? Was this in fact the case with your experiment?
Can you make any other comparisons between the expected and observed frequencies?

7 You have already investigated the make-up of families with various numbers of children.
Copy this table and enter your results for families with 1, 2, 3 and 4 children.

	No girls	Just 1 girl	Just 2 girls	Just 3 girls	Just 4 girls	Just 5 girls	Just 6 girls	Total number of families
1 child								2
2 children								4
3 children								8
4 children								16
5 children								32
6 children								64

Expected frequency of girls in a family with

Do you recognise the pattern of your results?
Can you complete the rows for five-children and six-children families?

Tree diagrams

Part 2 Unequal branches

1 An analogy

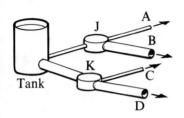

A plumber connects two sizes of pipes (narrow and wide) as in this diagram, where at each junction a narrow pipe takes $\frac{1}{6}$ of the water and a wide pipe takes $\frac{5}{6}$ of the water.

What fraction of the water leaving the tank reaches a junction J b junction K c end A d end B e end C f end D?

g If you have access to both end B and end C, what is the total fraction of water leaving the tank which reaches you?

2 The tree diagram on page 153 showing the outcomes when two dice are rolled has 36 branches. If we are only interested in scoring 6's, then many of these branches can be combined. If the scores of 1 to 5 are grouped together and called "not 6", the tree diagram now looks like this.

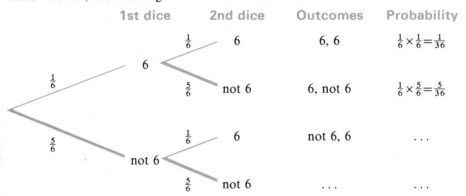

1st dice	2nd dice	Outcomes	Probability
6	6	6, 6	$\frac{1}{6} \times \frac{1}{6} = \frac{1}{36}$
	not 6	6, not 6	$\frac{1}{6} \times \frac{5}{6} = \frac{5}{36}$
not 6	6	not 6, 6	. . .
	not 6	. . .	. . .

Copy and complete the diagram. Note that as the branches are not equally likely, the probabilities are given. Check your working by adding the four probabilities in the final column.

A pack of 52 playing-cards is cut, shuffled and then cut again.
Copy and complete these three diagrams and find the probability of each outcome.

a

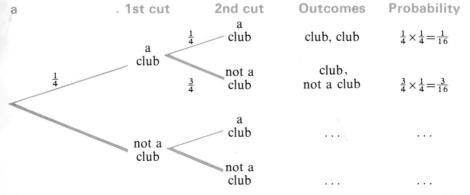

1st cut	2nd cut	Outcomes	Probability
a club	a club	club, club	$\frac{1}{4} \times \frac{1}{4} = \frac{1}{16}$
	not a club	club, not a club	$\frac{3}{4} \times \frac{1}{4} = \frac{3}{16}$
not a club	a club	. . .	. . .
	not a club	. . .	. . .

Tree diagrams

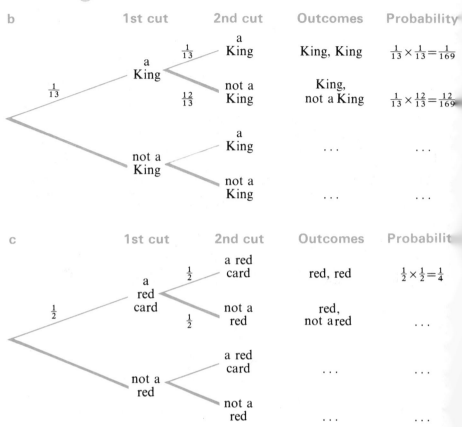

b

	1st cut	2nd cut	Outcomes	Probability

King, King: $\frac{1}{13} \times \frac{1}{13} = \frac{1}{169}$

King, not a King: $\frac{1}{13} \times \frac{12}{13} = \frac{12}{169}$

c

	1st cut	2nd cut	Outcomes	Probabilit

red, red: $\frac{1}{2} \times \frac{1}{2} = \frac{1}{4}$

4   This regular five-sided spinner is spun twice.

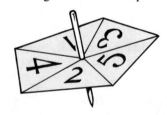

Copy and complete the two diagrams
to find the probability of each outcome.

a

	1st spin	2nd spin	Outcomes	Probabi

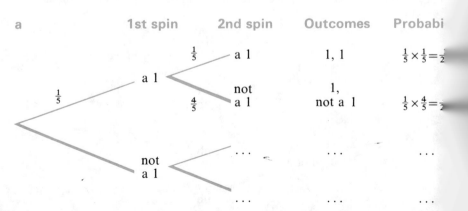

1, 1: $\frac{1}{5} \times \frac{1}{5} = \frac{}{2}$

1, not a 1: $\frac{1}{5} \times \frac{4}{5} = \frac{}{2}$

Tree diagrams

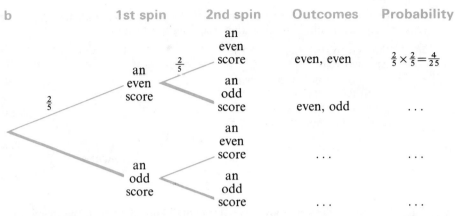

	1st spin	2nd spin	Outcomes	Probability

an even score — $\frac{2}{5}$ — an even score, even, even, $\frac{2}{5} \times \frac{2}{5} = \frac{4}{25}$

an even score — an odd score, even, odd, . . .

an odd score — an even score, . . . , . . .

an odd score — an odd score, . . . , . . .

$\frac{2}{5}$, $\frac{2}{5}$

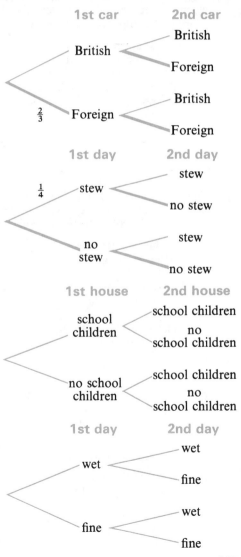

	1st car	2nd car

Two-thirds of the cars on British roads are of foreign manufacture. Copy and complete this tree diagram to find

a   P (the next 2 cars you see being British made)

b   P (the next two cars you see not being British made).

British — British

British — Foreign

$\frac{2}{3}$ Foreign — British

Foreign — Foreign

	1st day	2nd day

Some sort of stew is served for school dinner one day in every four at random. You have a school dinner on two successive days. Copy and complete this tree diagram to find

a   P (having stew on both days)

b   P (not having stew on either day).

$\frac{1}{4}$ stew — stew

stew — no stew

no stew — stew

no stew — no stew

	1st house	2nd house

If one-third of all British households has a child of school age and two houses are selected at random, copy and complete this tree diagram to find

a   P (both houses having children at school)

b   P (neither house having a child at school).

school children — school children

school children — no school children

no school children — school children

no school children — no school children

	1st day	2nd day

During winter it rains on $\frac{3}{5}$ of all the days. Copy and complete this tree diagram to find

a   P (two successive days having rain)

b   P (two successive days being fine)

c   P (the first day being wet, but the second day being fine).

wet — wet

wet — fine

fine — wet

fine — fine

157

Tree diagrams

9 A family go on holiday every summer and the probability that they go to the seaside is $\frac{2}{3}$. Copy and complete this tree diagram to find

a P (they go to the seaside for the next two years)

b P (they do not go to the seaside for either of the next two years)

c P (they go to the seaside this summer but not next summer).

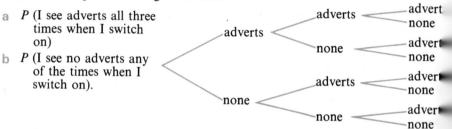

10 The probability that there are advertisements being shown on the television when I switch on is $\frac{1}{4}$. One evening I switch the television on three times. Copy and complete this diagram to find

a P (I see adverts all three times when I switch on)

b P (I see no adverts any of the times when I switch on).

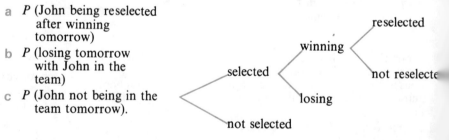

11 The probability of John being selected to play in tomorrow's football team is $\frac{1}{3}$. If he is selected, the probability of his team winning the match is $\frac{3}{4}$. If they win, the probability of John being reselected for the next match is $\frac{1}{2}$. Find

a P (John being reselected after winning tomorrow)

b P (losing tomorrow with John in the team)

c P (John not being in the team tomorrow).

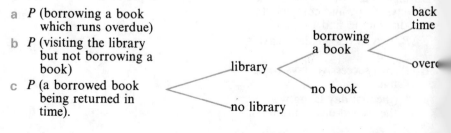

12 The probability of going to the library on Saturday is $\frac{1}{2}$. If I go, the probability of taking out a book is $\frac{4}{5}$. If I take a book out, the probability that I will take back overdue is $\frac{3}{4}$. Find

a P (borrowing a book which runs overdue)

b P (visiting the library but not borrowing a book)

c P (a borrowed book being returned in time).

Tree diagrams

13 Two ordinary dice are rolled, one after the other. Find

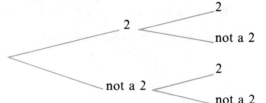

a P (a 2 on the first, not a 2 on the second)

b P (not a 2 on the first, a 2 on the second)

c P (just one 2 on either dice).

14 Two identical tetrahedra have their faces numbered 1, 2, 3 and 4. They are rolled separately, like dice, one after the other and the score is that on the bottom face in contact with the table. Copy and complete this tree diagram to find

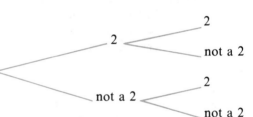

a P (a 2 on the first, not a 2 on the second)

b P (not a 2 on the first, a 2 on the second)

c P (just one 2 on either tetrahedron).

The probability of a fine day tomorrow is $\frac{1}{2}$ and if it is fine tomorrow, the probability that I shall take the dog for a long walk is $\frac{1}{4}$. If I take it for a long walk, the probability that it will chase rabbits is $\frac{2}{5}$. If it is wet, we shall definitely not go out. Copy and complete this diagram to find

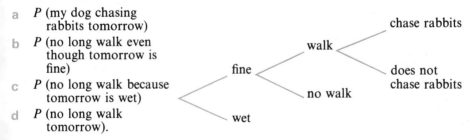

a P (my dog chasing rabbits tomorrow)

b P (no long walk even though tomorrow is fine)

c P (no long walk because tomorrow is wet)

d P (no long walk tomorrow).

When Joanne sees an advertisement for a job she likes, the probability that she will apply for it is $\frac{1}{20}$. If she applies, the probability of her being interviewed is $\frac{4}{5}$. If she is interviewed, the probability of her being offered the job is $\frac{5}{6}$. Draw your own tree diagram to find

a P (being offered the job she applied for)

b P (applying but not being interviewed)

c P (not being offered the job after being interviewed).

Tree diagrams

17 The probability that I stay up late on Saturday night is $\frac{3}{4}$.
If I stay up late, the probability that I shall lie in on Sunday morning is $\frac{2}{3}$.
But if I don't stay up late on Saturday night, the probability that I shall lie in is only $\frac{1}{3}$.
Draw your own tree diagram to find
a P (having a lie-in after a late night)
b P (having a lie-in but not after a late night)
c P (having a lie-in)   d P (not having a lie-in).

18 The probability that my family will go out in the car next Bank Holiday is $\frac{3}{4}$; otherwise we shall stay at home.
If we go out in the car, the probability that we shall drive on a motorway is $\frac{1}{3}$; and if we use a motorway, the probability of being delayed in a traffic jam is $\frac{2}{5}$.
But if we use ordinary roads, the probability of being in a traffic jam is $\frac{1}{5}$.
Draw your own tree diagram to find
a P (staying at home next Bank Holiday)
b P (being in a traffic jam on a motorway)
c P (being in a traffic jam on an ordinary road)
d P (being in a traffic jam on any kind of road)
e P (not being in a traffic jam on a motorway)
f P (not being in a traffic jam on an ordinary road)
g P (not being in a traffic jam on any kind of road).

Problems without replacement

19 You have ten coins in your pocket of which six are copper and the others are silver. You take two coins out at random, one after the other.
What is the probability of the first coin being
a copper   b silver?

Copy and complete this tree diagram and use it to find
c P (both coins being copper)
d P (both coins being silver)
e P (one coin of each type).

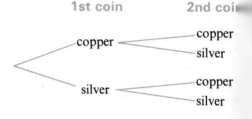

20 Five people, Mr Brown, Mr Black, Mrs White, Mrs Grey and Mr Green, stand for election to a committee which has two vacant places.
What is the probability that the first choice is
a a man   b a woman?

Copy this tree diagram to find
c P (both choices being male)
d P (both choices being female)
e P (one man and one woman being chosen).

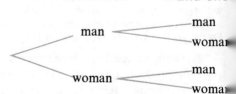

Tree diagrams

21 A shelf has 12 books on it, of which nine are fiction and the rest non-fiction.
You choose two books at random, one after the other.
Draw your own tree diagram to find
a P (your first choice being fiction)
b P (your first choice being non-fiction)
c P (both books being fiction)
d P (both books being non-fiction)
e P (one book being fiction and the other non-fiction).

22 A tube of fruit pastilles has two flavours placed at random down the tube. Ten
pastilles are flavoured orange and the other six are lemon. You take out the first
two pastilles.
Draw a tree diagram to find
a P (both pastilles being orange)
b P (both pastilles being lemon)
c P (one pastille of each flavour).

23 The probability of Jim getting up late in the morning is $\frac{1}{2}$. If he gets up late, he
certainly arrives late for work.
If he gets up on time, the probability of still being late for work is $\frac{1}{5}$.
Draw a tree diagram to find
a P (Jim getting to work on time)
b P (Jim being late for work after getting up on time)
c P (Jim being late for work after getting up late)
d P (Jim being late for work).

24 A fruit machine has the three drums shown here.
a Without drawing any tree diagram, calculate
the probabilities of these winning outcomes.

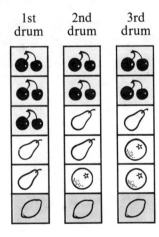

1st drum	2nd drum	3rd drum

Winning outcomes	Prize
(i) ▫▫▫	£5
(ii) ▫▫▫	£2
(iii) ▫▫▫	£1
(iv) 🍒🍒🍒	20p

b It costs 10 pence for each turn on the
machine. A man has 216 turns, one after the
other. What winnings might he expect from
the machine?
Will he expect to make an overall profit, and
if so, how much?

Statistics

Populations and samples

A **population** is the set of all the items which are being investigated and about which data is being collected.,
When collecting information in each of the following situations, would you investigate

    (i) every member of the whole population
or (ii) only a *sample* of the members of the whole population?

	Population	Data to be collected
a	Members of your class in school	their birthdays
b	Trees in the school grounds	distance around their trunks
c	Trees in a forest	distance around their trunks
d	Passengers on a bus	cost of their tickets
e	Rabbits on a farm	their weights
f	Cows on a farm	their milk yields
g	People in a town	how they will vote in an election
h	People in your family	their ages

Populations can be sampled in many ways.
Decide whether the methods below will give (i) a **biased** sample
                    or (ii) a **random** sample.
If biased, say why you think this is so.

	Investigation	Method of sampling
a	To find how pupils travel to your school.	Ask a group of pupils who arrive at school together.
b	To find how popular football is amongst the boys in a particular class.	Ask the first three boys who arrive on the football pitch at the start of the lesson.
c	To estimate how many oak trees there are in a certain area.	Divide a map of the area into six rows and six columns, shake a dice twice to select a square and then go to count the trees in that area. Repeat several times.
d	To find what the opinions of the townspeople are regarding a town bypass.	Deliver a questionnaire to every tenth house with a prepaid reply.

Write a few sentences to suggest in what ways these samples might be *biased*.

a A manufacturer gives a year's supply of washing powder to people who are willing to take part in an investigation into which washing powder is the most effective.

b To investigate the musical likes and dislikes of members of the public, a sample of the members of local youth groups is questioned.

c A porridge manufacturer wishes to estimate its popularity at breakfast in a certain city. People from two pages of the local telephone directory are contacted. All their surnames begin with Mc.

d An advertising agency wishes to find out which television advertisements are remembered most readily and asks a sample of people leaving the local supermarket.

e To decide whether stray dogs are particularly unhealthy, all those in one street are caught and inspected by a vet.

Populations and samples

f A garage investigates the defects in a certain model of car by questioning those customers who part-exchange that car for a new one of the same model.

4 When choosing a random sample, each member of the population must have equal chance of being chosen.

 a When choosing at random between *two* possibilities (such as starting a hockey match) what object is often used?

 b When choosing at random between *six* possibilities, what object can be used?

 c This regular octagon is used as a spinner to make a random choice. How many possibilities can it choose between?

 d If you sell a total of 100 tickets in a raffle, write a few sentences to descr how you would choose the one winning ticket at random.

 e If a television programme has 3648 correct entries to a competition on postcards, describe how they might televise choosing the *one* winning e

5 Here are some methods of choosing numbers from 0 to 9. Say whether you think they are *random* numbers. If you think they are *not* random, give a reason.

 a Choosing the last figure on house door numbers as you walk up one side a street.

 b Choosing the last figure on the number-plates of cars which pass you.

 c Using the score rolled on an ordinary dice.

 d Using the last figure of the ages of pupils in your class at school.

 e Choosing the last figure of telephone numbers from any page in a directe

 f Choosing the first figure of long-distance telephone numbers.

6 Without pause, write down a list of at least thirty whole numbers all lying in the range 0 to 9. Try to keep them random, but write them down as quickly as you can.
Copy this table and enter your results.

Number	0	1	2	3	4	5	6	7	8
Number of times written down									

Look at your results. Do you think your numbers *are* random numbers?

7 Here is a table of random numbers ready for use.

14 05	84 30	11 24	98 63	45 28	61 38	06 56	28 60	11 69	29 57
33 40	94 37	57 46	06 43	67 72	29 09	18 02	84 80	29 78	55 81
66 97	06 87	81 93	86 36	95 17	85 62	94 11	01 54	42 11	25 51
34 75	31 04	78 06	58 03	47 22	86 31	37 26	68 64	03 08	32 77
98 06	99 11	20 09	93 37	60 41	18 15	03 46	57 08	37 11	67 18
02 86	73 01	27 97	92 17	32 61	04 57	45 89	01 69	00 66	98 33
39 51	70 45	42 09	57 83	78 81	60 96	96 13	48 83	99 24	24 06
55 62	09 92	21 68	95 66	22 05	02 35	50 67	01 26	49 34	32 63
86 98	39 52	83 40	69 08	74 63	45 78	15 35	28 44	35 96	34 43
95 88	90 70	29 13	77 20	32 69	26 23	88 15	02 47	76 49	73 09
31 19	84 22	15 09	37 93	74 79	60 24	55 37	92 54	13 71	68 10
29 18	18 97	29 98	42 25	81 19	68 36	43 45	39 61	43 67	91 60
15 72	84 38	00 33	08 50	35 98	38 18	07 10	29 59	46 70	75 50
83 93	82 29	50 02	93 16	11 61	78 99	70 77	92 56	50 08	67 55
46 36	38 42	47 07	09 96	11 03	46 69	39 94	24 15	14 79	78 63

Populations and samples

To use them, (i) choose any number
            (ii) move from this number in any direction, left, right,
                up or down
           (iii) write each number which you pass.

a   999 tickets are sold in a raffle which has five prizes. Use the random number table to choose the five winning numbers.

b   Another raffle has sold only 568 tickets and there are five prizes. Use the table to choose the five winning numbers. Which random numbers will you have to ignore?

c   A primary school has 84 ten-year-old pupils. Four of them are to be chosen at random to present flowers to four lady guests. If the children are numbered from 01 to 84, use the table to select four of them.

d   The eleven boys in a cricket team can agree only on the two opening batsmen. If the other nine boys are numbered from 1 to 9, use the table to arrange them in a random batting order.

e   Seven soldiers numbered from 1 to 7 take turns to go on sentry duty. Use the table to arrange them in random order.

f   A machine automatically seals 8600 cartons of fruit juice each morning. The cartons are stamped with numbers from 0001 to 8600. A random sample of 15 cartons is taken in order to check their seals. Use the table to list the numbers of a possible sample.

g   52 major football matches are played during one weekend. A football pools firm has them numbered from 01 to 52. Select a random sample of 8 matches in which draws might occur.

24 school children are seated in four rows of 6 desks as shown. The school minibus can take only 15 of them on a trip and all of them would like to go. Use pairs of random numbers to choose those who go and write their names.

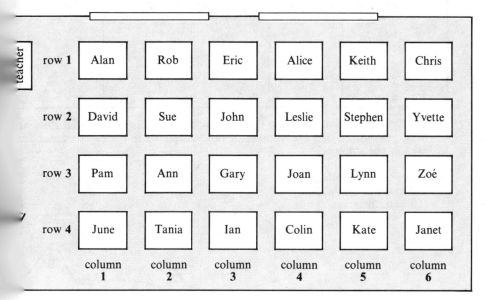

	row 1	Alan	Rob	Eric	Alice	Keith	Chris
teacher	row 2	David	Sue	John	Leslie	Stephen	Yvette
	row 3	Pam	Ann	Gary	Joan	Lynn	Zoé
	row 4	June	Tania	Ian	Colin	Kate	Janet
		column 1	column 2	column 3	column 4	column 5	column 6

Populations and samples

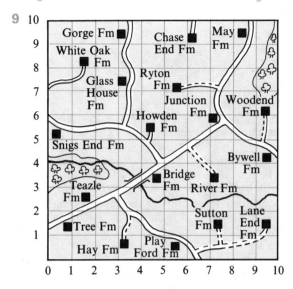

A survey is to be made of the chemicals which farmers use on the land in the area shown on this map. Time is too short to visit all the farms, so a random sample of six farms is chosen.

Use random numbers to select which six farms are visited and write their names.

Fm = Farm

10 a Take a sheet of squared paper ruled in 1 mm squares; draw and label both axes from 0 to 100 using a scale of 1 mm per unit.

b Take random numbers in groups of four from the random number table and use them to plot a point. For example, 2703 gives the point (27, 3).
Repeat this until you have 100 points plotted at random on your axis.

c A sample of these points can be taken as follows.
Draw a square of side 8 cm on tracing paper.
Place it at random on your axes (but not *outside* them) and count how many of your 100 points are inside the 8 cm square.
Repeat this ten times, copy this table and enter your results in the first row. Work out the *average* number of points inside the 8 cm square.

Length of side of square, cm	Area of square, cm²	Number of random points inside the square	Average number of points
8			
7			
6			
5			
4			

d Repeat these instructions for the other squares in this table. What do you notice about the average number of random points in the squares and the area of the squares?

e Trace these two shapes and use this method to estimate their areas.

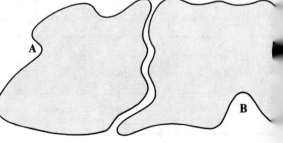

Populations and samples

1 A school sports field has an area of 10 000 m² and the biology teacher asks a class to estimate the number of dandelions growing in the field.
Ten groups of children each peg out at random one square metre with string and count the number of dandelions in the square, with these results.

4   5   8   6   3   7   5   4   5   8

a What is the total number of dandelions they count?
b Estimate the number of dandelions in the whole field.
c What should the class do to get a more accurate estimate?

2 The headmaster of a school of 1400 children wishes to estimate how many are not wearing school uniform one morning. He chooses three classes at random and finds the numbers without uniform are:

2 out of 20,   4 out of 24,   3 out of 26.

a How many children were inspected and how many were without uniform?
b Estimate the number without uniform in the whole school.

Stephen Davidson saves stamps. He bought a mixed bag of 1000 stamps and found that in the first 50 he looked at 13 were British. How many British stamps might he expect in the whole bag of 1000?

A sampling bottle contains a large number of white and coloured balls. When shaken and turned upside down, a random sample is taken in the hollow tube as shown.

a How large is the sample shown in this picture?
b How many of this sample are white and how many are coloured?
c If there are 1000 balls in the bottle altogether, make a rough estimate of the number of white and the number of coloured ones.
d It is usual to take many samples before making an estimate. If you have a sample bottle, take, for example, 100 samples, record your results in a table like this one, calculate the average (mean) number of coloured balls per sample and so estimate how many there are in the bottle.

a sampling bottle

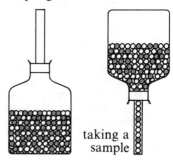

taking a sample

Number of coloured balls in the sample	0 1 2 3 4 . . .
Tally	
Frequency	

A mail-order catalogue has many items for sale in it. Take any catalogue and estimate the number of items as follows.

a Choose 20 pages at random and count the number of items on each page.
b Calculate the average (mean) number of items per page for your sample.
c Find how many pages there are in the catalogue.
d Estimate the number of items in the whole catalogue.
e How could your estimate be improved?

How many names in your local telephone directory have the same exchange as your own home town?

a Take a random sample of pages and count the number of names on each page with the exchange you want.

Populations and samples

b Find how many pages in the directory have names and exchanges listed on them.

c Hence, estimate the number of names with your exchange.

d How could your estimate be improved?

17 By using the above method, estimate the number of

a times the word "the" is used in a novel

b pupils in your school with surnames beginning with B

c capital letters used in a newspaper

d British entries in the index at the end of an atlas

e entries in the index of the atlas which are both *south* of the equator and *we* of Greenwich

f towns in an AA or RAC handbook with populations less than 10 000 people

g towns in an AA or RAC handbook which have just one recommended garage

h trains in the British Rail timetable which have a buffet service (⊑) on them

i trains in the British Rail timetable which start their journeys between midnight and 01.00 hours

j names in your local telephone directory which have five-figure telephone numbers

k names in your local telephone directory which have telephone numbers starting with an 8.

18 A sampling technique can be used to estimate the size of a population which cannot be easily counted.

Suppose you want to estimate the number of fish in a pond.

You catch 100 fish, mark each of them and then return them to the pond. So time later, after you think they have dispersed, you catch a second sample of : fish and count the number of marked ones.

If this second sample has 20 marked fish, estimate the total number n of fish the pond by copying and completing this table.

You assume that the *proportion* of fish in the second sample is the same as fo the whole pond.

	In the second sample	In the whole pond
Number of marked fish	20	100
Total number of fish	50	n

19 In a large lake, 250 marked frogs are released and allowed to disperse. In a l sample of 200 frogs, 40 are found to be marked. Estimate the number of fro in the lake.

20 A forester catches, marks and releases 500 deer. Several months later, he ca 360 deer and finds 140 marked ones amongst them. Estimate the total population of deer in the forest.

Collecting data

1 Data can be collected in several different ways:
  (i) by a census   (ii) by a questionnaire   (iii) by observation
  (iv) by experiment.
  Which of these four methods would you use to investigate
  a   details of each household throughout the country
  b   the voting intentions of the people in a particular town
  c   the choice of television programmes watched last week
  d   the number of cars which have to stop at a set of traffic lights
  e   the number of pupils wearing brown shoes
  f   the effect of sunlight on the rate of growth of bean shoots
  g   the effect of a fertilizer on the yield of a certain crop
  h   whether the employees in a firm wish to change the working hours of
      the day
  i   the number of pupils who bring their own lunch to school
  j   the number of defective parts produced automatically on a machine and
      delivered on a conveyor belt?

By questionnaire

2 When constructing a questionnaire, care must be taken so that the questions are
  clear, precise, unambiguous and require short answers.
  These questions for a questionnaire are not well written. Rewrite them in your
  own words so that they are clear, unambiguous and require short answers.
  a   How many pupils in your class usually have toast or a boiled egg or a
      cooked meal or nothing for breakfast?
  b   What time do you go to bed and does it depend on the day of the week
      and the school holidays?
  c   How many pupils in your class have bicycles, televisions and cassette
      recorders?
  d   Do you watch television programmes mostly on one channel or all channels
      or two channels?
  e   How many children live in your street and how many are too young to go
      to school and are boys?
  f   Would you say you were tall, very tall, short or of average height?

3 Here is a questionnaire which could be used to investigate various personal
  details of pupils in your class.

1 Are you a boy or a girl?	B or G ☐
2 How old are you?	☐ years
3 Is your hair blonde, red, brown or black?	☐
4 Are your eyes blue, grey, green or brown?	☐
5 How many brothers/sisters have you?	☐ brother(s) & ☐ sister(s)
6 How many first names do you have?	☐
7 At what time do you usually get up on a normal school day?	☐ a.m.
8 At what time do you usually go to bed on a normal school day?	☐ p.m.

Collecting data

   a   Decide whether any of these eight questions need altering to make them clearer and more easily understood.
Add any other questions of your own.

   b   Circulate the questionnaire around your class.

   c   Collect the data together and put the information into tables.
Here are some possibilities for questions 3, 5 and 8.

Hair colour	Blonde	Red	Brown	Black
Number of pupils				

Number of brothers	0	1	2	3	more than 3
Number of pupils					

Normal bedtime	Before 9 p.m.	9 p.m. up to 10 p.m.	10 p.m. up to 11 p.m.	After 11 p.m.
Number of pupils				

   d   Draw a bar graph for each table and write a sentence describing your findings.

4   Construct your own questionnaire to investigate various facts. Collect the data, tabulate it, draw bar charts and write about your findings. You could investigate school life, sporting interests, reading habits, holidays, music interests, etc.

By observation

5   You are to investigate traffic conditions outside your home or your school, perhaps with a view to requesting a zebra crossing. You will have to decide on what day, at what time, for how long and how often you will do a survey. You also need to decide how you will group your observations into vehicle types. Here is a possible format. Make any alterations to suit your own particular needs. Draw a bar chart of your results and write a few sentences about your findings.

SURVEY OF VEHICLES	carried out by..(name)
	on..(street/road)
	from...................to.......................(time of day)
	on..(date)

Type of Vehicle	Tally	Frequency
Cars		
Vans		
Lorries		
Buses/coaches		
Motor cycles		
Bicycles		
Others		

6 Here are other surveys which involve collecting data by observation.
For each one
  (i) decide where, how, for how long, when and by whom the survey is to be carried out
  (ii) decide the different categories that the survey will investigate
  (iii) construct a possible survey sheet to record the data
  (iv) carry out the survey, draw a bar chart of the results and comment on them.

a **Birds at breakfast**
A survey of the birds you see outside.

b **Colours of cars**
A survey to discover the popularity of different colours of cars.

c **People in cars**
A survey to investigate how many passengers are carried in cars.

d **Types of housing**
A survey of the different kinds of house near your home or your school.

e **Supermarket customers**
A survey of the different age groups and sexes of the customers who visit a supermarket in your area.

By experiment

7 You are to investigate the frequency of use of letters in the English language by choosing them at random from a book.
Open a book at random and point without looking at the page. Record the letter nearest to where you point in a table like this.

Letter	a	b	c	d	e	z
Tally						
Frequency						

Draw a bar chart of your results and write about your findings.

8 Here are other experiments which involve collecting data.
For each one   (i) design a frequency table to record your results
              (ii) do the experiment
              (iii) draw a bar graph of your results and comment on them.

a **Three dice**
Roll three dice and add the scores together. Repeat 50 times.

b **Spades**
Deal 13 cards from a pack of 52 playing cards and count the number of spades there are. Repeat 50 times.

c **Initials of surnames**
Take several class lists or registers for your school and record the initials of the surnames of 200 pupils.

d **First names**
Write down in order what *you think* are the five most popular boys' or girls' first names. Use the same class lists or registers and record how often they occur. (Ignore other names.)

e **Pairs of vowels**
The five vowels a, e, i, o, u can be paired in twenty different ways with the order of the pair being important, e.g. au and ua are different pairs. Can you list twenty pairs?
Open any book at any page and record the first 100 vowel pairs you meet as you read the book.

Tabulating data

There are two types of numerical data.
It can be either **discrete**, taking only certain values,
or **continuous**, taking any values within a given range.
Data found by *counting* is discrete; data found by *measuring* is continuous.

1 Which of these do you *count* and which do you *measure*?
   a goals in a football match   b peas in a pod
   c pips in an orange   d oil in an oil drum
   e the speed of a car   f windows in a house
   g the score on a dice   h cars in a car-park
   i the time to run 100 metres   j heights of people
   k shoe sizes   l colours of the rainbow
   m the temperature during the day   n people on a bus
   o houses on an estate   p workmen's weekly wages
   q your age   r grains of rice in 1 tonne
   Can you add eight more items to this list?
   Give *four* that you would count and *four* that you would measure.

2 One ordinary dice is rolled 80 times and the scores are as follows:

```
2 4 2 1 6 5 3 4 1 4 2 4 6 1 5 4 2 1 4 6
4 4 3 1 4 1 5 6 5 4 6 6 5 2 3 4 4 5 2 4
5 4 5 5 2 2 5 4 5 1 3 2 1 4 2 6 4 1 4 3
3 4 6 4 6 4 6 6 5 3 4 6 5 2 1 4 6 5 2 1
```

Copy this frequency table and use tally marks to complete it.

Score	1 2 3 4 5 6	
Tally marks		Total
Frequency		

   a Is the score on the dice *discrete* or *continuous*?
   b Would you say that this particular dice is *fair* or *biased*? Give your reasons.
   c Which score do you think is on the opposite face to that of the 4?
   d Repeat this experiment with a dice of your own, draw your own frequency table and comment on your results.

3 70 first-form pupils are asked how many siblings (brothers or sisters) they have. Their answers are:

```
1 2 1 2 1 1 0 0 1 1 1 3 2 1
2 1 7 0 0 0 1 1 2 5 1 1 1 3
0 1 0 1 1 3 2 1 0 1 1 1 4 2
0 8 1 1 1 0 0 2 1 0 2 2 1 1
1 2 2 4 2 1 1 3 1 3 1 3 1 7
```

Copy this table and use tally marks to complete it.

Number of brothers or sisters	0 1 2 3 4 5 6 7 8	
Tally marks		Total
Frequency		

Tabulating data

a   Does the number of brothers or sisters give *discrete* or *continuous* data?
b   How many children have *no* brothers or sisters?
c   How many children have just 3 brothers or sisters?
d   How many families have just 2 children?
e   How many families have more than 5 children?
f   Repeat this experiment with pupils from your own class (and maybe others too). Draw your own frequency table and comment on your results.

4   At the end of each month, a road haulage firm makes a note of the number of breakdowns it has had with its lorries during that month. Over a long period of time, these were the monthly breakdowns

1 0 3 1 0 2 3 2 1 4 0 0 1 3 2 5 2 1 0 2 1 4 1 2
1 2 0 1 6 2 0 1 3 1 2 2 0 1 2 5 1 0 3 0 1 3 2 1

Draw your own frequency table of this information, using these headings.

Number of breakdowns in a month	0 1 2 ...
Tally marks	
Frequency	

a   Is the number of breakdowns a *discrete* or a *continuous* variable?
b   For how long were results collected (i) in months   (ii) in years?
c   Which number of breakdowns occurred most often?

5   Each pupil in a class of 30 pupils is weighed, and their masses in kilograms are:

51.4   54.8   55.3   55.9   56.2   65.5   57.0   57.6   58.1   58.7
58.7   58.8   59.2   60.1   61.3   61.8   62.3   63.1   64.1   59.4
51.9   52.9   53.4   65.2   55.8   63.5   56.1   60.3   57.2   59.4

Copy this table and use tally marks to complete it.

Mass, kg	50–54	54–58	58–62	62–66	
Tally marks					Total
Frequency					

a   Is *mass* a discrete or continuous variable?
b   Which class of results in the table contains the most masses?
c   Repeat this experiment with the pupils in your group. You may decide to choose different class intervals for your results.

6   A group of 28 pupils were asked to draw a straight line without measuring so it had a length estimated at 10 cm. The pupils then measured their lines with a ruler. These are the results:

10.6   12.3   9.4   9.8   11.7   8.5   9.6   10.3   11.2   12.9   8.3   9.4   10.7   11.1
10.5   11.8   12.2   8.3   9.7   7.4   13.6   9.8   10.5   11.2   8.7   9.6   7.6   10.7

Copy this table and use tally marks to complete it.

Length, cm	7.0–8.0	8.0–9.0	9.0–10.0	10.0–11.0	11.0–12.0	12.0–13.0	13.0–14.0	
Tally marks								Total
Frequency								

Tabulating data

  a Is *length* a discrete or a continuous variable?

  b How many pupils made estimates greater than 10.0 cm but less than 11.0 cm?

  c Repeat this experiment with the pupils in your group. Use different class intervals if required.

7 A policeman has a machine which records the speeds of passing cars. He places it in a 30 mph built-up area, and the first 26 cars which pass him have these speeds.

```
31.2  23.5   7.2  29.4  36.3  42.8  31.7  35.4  27.2
30.3   9.5  48.6  26.6  38.8  15.9  22.3  31.1  37.4
39.8  47.0  32.1  38.0  30.2  20.7  35.0  38.1
```

Draw your own frequency table using these headings.

Speed, mph	0–10	10–20	20–30	30–40	40–50	
Tally marks						Total
Frequency						

  a Is *speed* a discrete or continuous variable?

  b How many cars exceeded the speed limit?

  c If the policeman stopped and cautioned those drivers travelling faster than 40 mph, how many did he stop?

  d How many cars do you suspect had either just set off or were just stopping?

For each of the following sets of data

  a decide whether you have a discrete or continuous variable

  b decide whether or not you need to group the data into classes

  c construct a frequency table

  d comment on your results.

8 Mrs Jenkins keeps six hens at the bottom of her garden. She collects the eggs each day and keeps a record of them. This is her record for the month of June.

```
4 5 4 3 6 5 3 4 2 2
4 3 2 4 5 6 6 5 3 3
2 1 1 0 1 0 0 2 2 3
```

9 Hartshead Town football club played 20 matches last season and scored these numbers of goals:

```
3 1 3 0 0 4 3 2 2 1
1 0 5 4 3 2 1 2 1 0
```

10 A butcher serves 18 customers one morning, all of whom buy sausage meat. They ask for various quantities, but this is what they receive in kilograms.

```
0.46  1.03  2.12  1.08  2.76  1.2
1.93  2.09  0.77  1.52  2.93  0.7
1.97  0.98  1.72  0.97  1.58  1.7
```

11 A weather ship in the Atlantic Ocean records the maximum strength of the wind each day on the Beaufort scale. Over a 40-day period its records show:

```
 5   6  5  7  8  7  6  4  4
 3   2  3  2  4  5  6  9  9
11  10  9  8  8  6  6  6  5
 4   4  3  5  4  5  6  7  7
```

Tabulating data

12 A weights & measures inspector selected a random sample of 30 packets of cheese, all labelled as 500 grams. Their masses, to the nearest gram, are as follows.

502	505	511	498	507	512
523	501	496	487	507	514
501	492	522	506	501	509
517	508	509	496	505	518
509	491	504	515	512	507

13 Mr Woollin is a salesman for a double-glazing firm, and he notes the mileage he travels every day during September.

74.2	61.7	12.5	23.6	37.8	50.9
41.7	65.3	47.2	31.8	52.2	43.9
26.7	17.4	20.9	41.3	55.8	37.8
78.4	13.6	26.6	81.4	37.6	45.8
54.4	41.8	39.2	53.3	35.4	27.7

14 A workman buys 50 packets of nuts and bolts and counts the number of defects in each packet.

0	2	4	1	3	2	0	6	2	2	0	1	3
3	2	2	1	2	4	3	0	1	0	2	5	1
1	2	1	0	0	1	1	2	1	0	2	1
3	4	3	2	5	3	0	1	2	0	1	1

15 A young boy is training for the 100-metre race at the school sports day. His friend times his practice runs with these results in seconds.

18.5	19.2	18.2	18.7	17.9	18.1
17.5	17.2	17.7	17.0	16.7	16.5
16.9	16.8	16.3	16.3	15.8	16.0
16.1	15.7	15.9	15.6	15.8	15.4
15.2	15.3	15.4	15.2		

16 Here are some experiments you can do, either by yourself or with friends. Decide how many items of data would be reasonable, collect the data by counting or measuring, construct a frequency table for your results and comment on them.

Telephone directories

a the frequency of certain telephone exchanges

b the number of pages of surnames for each letter of the alphabet

c the number of digits in telephone numbers

YHA handbook

d the number of beds in youth hostels

e whether the hostel serves evening meals and at what times

f the distance from the hostel to the nearest post office

Atlases

g the average (mean) annual rainfall for given locations

h the average (mean) annual range of temperature for given locations

i the populations of the countries of the world

j the areas of the counties of Britain

k the number of columns in the index for each letter of the alphabet

Dictionaries

l the number of pages for each letter of the alphabet

m the different languages from which the English words originated

Others

n estimates of an irregular area

o estimates of the capacity of a bottle

p estimates of the number of beads in a jar

q the time taken for pupils to come to school in a morning

r the length of pupils' "cubits" (fingertip to elbow)

Displaying data

Part 1 Pictograms

1 A supermarket manager notes the number of delivery vans which arrive each day.

   a On which weekday was the supermarket closed?

   b Which days were busier than Tuesday for deliveries?

   c On which day did least vans deliver? Can you suggest a reason why the manager arranged it so?

   d What was the total number of vans delivering that week?

Mon.	🚚
Tues.	🚚 🚚
Wed.	
Thurs.	🚚 🚚 🚚 🚚 🚚
Fri.	🚚 🚚 🚚
Sat.	🚚

🚚 = 6 vans

2 A family's monthly income is spent as shown by this pictogram.

   a How much is spent on food?

   b How much is left over for *other* items?

   c On which items do they spend more than what is taken in tax?

   d What is the total income for this month?

Tax	Housing	Fuel	Food	Travel	Clothes	Others

= £20

3 A building firm spends six months on a site where it is building a housing estate. This pictogram shows the number of men employed each month.

   a In which month were most men employed?

   b In which month were least men employed?

   c Can you suggest any reasons for the change in employment?

   d If the average monthly wage per man is £400, what is the wage bill for
     (i) July
     (ii) August
     (iii) the whole six months?

JULY	🚶 🚶 🚶 🚶
AUGUST	🚶 🚶 🚶 🚶 🚶
SEPT.	🚶 🚶 🚶 🚶 🚶 🚶
OCT.	🚶 🚶 🚶
NOV.	🚶 🚶
DEC.	🚶

🚶 = 10 men

4 A school investigates which television channels its pupils prefer.

   a How many pupils in the third year
     (i) prefer BBC to ITV
     (ii) prefer ITV to BBC?

   b In which years do more pupils prefer ITV channels to BBC channels?

176

Displaying data

c Which of these three statements does this pictogram illustrate?
  (i) Older pupils tend to prefer BBC channels.
  (ii) Older pupils watch more television than younger pupils.
  (iii) There is no tendency for age to determine which channels are preferred.

1st year	▬▬ ▬▬ ▭ ▭ ▭
2nd year	▬▬▬▬▬ ▪ ▭ ▭ ▭ ▱
3rd year	▬▬ ▬▬ ▬▬ ▪ ▭ ▭ ▭ ▭
4th year	▬▬ ▬▬ ▬▬ ▭ ▭ ▭ ▱
5th year	▬▬ ▬▬ ▬▬ ▬▬ ▬ ▭ ▭ ▭ ▭ ▱

▬▬ = 20 pupils prefer BBC   ▭ = 20 pupils prefer ITV

d Which year has the largest number of pupils?

e Copy this table and use the pictogram to complete it.

	1st year	2nd year	3rd year	4th year	5th year	Totals
Number preferring BBC channels	1	4	6	2	9	2
Number preferring ITV channels	4	5	9			
Totals						

f How many children are there in the school?

Draw a pictogram to illustrate each of these tables. Before you begin, decide on your symbol and what it will represent.

5 A car-park attendant records the number of cars using the car-park on each day of a week.

	Mon.	Tues.	Wed.	Thurs.	Fri.	Sat.	Sun.
Number of cars	200	250	150	175	275	300	75

6 Each year-group in a school raises money for charity.

	Year 1	Year 2	Year 3	Year 4	Year 5
Amount collected, £	350	325	200	250	310

7 A council have to decide whether to save money by closing a local youth club. They make a survey of the attendances for one week.

	Mon.	Tues.	Wed.	Thurs.	Fri.	Sat.	Sun.
Boys	15	20	22	26	40	88	0
Girls	10	15	25	22	33	41	0

8 A survey was made of the number of children killed on the roads in one year.

Age range, years	1–2	3–4	5–6	7–8	9–10	11–12	13–14
Number of boys	5	9	15	14	7	8	6
Number of girls	4	6	10	8	5	4	2

Displaying data

Part 2 Line graphs

1 A patient is admitted to hospital at 9 a.m. and her temperature taken every four hours.

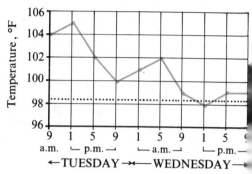

a She was given drugs as soon as she was admitted. How long did it take before the drugs started to reduce her temperature?

b How many degrees did her temperature then fall, and at what time did it start to rise again?

c Her parents visited her at 1 p.m. on Wednesday. What was her temperature then?

d Normal body temperature of 98.4°F is shown by the dotted line. How many degrees *above* normal was her temperature at 5 a.m. on Wednesday?

2 A garage in the country sells petrol and its takings at the pump are shown here for one week.

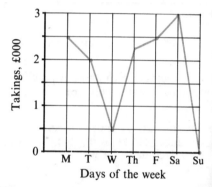

a On which day is the garage closed?

b Which day do you think it is open only in the morning?

c On which days was more petrol sold than on Thursday?

d On which day was most petrol sold? Can you suggest a reason for this?

3 In a certain part of Worcestershire, the area of land planted with various crops changes over the years.

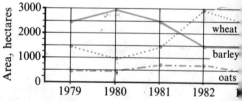

a Which crop has the least change of area during this period?

b Which was the most common crop in 1979?

c How many hectares were given to each crop in 1980?

d Between 1980 and 1982, the area of wheat increased. Suggest how some of this land became available for wheat.

4 During one week, children go to school by the methods shown on this graph.

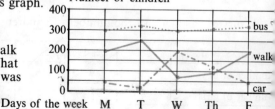

a Which form of transport shows the least variation?

b On which day did most walk and least come by car? What do you think the weather was like on this day?

Displaying data

c What do you think the weather was like on Wednesday?

d On Friday, 20 were absent and 10 came by bicycle. How many children attend this school altogether?

Draw a line graph to illustrate each of these tables.
Before you begin, decide on the scales of your axes.
In **6**, **7** and **8**, more than one line will be needed on the graph.

5 At the end of each month, Mr Hamilton receives a bank statement telling him the *balance* of his account, i.e. how much is left.

Month	Jan.	Feb.	March	April	May	June	July	August
Balance, £	50	75	110	95	120	85	20	15

6 Rentagleg Ltd has a shop which both rents televisions and sells them.
This table gives the details for two months.

Week ending	7 Jan.	14 Jan.	21 Jan.	28 Jan.	4 Feb.	11 Feb.	18 Feb.	25 Feb.
Number of sets rented	6	12	19	24	17	18	12	13
Number of sets sold	4	15	28	14	19	25	23	15

A small business makes both shirts and blouses. Their manager notes the number of garments made over several weeks.

Week ending	7 July	14 July	21 July	28 July	4 Aug.	11 Aug.	18 Aug.	25 Aug.
Number of shirts made	180	120	155	175	30	45	220	190
Number of blouses made	60	80	75	70	40	25	60	65

During the ten days of his Easter holiday, Gareth Evans records the maximum and minimum outside temperatures every day.

Day	M	T	W	Th	F	Sa	Su	M	T	W
Maximum temperature, °C	18	17	10	9	11	16	19	21	18	15
Minimum temperature, °C	5	4	6	5	6	2	0	−2	4	6

Displaying data

Part 3   Bar charts

Discrete variables

1 This bar chart gives the number of boys and girls in each year of a secondary school.

  a In which years are there more boys than girls?

  b How many girls are there altogether in the first three years of the school?

  c Which year below the sixth form has fewest pupils?

  d If each fifth-former on average sits six exams, what is the total number of exam entries for year 5?

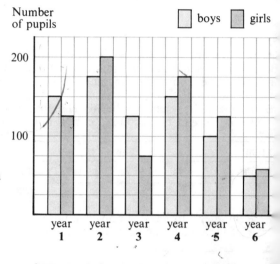

Number of pupils · boys · girls

2 A primary school serves dinners and also has some children bringing their own.

  a On which day was the number of those who ate school dinners and those who brought sandwiches nearest to being equal?

  b On which days did more children eat sandwiches than school dinners?

  c On which day was the school meal least popular?

  d How many school dinners were eaten throughout the whole week?

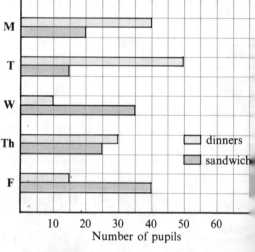

dinners · sandwich · Number of pupils

3 A chocolate factory in York sells its products in Britain, other Common Market (EEC) countries and beyond. This bar chart gives the sales, in millions of pounds, over recent years.

  a In which year was less sold in the EEC than elsewhere?

  b In which year did sales in Britain fall back?

  c What was the *total* amount sold in 1981?

  d How would you describe the sales in the EEC over these five years?

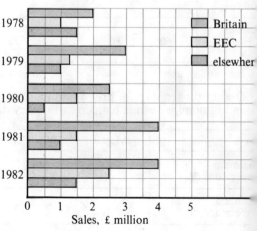

Britain · EEC · elsewher · Sales, £ million

Displaying data

e Copy and complete this table.

Year		1978	1979	1980	1981	1982	Totals
Sales in (£M)	Britain						
	EEC						
	elsewhere						
	Totals						

raw your own bar charts for the information in these tables.
raw some vertically and some horizontally.

This table gives the stopping distances for a car travelling at different speeds on wet and dry roads.

peed, mph		30	40	50	60	70
topping istance, feet	dry	75	120	175	240	315
	wet	165	265	385	530	690

A small business has a record of its income and expenditure for the first five months of the year.

onth	January	February	March	April	May
come, £000	6	9	12	18	·17
xpenditure, £000	5	7	15	12	10

The distribution of ages in the population of Britain has changed over the years.

ear		1930	1965	1980
umber of eople illions)	under 15	12	14	16
	15–64	32	35	37
	65 and over	4	7	8

ntinuous variables

The army has a recruiting campaign. The new recruits have heights as shown in this diagram.

a How many recruits have heights between 170 cm and 180 cm?

b What is the greatest possible height of the tallest recruit?

c How many recruits have heights less than 160 cm?

d How many recruits are there altogether?

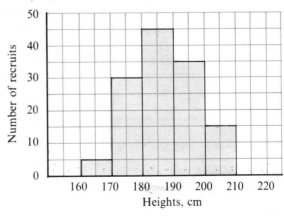

181

Displaying data

8 A survey is made in a
   supermarket of the masses of
   bags of sugar which are
   labelled 1 kg.
   a How many bags have a
      mass between 1000 grams
      and 1010 grams?
   b How many bags are
      "underweight"?
   c How many bags are
      more than 10 grams
      "overweight"?
   d How many bags altogether
      were weighed in the
      survey?

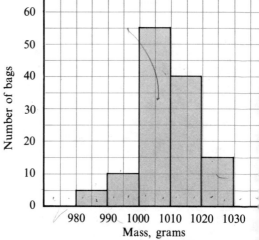

9 All the houses on a new estate
   receive their electricity bills at
   the same time.
   a How many houses received
      bills of between £150
      and £200?
   b How many houses received
      bills of less than £100?
   c What was the greatest
      possible amount of the
      most expensive bill?
   d How many houses are
      there on the estate?

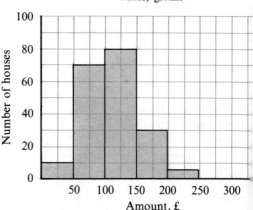

Draw your own bar charts for the information in these tables.

10 A young girl has a collection of LP records and she notes that they all play f
    different lengths of time.

Playing time, min	20–25	25–30	30–35	35–40	40–50
Number of records	2	8	13	18	6

11 A travel firm has a brochure advertising package holidays at these prices.

Cost per person, £	0–100	100–200	200–300	300–400	400–8(
Number of holidays	5	55	40	24	11

12 A hang-gliding club keeps a record of all flights lasting longer than 5 minute

Length of flight, min	5–10	10–20	20–30	30–60	60–12
Number of flights	36	48	24	18	9

Displaying data

Part 4 Pie charts

1 A survey of 600 people in a town asks each person which television channel, if any, they watched the previous evening. This pie chart shows the results.

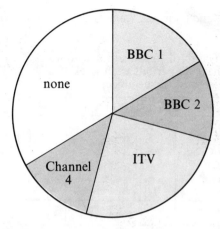

a Use a protractor to measure the angle of the sector labelled "ITV". What fraction of the circle is it? How many of the 600 people watched ITV?

b Measure the angle for BBC1, calculate the fraction of the circle, and so find how many people watched BBC1.

c Copy this table, enter your results for ITV and BBC1, and then complete the rest of the table.

Television channel	Angle	Fraction	Number of people
BBC 1			
BBC 2			
ITV			
Channel 4			
none			
Totals			

The working population of the town of Whitfield numbers 12 000 people who are employed in the various areas of industry shown in this pie chart.

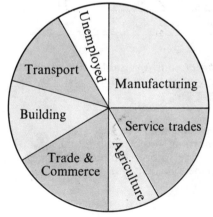

a Use a protractor to measure the angle of each sector on the pie chart.

b Find the fraction of the pie chart taken up by each sector, and so calculate the number of people employed in the various occupations.

c Enter your results in a copy of this table.

Occupation	Angle	Fraction	Number of people
Manufacturing			
Service trades			
Agriculture			
Trade & Commerce			
Building			
Transport			
Unemployed			
Totals			

Displaying data

Copy and complete each of these tables of data and use them to draw pie charts.

3 The third-formers in a school have 40 periods each week given to these subjects.

Subject	Periods	Fraction	Angle
Maths	5		
English	5		
Hist/Geog	8		
Craft	4		
Science	6		
Others	12		
Totals			

5 One hundred second-year pupils were asked where they spent their family holidays.

Place	Number of children	Fraction	Angle
England	60		
Scotland	5		
Wales	20		
Overseas	15		
Totals			

4 The 800 pupils at a school use these forms of transport when travelling to school in a morning.

Transport	Number of children	Fraction	Angle
Bus	400		
Car	100		
Bicycle	200		
Foot	100		
Totals			

6 Industrial goods in Britain are transported in the different ways given in this table.

Transport	Percentage	Fraction	Angle
Heavy lorries	35		
Small lorries	45		
Rail	10		
Coastal shipping	5		
Canals & pipelines	5		
Totals			

Construct your own tables of working to help you draw pie charts to illustrate the following information.

7 A newspaper boy has a morning and evening round and he records the number of papers he delivers.

Newspaper	Number of house
Morning only	120
Evening only	40
Morning & evening	10
None	30
Total	200

8 A workman's typical day is spent in these activities.

Activity	Sleeping	Working	Travelling	Eating	At leisu
Time spent, h	8	8	1	1	6

9 A traffic survey notes the "country-of-origin" of the cars parked in a factory parking area.

Country-of-origin	Britain	France	Germany	Japan	Elsewh
Number of cars	250	50	75	100	25

Displaying data

You will need to use a calculator to help you work out the angles required for drawing the pie charts for these tables.

10

Country	England	Wales	Scotland	N. Ireland	Total
Area, 000 km²	130.4	20.8	77.2	14.1	242.5

11

Continent	Asia	Europe	Africa	North America	South America	Oceania	Antarctica
Population, millions	2693	695	484	382	262	25	0

12

Continent	Asia	Europe	Africa	North America	South America	Oceania	Antarctica
Area, millions of km²	44.4	10.5	30.3	24.2	17.8	8.5	13.2

13

Services offered by local authority	Education	Social Services	Environment	Police	Others
Expenditure, £000	15 525	4 281	5 510	2 557	4 561

14 Collect your own information about each of these situations and represent your findings in a table and on a pie chart.
   a how you spend the 24 hours of a typical day
   b the different types of programme shown on television during one week
   c the number of lessons you have each week in different subjects
   d the amount of newsprint in a paper given to home news, overseas news, sport, advertisements, etc.
   e the number of pages given to the various topics in this book

Part 5   Other diagrams

1 This special type of bar graph is called an **age and sex pyramid**.
It shows the distribution of the ages of the population of a country.
   a Approximately how many girls are there aged 15–19 in
     (i) country A
     (ii) country B?
   b What is the approximate total number of children aged 0–4 in
     (i) country A
     (ii) country B?

(i) Country A

185

Displaying data

c What is the approximate total population aged 30–34 in
  (i) country A
  (ii) country B?

d Which one of these two countries do you think has an effective "family planning" programme?

e One of these countries is an industrialized Western nation, the other a developing Third World nation. Which is which?

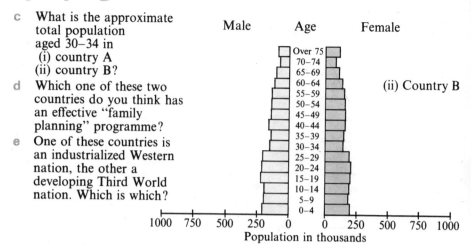

(ii) Country B

Population in thousands

2 Draw an age and sex pyramid for the United States in the early 1960s.

Age range, years	0–4	5–9	10–14	15–19	20–24	25–29	30–34
Male population, millions	10.4	9.8	8.5	7.0	5.6	5.7	6.1
Female population, millions	9.8	9.0	8.0	6.2	5.2	5.1	5.7

35–39	40–44	45–49	50–54	55–59	60–64	65–69	70–74	75–80	Over 80
6.5	6.0	5.9	5.4	4.7	4.0	3.5	2.8	2.0	0.9
6.3	5.5	5.3	5.0	4.3	3.8	3.4	2.9	2.6	1.0

a In which age ranges does there appear to be a "shortage" of people?
b In which age ranges are there more females than males?

3 **Clock graphs** use the 12 hours on a clock face to illustrate the 12 months of the year.
This clock face shows the various seasons for growing potatoes.

a For how many months does the ground lie fallow during the winter?

b When should potatoes be planted?

c During which months are potatoes lifted and ready for eating or storing?

d When should manure or compost be dug into the soil?

4 Draw a clock graph to illustrate the growing of wheat.
April and the first half of May is the time for sowing wheat. From then until the middle of August is the growing season. Harvesting takes place until the end of September. From October until mid-November, the fields are ploughed and they then lie fallow through the winter until April.

Displaying data

5 The diagram below, called a **divided rectangle**, illustrates the areas of the United Kingdom by vertical strips in proportion to the areas of the four countries. Each vertical strip is then divided to show land use.
Copy this table and complete it by taking readings from the diagram as accurately as you can.

Country	Area 000 km²	Land used as a percentage of total area				
		Rough grazing	Woodland	Pasture	Arable	Urban
England						
Scotland						
Wales						
Northern Ireland						

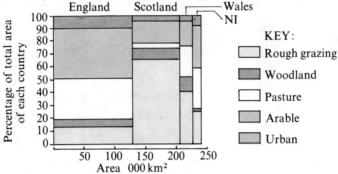

6 A **flow map** is a method of representing amounts of movement. This one shows the number of passenger trains per week from York station during the summer.

a How many passenger trains go from York to
 (i) Harrogate
 (ii) Bradford?

b (i) How many trains go from York to Sheffield, and how many of these continue to Birmingham?
 (ii) How many of these trains to Sheffield do not go on to Birmingham?

c How many of the trains from York to Huddersfield do *not* continue to Manchester?

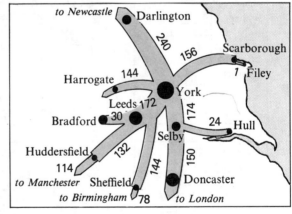

d The one weekly train from York to Filey is on a Saturday. Can you give any reason why this train should run?

e Many of these passenger trains do not *start* at York. By looking at the flow map, can you suggest any through-routes which pass through York? Where do you think main-line trains are coming from and going to?

Design a survey to ask pupils in your school which primary school they attended. Design a flow map to illustrate your findings.

Design a survey to find by which routes pupils come to your school. Draw a flow map to illustrate your findings.

Displaying data

Part 6 Misrepresenting information

Statistics should give a fair picture of a situation for which data has been collected, but they can be used to misrepresent and distort the true situation in order to mislead people.

Advertisers and political parties will often use statistics in ways which can encourage misunderstandings.

Examine these statements and their diagrams. Criticise each one and say why it might be misunderstood.

1

4
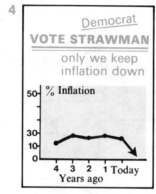

7
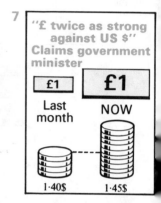

2

5

8

3

6

9

10 Draw the information in **9** on conventional axes and make further comment about the claim of costs rising fast.

Averages

A single value which is used to represent a distribution is called an **average**. It is usually near the centre of the distribution and is a measure of the central location.

Three averages are in common use.

The **mode** is that value which occurs most often.

The **median** is the middle value when all the values are arranged in order of size. If there is no middle value, i.e. when there is an even number of values, the median is midway between the two middle values.

The **mean** is found by calculating $\dfrac{\text{the total of all the values.}}{\text{the number of values.}}$

Part 1   Three kinds of average

Find the mode, the median and the mean of these sets of results.

1   A dice is rolled seven times and these scores are recorded.
    2   4   5   3   3   2   2

2   A second dice is rolled nine times to get these scores.
    4   6   2   3   2   4   1   1   4

3   Eleven children are asked how many brothers or sisters they have.
    1   3   2   3   1   1   1   2   1   3   4

4   A hockey team plays ten matches and scores these numbers of goals.
    0   3   2   1   4   1   0   4   2   1

5   A bus route is served by 12 buses during the day. The number of passengers on each bus is
    6   18   23   19   29   35   12   8   14   27   39   28.

6   Eight crates of peaches are delivered to a shop. The bad peaches in each crate are taken out and counted.
    1   2   0   5   1   4   5   2

7   During one week, a family has nine newspapers delivered. The young boy of the house makes a note of the number of pages in each paper.
    14   16   22   12   14   12   16   24   26

8   A car-park attendant makes a record every hour of the number of cars in the car-park.
    2   32   25   17   14   17   26   24   12   3

9   The number of aircraft taking off from an airport is noted each hour over a 12-hour period.
    3   6   8   9   12   9   15   10   15   8   8   5

10   The 14 fifth-formers in a class are asked how many exams they will sit at the end of the year.
    4   4   6   7   6   9   9   4   5   8   6   8   6   8

Averages

11 A football team displays the number of goals they have scored during the season on a bar chart.
    a Write out a list of the number of goals scored in each match.
    b Use your list to find
       (i) the mode
       (ii) the median
       (iii) the mean of the scores.

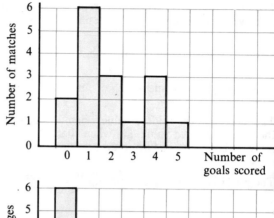

12 A mother buys a large bag of supposedly seedless oranges. Her children count the pips when they eat them. This bar chart shows their results.
    Write out a list of the numbers of pips and find
    (i) the modal number of pips per orange
    (ii) the median number of pips
    (iii) the mean number of pips.

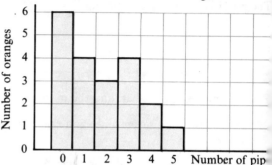

13 If the mode of these numbers is 2, what is the value of the missing number x?
    1 2 2 3 3 4 1 4 3 2 x

14 If the median of these numbers is 4, what is the value of the missing number x?
    1 2 x 5 6 7

15 If the mean of these numbers is 5, what is the value of the missing number x?
    2 4 8 5 x

16 These six numbers have a mean of $8\frac{1}{2}$. Four of them are known and one of the unknown numbers is twice the other. Find the value of x.
    4 6 8 12 x 2x

Part 2   Averages and frequency tables

Discrete data

For each of these distributions,
a write the **modal value**
b find the **median value** by writing out the individual values in order of size
c calculate the **mean value**.

1 Ten people get on a bus and the price of their tickets is given by this table.

Price of ticket, pence	5	10	15	20
Frequency	2	4	3	1

Averages

2 Eleven families live on an estate. The number of children in each family is recorded.

Number of children in a family	0	1	2	3	4	5
Frequency	2	2	4	1	1	1

3 A dice is thrown fifteen times and the results are tabulated.

Score on dice	1	2	3	4	5	6
Frequency	4	3	2	3	1	2

4 The number of passengers in twelve cars arriving in an office car-park are noted.

Number of passengers in a car	0	1	2	3	4
Frequency	3	5	0	3	1

Each pupil in a class of 22 children is asked for their shoe size.

Shoe size	2	3	4	5	6	7
Frequency	1	3	5	10	3	0

A class of 25 pupils is given a test with these results.

Mark out of 10	1	2	3	4	5	6	7	8	9	10
Frequency	0	0	0	2	4	7	8	2	2	0

Thirty bushes are planted and after a few weeks the number of flowers on each is counted.

Number of flowers per bush	0	1	2	3	4	5	6	7
Number of bushes	4	2	2	4	10	8	0	0

The number of matches in each of twenty full matchboxes is counted.

Number of matches per box	38	39	40	41	42
Number of boxes	1	6	7	4	2

A survey is made of traffic on a road. The number of cars which pass each minute is recorded over a period of 100 minutes.

Number of cars per minute	0	1	2	3	4	5	6
Frequency	12	14	18	21	15	13	7

each of these distributions,
write the modal value
find the median value by calculating the position of the middle of the distribution
calculate the mean value by using the third row of each table.

Averages

10 A dice is thrown 100 times with these results.

Score, x	1	2	3	4	5	6	Totals
Frequency, f	12	15	17	18	20	18	
fx							

11 A housewife buys 100 kg of old potatoes during the winter. Her son counts how many potatoes there are in each kilogram which she buys.

Number of potatoes, x	3	4	5	6	7	8	Totals
Frequency, f	2	12	38	24	18	6	
fx							

12 A carton contains 200 boxes of matches and the number of matches in each box is counted.

Number of matches, x	50	51	52	53	Totals
Frequency, f	81	46	45	28	
fx					

13 The length of each rally in the men's Wimbledon tennis final is recorded.

Number of hits, x	1	2	3	4	5	6	7	8	Totals
Frequency, f	4	12	63	62	23	12	15	9	
fx									

14 100 young people are selected at random and asked at what age they finished their full-time education.

Age, x years	16	17	18	19	20	21	22	23	Totals
Frequency, f	31	12	21	13	11	2	8	2	
fx									

Continuous or grouped data

For each of these distributions,
a write the modal class
b estimate the mean by approximating each class with its mid-value x and using a table as before.

The median for grouped data will be found using a method given in the next section on page 203.

15 A gardener plants ten young trees and measures their heights.

Height, m	1–3	3–5	5–7
Frequency	6	3	1

16 A ferry can take 50 vehicles at a time across a lake. On one particular trip, the masses are recorded.

Masses, tonnes	0–2	2–4	4–6	6–8
Frequency	26	15	7	2

Averages

7 A group of 16 people set off on a sponsored walk. They cover the first mile in the following times.

Time, min	0–12	12–24	24–36	36–48
Frequency	0	8	6	2

8 Fifty teenage boys run 100 metres in the following times.

Time, s	10–12	12–14	14–16	16–18	18–20
Frequency	2	18	21	6	3

9 Sixty recruits for the army are weighed and the results tabulated.

Mass, kg	50–60	60–70	70–80	80–90	90–100
Frequency	5	12	19	18	6

10 The same sixty recruits are now measured and their heights recorded.

Height, cm	150–160	160–170	170–180	180–190	190–200
Frequency	1	13	18	22	6

11 A shop assistant weighs 50 bags of potatoes and records the results in a table.

Mass, kg	9–10	10–11	11–12	12–13	13–14
Number of bags	8	12	10	14	6

12 The distances thrown by 20 competitors in the javelin on sports day are:

Distance, m	20–30	30–40	40–50	50–60	60–70
Number of throws	3	8	5	3	1

Practical work

The instruction leaflet issued with a film for a camera is often written in several languages. Here is part of such a leaflet.

ld the film be faulty in
ufacture, labelling or
ing, or be damaged during
it, or be lost through our
or the fault of our agents,
iability is restricted to the
cement of the same amount
exposed film. We are not
nsible for shortcomings
h arise during the sale,
ling or use of the film or
aused by carelessness or
ther reason. Since dyes can
ge in the course of time, we
t provide a guarantee
st changes in dye and will
eplace a film for this
n.

Si la pellicule présente un défaut
de fabrication, d'étiquetage ou
d'emballage, ou si elle est
endommagée au cours du
transport, ou perdue par nous
ou nos filiales, notre
responsabilité se limitera au
remplacement d'une quantité
équivalente de pellicule vierge.
Exception faite de ce
remplacement, la vente,
le traitement ou la manipulation
de cette pellicule, pour quelque
cause que ce soit, sont faits sans
aucune garantie, meme à la suite
d'une negligence, ou pour tout
autre motif, les matieres
colorantes pouvant se modifier
à la longue, notre garantie ne
pourra être engagée en cas de
modification des couleurs, et
cette pellicule ne sera pas
remplacée pour ce motif.

Sollte der Film einen
Fabrikations-, Beschriftungs-
oder Verpackungsfehler
aufweisen, oder sollte er
während des Transports
beschädigt worden oder durch
unsere Schuld oder die unserer
Vertretungen verloren gegangen
sein, beschränkt sich unsere
Haftung auf den Ersatz der
gleichen Menge unbelichteten
Films. Wir haften nicht für
Mängel, die beim Verkauf, der
Bearbeitung oder der
Verwendung dieses Films aus
irgendeinem Grund entstehen,
auch infolge einer
Nachlässigkeit oder aus
Irgendeinem anderen Grund. Da
sich die Farbstoffe im Laufe der
Zeit verändern können, leisten
wir bei Farbveränderungen
keine Garantie und können den
Film aus diesem Grund nicht
ersetzen.

Averages

Construct three frequency tables for the number of letters in the words of these languages.

Word length, x	1	2	3	4	〜	17	18
Frequency, f					〜		

a What is the modal word length for each language?

b Use a calculator to help you find the mean word length for each language.

c Can you make any comment on your results?

24 a The method of **23** can be used to investigate the length of the words used i national newspapers. Take three different newspapers, choose any article and count the lengths of the first 200 words in each paper. State the modal word length and calculate the mean word length for each paper. Comment on your results.

b Use the same method to investigate the number of words in sentences written by different authors. Find the modal and mean "sentence length" i each case and comment on your results.

25 Draw a straight line on a sheet of paper. Place a ruler some distance away and let several people look at both the ruler and the line. Ask each one to estimate the length of the line. (Should you allow them to listen to each others' estimates?)
Tabulate your results and calculate the mean of the estimates.
How does this mean compare with the actual length of the line?

26 This square has an area of 1 cm^2.
Ask every member of your class to estimate the area (in cm^2)
of the shaded region in **27** below.
Tabulate the estimates and calculate their mean.
How does this mean compare with the actual value of the area?

27 Here are the English football results for the first Saturday of the 1984–85 season.

DIVISION ONE
Arsenal ....1–1 ....Chelsea
A. Villa.......1–0 ..... Coventry
Everton ....1–4 ...Tottenham
Leicester ......2–3 ... Newcastle
Luton..........2–0 ....Stoke
Man U.........1–1 ..... Watford
Norwich ....3–3 .....Liverpool
QPR.............3–1 ..West Brom
Sheff Wed...3–1 ......Nottm F
Sunderland...3–1 ....Soton
West Ham ...0–0 ....Ipswich

DIVISION TWO
Cardiff ....0–3 ..... Charlton
Carlisle ....0–3 ...... Brighton
C Palace ......1–1 ...Blackburn
Fulham.........1–2 ..Shrewsbury
Grimsby ......1–0 ...... Barnsley
Huddersfield.0–3 .... Oxford
Notts Co......1–2 ....Leeds
Oldham.........0–1 .Birmingham
Portsmouth ..1–0 ..Middlesbro
Wimbledon...2–2 .... Man City
Wolves.........2–2 ..... Sheff U

DIVISION THREE
Bournemth ...1–0 ....Derby
Bolton ....0–1 ..... Bristol R
Bradford ......2–0 ...Cambridge
Brentford .....0–1 .... Orient
Bristol C......2–0 .... Wigan
Burnley ....1–1 ....Plymouth
Gillingham ...1–1 ...... Newport
Lincoln.........0–0 ....Hull C
Millwall ....2–0 ...... Swansea
Preston.........2–0 ....Doncaster
Reading........1–0 .. Rotherham
York ....1–1 ......Walsall

DIVISION FOUR
Chester ....1–1 ..Scunthorp
Chesterfld....2–1 ....Aldershc
Colchester ...3–3 ..... Southen
Crewe..........3–0 .... Torqua
Darlington....1–1 .... Bu
Exeter..........5–0 ...Northmp
Halifax ....0–2 .... Blackpo
Peterboro.....1–0 .... Tranme
Port Vale......0–1 .... Mansfie
Rochdale ......0–1 ..... Herefo
Stockport.....4–1 ...Hartlepo
Swindon.......2–1 .... Wrexha

a For each division, tabulate the number of goals scored in each match. Fir the mode, median and mean of these numbers for each division separately

b Find these three averages for all the divisions combined into one table.

28 Ask the members of your class for the following information and find suitab averages for your results.

a their mass   b their height

c their armspan   d their handspan

e the time taken to reach school

f the number of letters in their names

g the number of used pages in their current maths exercise books

h the number of houses on the same road as their home

Averages

art 3   Using a guessed mean

his method reduces the amount of calculation required when finding the mean of a
stribution, provided the **guessed mean** is a sensible one.

Mean value = Guessed mean + mean of the differences

$$= \text{Guessed mean} + \frac{\text{total of all the differences}}{\text{number of values}}$$

$$= g + \frac{\sum fd}{\sum f}$$

The number of pupils in fifty primary school classes in each of the towns of
Granchester and Bradfield are counted, and the results tabulated as shown.
Copy and complete these tables to find the mean number of pupils per class for
each town. Start your calculation by writing down your *guessed mean*.

a   Granchester
Guessed mean, $g = \ldots$

b   Bradfield
Guessed mean, $g = \ldots$

umber of pupils in class x	Frequency f	$d = x - g$	fd
25	5		
26	6		
27	9		
28	10		
29	8		
30	6		
31	4		
32	2		
als $\sum f =$		$\sum fd =$	

Number of pupils in class x	Frequency f	$d = x - g$	fd
25	2		
26	5		
27	7		
28	8		
29	11		
30	9		
31	5		
32	3		
Totals $\sum f =$		$\sum fd =$	

culate the mean of each of the following distributions.
ose a sensible guessed mean and construct your own tables.

A consumer-protection group surveys the number of matches in 200 boxes to
see if the claim on the label is fair. The label states that each box holds an
average of 48 matches. Calculate the mean number of matches per box and say
whether or not you think it is a fair claim.

Number of matches in a box, x	45	46	47	48	49	50	51	52
Number of boxes, f	6	8	16	69	72	14	10	5

A large company makes a record of the ages of those employees who retire
during the year. Calculate the mean retirement age.

Age, x years	58	59	60	61	62	63	64	65
Frequency, f	6	12	33	12	8	12	15	52

Averages

4 The inspectors for a bus company note the number of passengers carried by 42-seater buses in the morning rush-hour. Calculate the mean number of passengers per bus.

Number of passengers, x	38	39	40	41	42	43	44	45	46	47	48
Number of buses, f	2	5	4	6	4	8	10	12	20	17	32

5 An automatic machine seals packets containing 20 light bulbs. Some of the bulbs are defective. Use this table to calculate the mean number of good bulbs per packet.

Number of good bulbs in a packet, x	14	15	16	17	18	19	20
Frequency, f	2	0	4	3	5	8	28

6 For grouped data, the mid-value of each class is used. Copy and complete this table to estimate the mean height of 60 fifth-formers.

Guessed mean, $g = \ldots$ cm

Heights, cm	Mid-value x	Frequency f	$d = x - g$	fd
150–160		3		
160–170		12		
170–180		22		
180–190		18		
190–200		5		
Totals $\sum f =$			$\sum fd =$	

In each of the following, estimate the mean of the distribution. Choose a suitable guessed mean and construct your own table.

7 A small factory employs 100 people who earn weekly wages as given in this table.

Weekly wage, £	50–70	70–80	80–90	90–100	100–120	120–1
Number of employees	4	24	35	27	9	1

8 Fifty beans are planted and the heights of their shoots are measured some ti⊁ later.

Height, mm	0–20	20–30	30–40	40–50	50–60	60–1
Frequency	1	5	14	21	8	1

9 An estate agent records the prices of all the houses he has on his files.

Price of house, £	0–10 000	10 000–20 000	20 000–30 000	30 000–40 000	40 000–60 000
Number of houses	2	14	26	15	3

10 The station-master of a British Rail station notes how punctual each train is. His observations are shown in this table.

Number of minutes late	0–2	2–5	5–10	10–20	20–30	30–60	60–120
Frequency	125	35	7	16	11	5	1

Part 4 Weighted means

The word **weight** can refer not only to the "heaviness" of an object, but also to its importance generally.

a A shop sells packets of different teas which cost 40p, 50p, 55p and 75p. Calculate the mean of these four prices.

b The answer in **a** is not a fair representation of the prices of these teas if the cheaper brands are more popular. If the "weights" are taken into account, use the data in this table to calculate the **weighted mean** of the prices of the teas.

Price of tea pence x	Number of packets sold per week w	wx
40	460	
50	380	
55	110	
75	50	
Totals		

A school gives its pupils examinations in English, Maths, Science, Geography, History and French.

a Robert Fowler scored 60%, 62%, 58%, 75%, 72% and 69% respectively. Calculate his mean score.

b However, the school weights these marks according to the number of periods per week for each subject. Copy and complete this table to calculate Robert's weighted mean score.

Subject	Score, % x	Number of periods w	wx
English	60	6	
Maths	62	5	
Science	58	6	
Geography	75	4	
History	72	4	
French	69	5	
Totals			

197

Averages

c His friend, Chris Parry, scored 75%, 74%, 56%, 64%, 52% and 66% respectively.
   (i) Calculate his mean score.
   (ii) Construct a table to calculate his weighted mean score.

3 The personnel officer of a firm interviews three young men for a job. She assesses each of them on a "5-point scale" from 0 = poor, to 5 = excellent on certain qualities which are weighted.

a Calculate the weighted mean score for each candidate.
b Who do you think was offered the job?

Stuart Harris

Quality	Weight w	Score x	wx
Dress	1	0	
Speech	3	1	
Manner	4	2	
Initiative	2	2	
Interest in job	3	3	
Qualifications	3	3	
$\sum w =$		$\sum wx =$	

John Glenn

Quality	Weight w	Score x	wx
Dress	1	4	
Speech	3	2	
Manner	4	3	
Initiative	2	0	
Interest in job	3	2	
Qualifications	3	2	
$\sum w =$		$\sum wx =$	

Kevin Brown

Quality	Weight w	Score x	w
Dress	1	3	
Speech	3	4	
Manner	4	3	
Initiative	2	1	
Interest in job	3	3	
Qualifications	3	3	
$\sum w =$		$\sum wx =$	

4 Three performers in an ice-skating championship have to do four routines, each marked out of 10, but given different weights. Calculate the weighted mean score for each performer and so find the winner.

Janice Symonds

	Weight	Score
1st routine	2	6
2nd routine	2	6
3rd routine	3	5
4th routine	5	7

Sonia Heaney

	Weight	Score
1st routine	2	7
2nd routine	2	4
3rd routine	3	6
4th routine	5	6

Kate Smith

	Weight	Sc
1st routine	2	
2nd routine	2	
3rd routine	3	
4th routine	5	

Averages

Part 5   Moving averages

Many quantities vary over a period of time. The set of values of such a quantity over a time period is called a **time series**. The variations in these values can be smoothed out by calculating the **moving averages**. This enables any general **trend** to be seen.

1   This table and graph shows the profits of a firm over a ten-year period. A director of the firm wants to know if the profits have been decreasing, increasing or staying fairly steady.

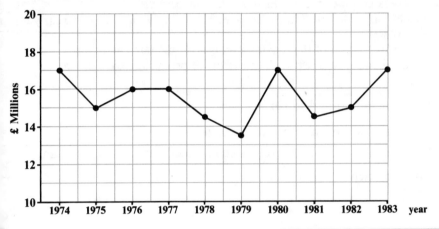

ear	1974	1975	1976	1977	1978	1979	1980	1981	1982	1983
ofit, £M	17	15	16	16	14.5	13.5	17	14.5	15	17
oving total										
oving average										

a   Draw your own graph from this table.
b   Copy the table and complete it by finding the moving totals in groups of three (called a *three-yearly moving total*) and hence the *three-yearly moving averages*.
c   Plot the moving averages on the same graph, and join them by dotted lines.
d   How would you describe the *trend* to the director of the firm?

A local Rugby League team have the attendances given in this table for the first 12 matches of the season.

tch	1	2	3	4	5	6	7	8	9	10	11	12
endance	520	630	520	590	740	820	930	770	840	1040	920	1130
ving total												
ving average												

a   Draw a graph of attendances against the number of matches.
b   Copy and complete the table by finding the moving totals of *order 5* and moving averages of *order 5*.
c   Draw a graph of the moving averages on the same diagram.
d   How would you describe the *trend* in the number of people attending the matches?

Averages

3 A gravel pit's yearly production over several years is shown in the table in thousands of tonnes.

Year	1974	1975	1976	1977	1978	1979	1980	1981	1982	1983	1984
Production (000 tonnes)	100	72	86	89	78	75	67	76	84	83	65
Moving total											
Moving average											

a Draw a graph of the production over this period.

b Copy the table and find the five-yearly moving totals and five-yearly moving averages.

c Draw the graph of the moving averages on the same diagram.

d How would you describe the *trend* in the production over this period?

For each of the problems **4** to **10**:

a draw a graph of the data given in the table

b calculate the moving averages requested and plot them on the same graph

c describe any trends.

4 This table gives the percentage unemployment rate of 18-year-olds in a certain town every three months.

Month	Jan.	April	July	Oct.	Jan.	April	July	Oct.	Jan.	April
Percentage unemployed	65	72	58	62	57	64	47	54	55	47

Calculate moving totals of order 3 and moving averages of order 3.

5 A shoe shop records the number of pairs it sells every week over a period of twelve weeks.

Week	1	2	3	4	5	6	7	8	9	10	11	1?
Number of pairs sold	77	92	86	98	92	101	104	89	116	98	122	11?

Calculate the three-weekly moving totals and three-weekly moving averages.

6 A new youth group, twelve weeks after opening, wants to see if there is any trend in its attendances.

Week	1	2	3	4	5	6	7	8	9	10	11
Number of members attending	42	38	57	46	32	47	53	37	51	27	67

Calculate the five-weekly moving averages.

Averages

These next problems involve moving averages of an *even* order.
In your table, centre moving totals and moving averages *between* successive values given in the table.
In your graph, plot the moving averages at *mid points* of the time intervals.

7 The quarterly electricity bills for one family over a three-year period are given in this table.

Year	1982				1983				1984			
Month	March	June	Sept.	Dec.	March	June	Sept.	Dec	March	June	Sept.	Dec.
Cost of electricity, £	82	46	48	60	74	48	50	58	86	46	52	56

Calculate the four-monthly moving averages.
What is the *trend* in the payments over this period?
Do you notice any *seasonal variations* in the payments?

The inflation figures released by a government every month are shown in this table for one year.

Month	Jan.	Feb.	March	April	May	June	July	Aug.	Sept.	Oct.	Nov.	Dec.
Inflation rate, %	8.5	9.6	8.7	9.0	8.6	9.6	9.9	9.4	9.8	9.0	9.8	9.4

Calculate the four-monthly moving average.
How would you describe the *trend* in these inflation figures?
Would you agree with the comment that "the rate at which inflation was increasing slowed down towards December"?

Over a period of 15 weeks, a firm notes how much it spends on telephone calls.

Week	1	2	3	4	5	6	7	8	9	10	11	12	13	14	15
Cost of telephone calls, £	88	90	82	85	79	80	82	78	82	79	85	74	82	75	76

Calculate the six-weekly moving averages.
Describe the trend in the data.
Would you agree with the statement that "the firm is having some success in reducing the amount spent on telephone calls"?

A scientist records the temperature of a liquid every minute for 14 minutes.

Time from start, min	0	1	2	3	4	5	6	7	8	9	10	11	12	13	14
Temperature,	0	10	5	14	9	10	18	13	21	19	16	24	13	18	19

Calculate the moving averages of order 6.
Describe the trend.
Would you agree with the statement that "the temperatures are tending to oscillate about a fixed temperature"?
If you agree, can you suggest what this fixed temperature might be?

Cumulative frequency

Part 1 Medians and quartiles

1 Twenty-four pupils took a history exam which was marked out of 20. Here are the results arranged in order, altogether, in halves and in quarters.

5	6	8	12	12	12	14	15	15	15	15	16	16	16	16	16	17	17	18	18	18	19	19	20

| 5 | 6 | 8 | 12 | 12 | 12 | 14 | 15 | 15 | 15 | 15 | 16 ‖ 16 | 16 | 16 | 16 | 17 | 17 | 18 | 18 | 18 | 19 | 19 | 2 |

| 5 | 6 | 8 | 12 | 12 | 12 ‖ 14 | 15 | 15 | 15 | 15 | 16 ‖ 16 | 16 | 16 | 16 | 17 | 17 ‖ 18 | 18 | 18 | 19 | 19 | 2 |

        ↑   ↑   ↑

    lower   median   upper
    quartile   quartile

Write the median, the lower quartile and the upper quartile.

2 A geography teacher marks five exams at the end of the school year for five different classes.
Find the median mark, the lower quartile and the upper quartile for each exam.

  a **Class 1M** (maximum mark 40)
    18 19 20 20 21 21 24 25 29 31 34 36 36 36 36
    37 37 37 38 39 39

  b **Class 2T** (maximum mark 50)
    24 25 25 25 27 29 30 31 32 32 35 35 38 40 40
    42 42 42 44 45 46 46 47 47 48

  c **Class 3J** (maximum mark 80)
    43 47 50 50 51 52 54 54 56 58 58 60 60 62 65
    67 68 72

  d **Class 4C** (maximum mark 100)
    50 50 51 55 57 57 58 58 59 61 63 63 65 67 69
    71 75 75 76 78

  e **Class 5L** (maximum mark 120)
    80 81 83 84 84 85 87 87 90 91 95 96 97 98 98
    100 101 101 102

3 A French teacher marks three exams with these results, which are *not* yet arranged in order.
Find the median mark and the two quartiles.

  a 36 39 40 57 35 36 37 58 51 48 39 46 38 49

  b 24 26 20 18 24 27 30 19 23 19 24 26 30 28 25 25

  c 13 11 20 19 18 12 13 16 19 18 14 12 13 14 17

4 **Discrete** data which has been *counted* can be tabulated.
Find the median and the two quartiles for each of these tables by writing out the individual results in order.

  a The number of goals scored in   b The scores on a dice which has
     20 football matches.   been rolled 18 times.

Number of goals	0	1	2	3	4	5	6
Frequency	8	6	2	1	0	2	1

Score	1	2	3	4	5
Frequency	4	5	2	1	3

Cumulative frequency

c   The number of girls in 14 families living in the same street.

Number of girls	0	1	2	3	4	5
Frequency	6	4	1	2	0	1

d   The number of passengers carried by the 23 cars which park outside an office block.

Number of passengers	0	1	2	3	4
Frequency	12	5	3	1	2

e   The number of defective bolts in 25 packets delivered to a shop.

Number of defects	0	1	2	3	4	5	6
Frequency	9	8	1	3	0	3	1

f   The number of passengers carried by 17 consecutive buses leaving the bus station.

Number of passengers	20	21	22	23	24	25	26
Frequency	4	2	3	2	4	1	1

Continuous data which has been found by *measurement* can be tabulated in groups or classes. The median and quartiles can only be *estimated* as the individual results within each class are not known.
A **cumulative frequency table** is completed and a graphical method used.

A gardener has 60 tomato plants and their yields are given in this table.

Yield, kg	from 1 – 3	from 3 – 5	from 5 – 7	from 7 – 9	from 9 – 11
Frequency	5	11	25	13	6

Copy and complete the following **cumulative frequency table** by answering these questions.
How many tomato plants have yields of

a   1 kg or less
b   3 kg or less
c   5 kg or less
d   7 kg or less
e   9 kg or less
f   11 kg or less?

Yield, kg	⩽ 1	⩽ 3	⩽ 5	⩽ 7	⩽ 9	⩽ 11
Cumulative frequency						

Confirm that the graph shown here gives the cumulative frequency polygon.
Take readings from the graph to find

g   the median yield
h   the lower quartile
i   the upper quartile.

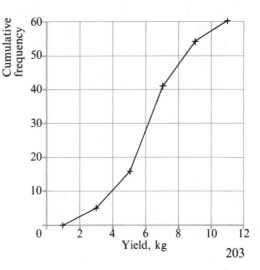

Cumulative frequency

6 An examination is taken by 240 pupils and the percentage marks are awarded as follows.

Marks (%)	0–20	21–30	31–40	41–50	51–60	61–70	71–80	81–100
Frequency	2	4	21	62	73	45	18	15

a Copy and complete the cumulative frequency table below.

Marks (%)	⩽ 20	⩽ 30	⩽ 40	⩽ 50	⩽ 60	⩽ 70	⩽ 80	⩽ 100
Cumulative frequency								

Draw the cumulative frequency curve and find
b the median mark   c the lower quartile   d the upper quartile.

7 This table gives the distribution of the girth of 600 twenty-year-old trees in a plantation, where measurements were taken to the nearest cm.

Girth (cm)	0–20	21–30	31–40	41–50	51–60	61–80
Frequency	24	95	202	214	61	4

a Copy and complete the cumulative frequency table below.

Girth (cm)	⩽ 20	⩽ 30	⩽ 40	⩽ 50	⩽ 60	⩽ 80
Cumulative frequency						

Draw the cumulative frequency curve and find
b the median girth   c the lower quartile   d the upper quartile.

8 The size of a house can be measured by the total area of all its floors. A survey is made of the housing in a village of 280 houses. The results are shown in this table.

Floor area, m²	0–100	101–150	151–200	201–250	251–300	301–5
Frequency	4	86	20	105	60	5

a Copy and complete this cumulative frequency table.

Floor area, m²	⩽ 100	⩽ 150	⩽ 200	⩽ 250	⩽ 300	⩽ 5
Cumulative frequency						

Draw a graph of cumulative frequency and find
b the median area   c the lower quartile   d the upper quartile.

Cumulative frequency

9   After a week's holiday from school, a class of 32 children are asked how much money they spent during the holiday. The results are tabulated below.

Amount spent, £	0–1	from 1–2	from 2–5	from 5–10	from 10–15	from 15–20
Number of children	6	9	12	2	2	1

a   Copy and complete this cumulative frequency table.

Amount spent, £	⩽ 1	⩽ 2	⩽ 5	⩽ 10	⩽ 15	⩽ 20
Cumulative frequency						

Draw a cumulative frequency graph and find
b   the median amount spent   c   the lower quartile   d   the upper quartile.

art 2   Spread or dispersion

Eleven pupils sit a chemistry and a biology exam with these results which are arranged in order.

Chemistry   45 49 52 54 54 55 57 59 60 60 62
Biology   25 29 36 37 48 55 63 72 79 83 90

a   What is the *median* mark for each exam?
b   Which exam has its results more scattered about its median?
c   The **range** is the difference between the highest and lowest scores.
    Find the range of
    (i) the chemistry marks   (ii) the biology marks.

The first three batsmen in a cricket team make these scores in nine innings.

John Davies   0   0   10   21   36   48   74   90   102
Richard Hopkinson 28   29 32   35   36   40   43   47   50
Peter Price   2   25 25   28   36   36   38   39   39

a   Find the *median* number of runs for each batsman.
b   Find the *range* of the scores for each batsman.
c   Which batsman has scores with
    (i) the greatest spread   (ii) the least spread?

Five apprentices spend three weeks making metal parts for certain machines. These figures give the number of parts made each day by each apprentice.

Gary
21 24 18 17 22 27 17 25 19 32 30 26 38 29 36
Leslie
17 14 12 23 27 21 16 19 25 27 26 19 20 21 24
Malcolm
22 27 23 30 29 21 27 38 40 41 39 40 37 42 39
Tom
24 26 23 24 25 25 26 25 27 26 27 24 · 25 26 25
William
 3 24 32 37 42 46 41 48 51 42 39 52 54 48 51

205

Cumulative frequency

a Find the range of each set of figures.

Which apprentice has

b the greatest spread of results

c the least spread of results?

d One apprentice was taken ill on the first day of this 3-week period. Who wa it and is the range calculated for his work a fair measure of the spread of his results? Give your reasons.

e What would his range have been if his first day was not included?

4 Eleven candidates take cookery and needlework examinations with these results which are arranged in order.

| Cookery | 0 | 35 | 38 | 42 | 47 | 50 | 52 | 59 | 63 | 64 | 100 |
| **Needlework** | 0 | 10 | 19 | 28 | 36 | 50 | 62 | 73 | 81 | 90 | 100 |

a Find the median score in each examination.

b Find the range of the scores in each examination.

c Do you think that the *range* is a good measure of the *spread* or *dispersion* c the marks about the median? Give your reasons.

5 Each of 160 fourth-form pupils in a school takes a maths and an English exam The results are shown in this table.

Maths mark, %	0–30	31–40	41–50	51–60	61–70	71–80	81–90	91–1C
Frequency	2	16	28	41	32	24	15	2

English mark, %	0–30	31–40	41–50	51–60	61–70	71–80	81–90	91–1C
Frequency	0	2	25	58	54	18	3	0

The results are illustrated by these two bar charts.

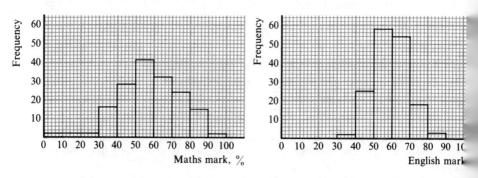

a The modal class is the same for both exams. Which class is it?

b Which exam gives marks which have a greater *spread* or *dispersion* about modal class?

c If a boy scored 35 % in both exams, which do you think was the better mark? Give your reason.

d If the teachers use these marks to divide the pupils into five grades A to l which exam results allow them to do this the more easily? Give your reas (This exam is said to *discriminate* better between the pupils.)

Cumulative frequency

e   Copy this table twice and complete one table for each of the two exams.

Mark, %	⩽ 30	⩽ 40	⩽ 50	⩽ 60	⩽ 70	⩽ 80	⩽ 90	⩽ 100
Cumulative frequency								

f   Draw two cumulative frequency curves on the same axes. For each exam,
find   (i) the median mark
       (ii) the lower and the upper quartiles
       (iii) the interquartile range.

g   Note that the **interquartile range** is a measure of *spread* or *dispersion* which is
not affected by exceptional or freak results.

6   Five hundred children sat an intelligence test with these results.

IQ	81–85	86–90	91–95	96–100	101–105	106–110	111–115	116–120
Frequency	9	34	69	120	112	76	53	27

Copy and complete this cumulative frequency table.

IQ	⩽ 80	⩽ 85	⩽ 90	⩽ 95	⩽ 100	⩽ 105	⩽ 110	⩽ 115	⩽ 120
Cumulative frequency									

Draw a cumulative frequency graph and find   a   the median score
                                             b   the lower and upper quartiles
                                             c   the interquartile range.

7   All the 40 boys who take games together have their heights measured to the
nearest centimetre.

Height, cm	121–130	131–140	141–150	151–160	161–170	171–180
Frequency	4	8	12	8	4	4

Copy and complete this cumulative frequency table.

Height, cm	⩽ 120	⩽ 130	⩽ 140	⩽ 150	⩽ 160	⩽ 170	⩽ 180
Cumulative frequency							

Draw a cumulative frequency curve and find   a   the median height
                                             b   the lower and upper quartiles
                                             c   the interquartile range.

A gardener plants 100 seed potatoes and when he digs the plants up, he weighs
the potatoes from each one to the nearest 0.1 kg.

Mass, kg	0–1.0	1.1–2.0	2.1–3.0	3.1–4.0	4.1–5.0	5.1–6.0	6.1–7.0	7.1–8.0	8.1–9.0	9.1–10.0
Number of plants	3	6	9	16	25	17	9	7	6	2

Cumulative frequency

Copy and complete the following table and use it to draw a cumulative frequency curve. Find
a   the median yield per plant
b   the lower and upper quartiles
c   the interquartile range.

Mass, kg	≤ 1.0	≤ 2.0	≤ 3.0	≤ 4.0	≤ 5.0	≤ 6.0	≤ 7.0	≤ 8.0	≤ 9.0	≤ 10.0
Cumulative Frequency										

9   On an estate of 100 houses, the annual incomes of the householders are as in this table.

Income, £	0–2000	2001–4000	4001–6000	6001–8000	8001–10 000	10 001–12000	12 001–1500
Number of houses	8	24	31	19	12	4	2

Construct your own cumulative frequency table and use it to draw a curve. Use your graph to estimate
a   the median income
b   the lower and upper quartiles
c   the interquartile range.

10   A firm wishes to buy a machine which will automatically cut copper pipe into lengths of about 3 metres with as little variation between lengths as possible. There are two machines available, the Accrocut and the Pipeholme, which the firm tests by having each cut 600 lengths, with these results.

Length cut, cm	297.1–298.0	298.1–299.0	299.1–300.0	300.1–301.0	301.1–302.0	302.1–303
Frequency						
"Accrocut"	4	69	237	228	53	9
"Pipeholme"	15	102	341	128	14	0

Construct your own cumulative frequency table for each machine and draw two curves on the same axes.
For each machine, find
a   the median length
b   the lower and upper quartiles
c   the interquartile range.
d   Remembering that the firm wants the lengths of cut pipe to vary as little a possible, which machine should they choose?

Part 3   Percentiles

The nth percentile of a set of results is that result in the set which has n % of all th results below it.
So, for example, the median is the 50th percentile and the upper quartile is the 75 percentile.

Cumulative frequency

1 An examination is taken by 400 candidates and this cumulative frequency graph relates to the marks they obtain.

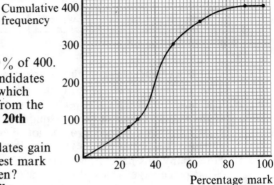

a Use the graph to find
(i) the median mark
(ii) the lower quartile
(iii) the upper quartile.

b Calculate 10 % of 400 and 20 % of 400.

c If the weakest 20 % of the candidates fail the exam, find the mark which separates the highest failure from the lowest pass. This mark is the **20th percentile**.

d If the best 10 % of the candidates gain a distinction, what is the lowest mark for which a distinction is given? This mark is the **90th percentile**.

An ornithologist captures 200 birds of a certain species and measures the length of their wing spans to the nearest millimetre.

Wing span, cm	10.1–12.0	12.1–13.0	13.1–14.0	14.1–15.0	15.1–16.0	16.1–18.0
Number of birds	14	39	67	48	22	10

a Copy and complete this cumulative frequency table and draw a graph of cumulative frequency.

Wing span, cm	≤ 10.0	≤ 12.0	≤ 13.0	≤ 14.0	≤ 15.0	≤ 16.0	≤ 18.0
Cumulative frequency							

b The 15 % of the birds which have the shortest wing span are kept for observation on a special diet. Up to what length of wing span will these birds have? (This is the 15th percentile.)

c The 30 % of the birds which have the longest wing span are released immediately. How long has a bird's wing span to be for it to be released straight away? (This is the 70th percentile.)

To find out which boys in the third year are to be entered for the discus event on sports day, each of 120 boys has one throw with these results.

Distance, m	from 10–15	from 15–20	from 20–25	from 25–30	from 30–35	from 35–40
Number of boys	8	26	48	29	7	2

a Construct your own cumulative frequency table and draw its graph.

b The 10 % of the boys with the longest throw are automatically selected for sports day. What is the least distance a boy has to throw to qualify? (This is the 90th percentile.)

c The 60 % of the boys with the shortest throw are not considered at all. What is the furthest throw of a boy who is not considered? (This is the 60th percentile.)

209

Cumulative frequency

4 A supermarket has a delivery of 600 tins of rice pudding. When weighed individually, the masses of the tins (to the nearest gram) are found to be:

Mass of tin, grams	471–480	481–490	491–500	501–510	511–520	521–530
Number of tins	5	25	35	337	153	45

a Construct your own cumulative frequency table and draw its graph.
b Find (i) 10% of 600, and (ii) the 10th percentile of this distribution.
c The mass of each tin is printed on the label as 500 grams.
   If the manufacturer of the rice pudding has 10% of the tins with masses less than 500 grams, it risks prosecution. Do the tins delivered to the supermarket provide any evidence for prosecution?
d How many tins have a mass greater than 510 grams?
   What percentage is this of all the 600 tins delivered?
e How much "overweight" is the median size of tin?

5 1600 candidates sit a science exam and the results are given in this table.

Mark, %	0–20	21–30	31–40	41–50	51–60	61–70	71–80	81–90	91–10
Frequency	20	90	157	205	379	356	238	124	31

Construct a table and draw a graph of cumulative frequencies.
All the candidates are to be divided into five grades A to E.
The divisions between the grades are as follows:
the 10th percentile divides grades D and E,
the 30th percentile divides grades C and D,
the 70th percentile divides grades B and C,
the 95th percentile divides grades A and B.

a What mark separates grades D and E?
b What mark separates C and D?
c Find the marks which separate grades B and C and also grades A and B.
d If Amanda Nicholson scored 78%, what grade did she get?
e If Robert Birkenshaw needed at least a grade C for a job application, what was the lowest mark which he had to get?

6 240 typists apply for 48 jobs with an insurance firm. They all have their typing speeds in words per minute tested by the firm, with these results.

Speed, w.p.m.	21–30	31–40	41–50	51–60	61–70	71–8
Number of typists	24	87	102	21	4	2

a Construct a table and draw a graph of cumulative frequencies.
b The firm keeps a record of the names and addresses of the fastest 30% of the applicants. Find (i) 30% of 240, and
                      (ii) the speed above which a record of the typist is m
c The firm offers the jobs to the fastest 48 typists.
   What percentage is this of the 240 applicants and what is the speed of th slowest successful applicant?
d How many typists have their names and addresses recorded but are not offered a job?

Correlation

Introduction

1 Would you expect any connection between
  a the amount of rain which falls and the depth of mud in a ploughed field
  b the number of vehicles on the roads near school and the number of pupils late for school
  c the standards of hygiene in a country and the number of infant deaths
  d the number of televisions bought at shops in a town centre and the number of passengers on the town's public transport
  e the number of children attending a primary school and the number of times chips are served for school dinner
  f the number of people in a household and the amount of electricity which the household uses
  g the amount of insecticide used in agriculture and the thickness of the shells of certain birds' eggs?

2 If one variable increases as another variable increases, then there is **positive correlation** between them.
If one variable increases as another variable decreases, then there is **negative correlation** between them.
Would you expect *positive* or *negative* correlation between
  a the number of flowers and the number of bees in a garden
  b the number of cars on the roads and the number of road accidents
  c the number of policemen patrolling the streets and the number of burglaries
  d the number of cigarettes smoked and the number of deaths from lung cancer
  e the amount of pollution in a river and the number of fish caught in it
  f the heights of children and their ages
  g the mileage which a car has done and the depth of tread on its tyres
  h the number of frosty days in winter and the number of wrens in your garden in spring?

Which variable in each of these pairs is the one which you suspect might *cause* changes in the other variable?

The value of one variable when paired with the value of another variable can be illustrated on a graph by a point. As the pair of values change, so several points can be plotted. The **scatter** of points indicates the degree of **correlation** between the two variables.
The scale of correlation runs from $+1$ to -1.

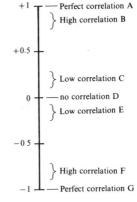

Correlation

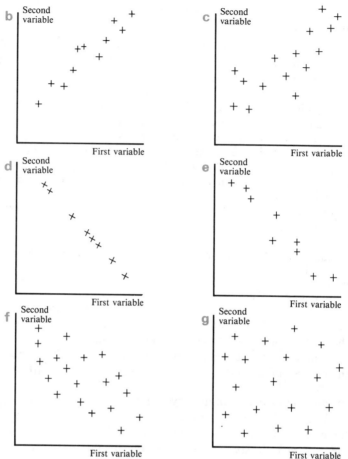

4 Which of the seven scatter diagrams in **3** might you expect from your results if you investigate

   a the ages of cars and their second-hand selling prices

   b the temperature in a room and the length of the mercury column in a thermometer

   c the heights of people and their shoe sizes

   d the amount of tea drunk from a cup and the amount of tea left in it

   e marks in a history exam and the distance which the pupils travel to school

5 Which of these statements do you agree with? If you *disagree* with any, then say why you disagree.

   a A high correlation between two variables *proves* that changes in one variable *cause* changes in the other.

   b A high correlation between two variables indicates that there *might* be a connection between them.

   c No correlation between two variables *proves* that the two variables are definitely not related to each other in any way.

   d A low correlation between two variables *proves* that the two variables are only occasionally related to each other.

   e A low correlation between two variables indicates that changes in one variable *might* affect the other variable slightly.

Correlation

Part 1   Scatter diagrams

For each problem, draw a scatter diagram of the data.
Say whether there is positive, zero or negative correlation.
Say whether any correlation is high, medium or low.
Draw a **line of best fit** through your points, if appropriate, and answer any questions.

Pupils in a class are asked their heights and masses.

John	175 cm, 70 kg	Graham	140 cm, 57 kg	Yvette	138 cm, 54 kg
David	160 cm, 63 kg	Kate	165 cm, 66 kg	Malcolm	171 cm, 67 kg
Angela	156 cm, 63 kg	Lynn	140 cm, 50 kg	Douglas	175 cm, 62 kg
Francis	150 cm, 60 kg	Jeanette	130 cm, 50 kg	Debbie	132 cm, 52 kg
Gerald	154 cm, 60 kg	Robin	155 cm, 57 kg	Helen	166 cm, 62 kg
Robert	145 cm, 55 kg	Stephen	145 cm, 62 kg	Kathleen	138 cm, 53 kg

a   Keith is absent from the class but he is known to have a mass of 64 kg. What would be your best estimate of his height?

b   Christine refuses to give her mass. If she is 152 cm tall, how much do you estimate her mass to be ?

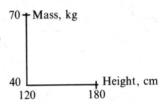

A garage sells 14 different types of car whose advertisements give details of engine size and petrol consumption.

Aurora	2000 cc, 40 mpg	Silvestrine	2400 cc, 35 mpg
Vespera	1000 cc, 50 mpg	Walder GT	3200 cc, 20 mpg
Nocturne	1500 cc, 40 mpg	Floresta	2400 cc, 28 mpg
Polonaise	2000 cc, 35 mpg	Bosquetta	3500 cc, 20 mpg
Prelude	950 cc, 55 mpg	Foret Estate	1300 cc, 36 mpg
Ludo Maxi	3000 cc, 25 mpg	Woodlander	1300 cc, 42 mpg
Ludo Mini	1000 cc, 45 mpg	Madera	2000 cc, 28 mpg

Two new models are introduced.

Estimate

a   the engine size of the first model if it has a petrol consumption of 35 mpg

b   the petrol consumption of the second model if it has an engine size of 2800 cc.

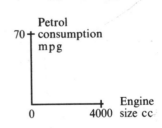

Fifteen children who all live on the same estate are asked two questions: "How old are you?" and "What time do you usually go to bed?" Their answers are given in this table.

Age, years	6	6	7	9	9	7	7	10	14
Bedtime	7.00	7.30	7.30	8.00	8.45	8.00	8.30	8.30	9.45

14	13	10	11	12	13
10.00	9.30	9.00	9.15	9.00	10.00

a   A new family with two children moves into the estate. What would you estimate the bedtime of the 8-year-old daughter to be?

b   If the son goes to bed at 7.45 p.m., how old do you expect him to be?

Correlation

4   A gardener plants twenty tomatoes and after some time he gauges his success by counting their leaves and measuring their heights.

Height, cm	2	6	4	8	14	12	8	6	24	22	18	16
Number of leaves	0	1	2	3	5	6	4	5	14	12	11	6

10	20	18	24	22	16	14	18
7	7	8	11	10	9	10	13

a   How many leaves would you expect on a plant 15 cm high?
b   Estimate the height of a plant which has ten leaves.

5   After a biology test, a group of twenty pupils were asked what size of shoe they take. Their test scores and shoe sizes are recorded in this table.

Mark in test, %	40	70	80	80	60	50	40	60	90	60	40	70
Shoe size	2	$2\frac{1}{2}$	$3\frac{1}{2}$	$5\frac{1}{2}$	3	$3\frac{1}{2}$	4	$4\frac{1}{2}$	$6\frac{1}{2}$	5	$2\frac{1}{2}$	8

60	60	30	30	20	40	70	50
$7\frac{1}{2}$	6	8	$5\frac{1}{2}$	$4\frac{1}{2}$	7	7	5

a   Do children with big feet do better at biology?
b   Would you say that there is any correlation between shoe size and success in biology tests?

6   A youth group has fifteen army cadets. Their shooting instructor has a record of their ages and the results they obtained in a recent shooting test.

Age, years	12	$13\frac{1}{2}$	15	$12\frac{1}{2}$	$16\frac{1}{2}$	16	14	$18\frac{1}{2}$	20	17	$19\frac{1}{2}$	19
Shooting score	30	40	60	30	70	60	60	80	90	60	90	70

$17\frac{1}{2}$	13	17
70	40	80

a   What would you expect the average 15-year-old cadet to score in this test?
b   If a boy had scored 65 in the test, how old would you expect him to be?

7   At a seaside holiday camp, there are 15 entries in a beauty contest where the girls are awarded points by the judges. During the competition they are also given an intelligence test.

IQ test score	90	120	95	110	105	100	115	100	105	93	118	116	112	98	10
Competition score	50	40	25	30	40	55	50	32	28	35	25	38	45	45	

a   A late entry to the contest was awarded 45 marks in the beauty competition but she did not take the intelligence test. Is it possible to estimate her IQ test score?
b   Would you say that there is any correlation between the two scores?

Correlation

In a particular school, 18 pupils study both French and German. Their results in an end-of-term exam are as follows:

German mark, %	30	35	60	75	40	55	15	65	50	40	75	45	20	80	45	25	55	65
French mark, %	40	50	75	80	60	70	30	80	65	50	85	70	40	95	55	45	60	70

a Jennifer scored 55 % in the German exam but was absent for the French exam. What mark might she have been expected to receive in French?

b Alan scored 82 % in the French exam but he was absent for the German exam. Estimate the mark he might have got in German.

c Which exam did the pupils find harder?

Many national newspapers print details about the amounts of sunshine and the maximum temperatures at various places throughout Britain on the previous day. Here is the data for Scotland on 7th June 1983, as given by *The Guardian* newspaper.

Dunbar	10.7 h, 13°C	Lerwick	7.5 h, 12°C
Eskdalemuir	15.7 h, 21°C	Wick	3.3 h, 13°C
Prestwick	16.2 h, 21°C	Kinloss	7.7 h, 14°C
Glasgow	13.8 h, 25°C	Aberdeen	6.8 h, 13°C
Tiree	15.1 h, 15°C	St. Andrews	15.5 h, 15°C
Stornoway	3.6 h, 11°C	Edinburgh	14.7 h, 17°C

a If the maximum temperature in Perth was 14°C, can you estimate how many hours of sunshine Perth had that day?

b If Inverness had $10\frac{1}{2}$ hours of sunshine, estimate its maximum temperature on 7th June 1983.

In the 1950s, when public broadcasting on television was being introduced in the Central European state of Erfundenland, a record was kept every three months of the number of new televisions which were sold and the number of people going to the cinema.

Number of TVs sold (per thousand homes)	10	10	30	30	40	70	70	60	90	100	110	120
Cinema attendances (millions of people)	$10\frac{1}{4}$	11	$10\frac{1}{2}$	10	$9\frac{3}{4}$	$9\frac{3}{4}$	$9\frac{1}{4}$	9	$8\frac{3}{4}$	9	$8\frac{1}{2}$	8

a Would you agree that cinema admissions fell as the television audience grew?

b Does this *prove* that the fall in cinema attendance was *caused* by the growth of the television audience?

A midwife in a hospital makes a record of the masses of the 30 babies born during one week and she asks the mothers how many cigarettes they smoke on average each day. These are her results.

Number of cigarettes smoked each day	0	5	8	10	15	20	30
Masses of babies, kg	4.30	3.90	3.80	3.65	4.10	3.35	2.80
	4.25	3.60	3.55	3.40	3.25	3.00	2.20
	4.10	3.30	3.20	3.10	2.85	2.70	2.10
	3.80		2.70	2.80	2.50	2.50	
	3.30			2.20		2.05	
	3.05						

STATISTICS

Correlation

a   Would you say there is any correlation between the mass of a new-born baby and the number of cigarettes its mother smokes?

b   Would you say there is a high, medium or low correlation?

c   Estimate how much lighter babies are on average if their mothers smoke 30 cigarettes each day than if their mothers did not smoke at all.

12   Class experiments
It is interesting to collect data yourself and draw your own scatter diagrams to investigate any correlation. Here are several possible investigations.

a   **Height–mass**
Members of your class give their heights in centimetres and their masses in kilograms.

b   **Height–shoe size**
Members of your class give their heights in centimetres and the sizes of their shoes.

c   **Length of foot–shoe size**
Class members measure the length of one of their feet and state the size of shoe which they wear.

d   **Height–arm span**
Class members measure their height and the distance between the tips of their longest fingers when arms are stretched out fully sideways.

e   **Hand span–arm span**
Class members measure their arm spans as in d and also the distance between the tips of their thumb and little finger when the hand is outstretched.

arm span

hand span

f   **Maths mark–science mark**
Class members give their marks in their most recent maths and science test. You could investigate for any pair of subjects to find where the correlation is greatest and least.

g   **Distance–time**
Class members say how far they have to travel to get to school and how long it takes them.

Other experiments might include:

h   taking a selection of leaves from one species of tree and measuring the overall width and length of each leaf

i   noting the mass and cost of the many different makes and sizes of packet of soap powder in several supermarkets

j   noting the attendances at First Division football matches one Saturday and the number of points each team has scored

k   the number of lines of print on a full page of a book and the average number of words on a line.